Translation and Community

Community, or public service, translation contributes to a more equitable and sustainable community by empowering minority groups such as migrants and refugees and is a growing area for both teaching and research within translation studies.

Written by a leading authority with over 20 years of teaching experience and in consultation with a range of academics running major courses across the globe, this is the first accessible and interactive introductory textbook to this growing area. It provides step-by-step guidance to students undertaking an undergraduate or postgraduate course covering community translation, public service translation, translation as social action or translation as a social service in multilingual and multicultural societies. The book covers key issues in this area of translation practice, including its distinctive features, challenges and requirements, role and ethical issues, common text types, translation strategies, translation revision and quality assurance and relationships with end users.

Including examples of a range of different text types, suggested activities and readings at the end of each chapter and additional resources and activities on the Routledge Translation Studies portal, this is the essential introduction for all students of community and public service translation.

Mustapha Taibi is an associate professor in interpreting and translation at Western Sydney University, the leader of the International Community Translation Research Group and editor of *Translation & Interpreting*. His books include *Community Translation, New Insights into Arabic Translation and Interpreting, Translating for the Community, Multicultural Health Translation, Interpreting and Communication* and *Translating Cultures*.

Routledge Introductions to Translation and Interpreting

Series Editor:
Sergey Tyulenev is Professor of Translation Studies and Director of
Postgraduate Research at the School of Modern Languages and Cultures,
Durham University, UK

<u>Advisory Board</u>
Luise von Flotow, University of Ottawa, Canada
Ricardo Munoz Martin, University of Bologna, Italy
Kobus Marais, University of the Free State, South Africa
Nike K. Pokorn, University of Ljubljana, Slovenia
James St André, Chinese University of Hong Kong, China
Michaela Wolf, University of Graz, Austria

Routledge Introductions to Translation and Interpreting is a series of textbooks,
designed to meet the need for teaching materials for translator/interpreter training.
Accessible and aimed at beginning students but also useful for instructors designing
and teaching courses, the series covers a broad range of topics, many of which
are already core courses while others cover new directions of translator/interpreter
teaching.

The series reflects the standards of the translator/interpreter training and professional practice set out by national and international competence frameworks and
codes of translation/language service provision and are aimed at a global readership.

All topics combine both practical and theoretical aspects so as to ensure a
bridging of the gap between the academic and professional world and all titles
include a range of pedagogical support: activities, case studies etc.

Most recent titles in the series:

Localization in Translation
Miguel A. Jiménez-Crespo

Automating Translation
Joss Moorkens, Andy Way, Séamus Lankford

Translation and Community
Mustapha Taibi

For more information on any of these and other titles, or to order, please go to www.routledge.com/
Routledge-Introductions-to-Translation-and-Interpreting/book-series/RITI

Additional resources for Translation and Interpreting Studies are available on the Routledge
Translation Studies Portal: http://routledgetranslationstudiesportal.com/

Translation and Community

Mustapha Taibi

LONDON AND NEW YORK

Designed cover image: Belitas, Getty

First published 2025
by Routledge
4 Park Square, Milton Park, Abingdon, Oxon OX14 4RN

and by Routledge
605 Third Avenue, New York, NY 10158

Routledge is an imprint of the Taylor & Francis Group, an informa business

© 2025 Mustapha Taibi

The right of Mustapha Taibi to be identified as author of this work has been asserted in accordance with sections 77 and 78 of the Copyright, Designs and Patents Act 1988.

All rights reserved. No part of this book may be reprinted or reproduced or utilised in any form or by any electronic, mechanical, or other means, now known or hereafter invented, including photocopying and recording, or in any information storage or retrieval system, without permission in writing from the publishers.

Trademark notice: Product or corporate names may be trademarks or registered trademarks, and are used only for identification and explanation without intent to infringe.

British Library Cataloguing-in-Publication Data
A catalogue record for this book is available from the British Library

Library of Congress Cataloging-in-Publication Data
Names: Taibi, Mustapha, author.
Title: Translation and community / Mustapha Taibi.
Description: Abingdon, Oxon ; New York, NY : Routledge, 2025. | Series: Routledge introductions to translation and interpreting | Includes bibliographical references and index. |
Identifiers: LCCN 2024029120 | ISBN 9781032435305 (hardback) | ISBN 9781032424262 (paperback) | ISBN 9781003367741 (ebook)
Subjects: LCSH: Public service interpreting. | LCGFT: Introductory works.
Classification: LCC P306.947 .T35 2025 | DDC 418/.02--dc23/
    eng/20240925
LC record available at https://lccn.loc.gov/2024029120

ISBN: 978-1-032-43530-5 (hbk)
ISBN: 978-1-032-42426-2 (pbk)
ISBN: 978-1-003-36774-1 (ebk)

DOI: 10.4324/9781003367741

Typeset in Times New Roman
by Apex CoVantage, LLC

Access the Support Material: www.routledgetranslationstudiesportal.com

Contents

Series editor's foreword		*vi*
Acknowledgements		*vii*
Introduction		1
1	What is special about community translation?	8
2	Your role as a community translator	25
3	Text types, translation brief and translation strategies	42
4	Translating public messaging	59
5	Translating regulatory texts	81
6	Translating culturally sensitive texts	99
7	Translating for different dissemination media	119
8	Translating personal official documents	135
9	Locating and using resources	154
10	Revising your and another translator's work	171
11	Teamwork and community engagement	188
Author index		*202*
Subject index		*204*

Series editor's foreword

I am pleased to introduce a new addition to the Routledge Introductions to Translation and Interpreting series. This series is becoming increasingly popular among both translator/interpreter trainees and trainers because it addresses the needs of translator/interpreter training by providing ready-made teaching and learning materials. The thematic range encompasses courses designed for budding translators and interpreters as well as the skills and competencies essential for any professional translator/interpreter or translation and interpreting studies researcher.

Community translation, also known as public service translation, plays a significant social role. It contributes to creating more equitable and sustainable communities by empowering minority groups, particularly migrants, refugees and other individuals facing language barriers. Despite its importance, this area of translation and interpreting studies is relatively new in both teaching and research contexts.

Therefore, it is crucial for the younger generation of translators and interpreters to be introduced to community translation early in their professional training. This textbook, authored by Dr Mustapha Taibi, a leading scholar in community translation research and teaching, takes a distinct pedagogical approach. It provides structured, step-by-step guidance for students in undergraduate or postgraduate programs covering community translation, public service translation, translation as social action and translation as a social service in multilingual and multicultural societies. The textbook includes discussions on various text types and features suggested activities at the end of each chapter.

Sergey Tyulenev
2024

Acknowledgements

First, I would like to thank Prof. Sergey Tyulenev, the Series Editor, for inviting me to write this textbook.

While planning and writing it, the encouragement, insights and feedback of my colleagues in the International Community Translation Research Group were invaluable. Special thanks go to Ineke Crezee, Alicia Rueda-Acedo, Erika González, Wei Teng, Tatjana Radanovic Felberg, Harold Lesch, Marija Todorova, Brooke Townsley, Anne Beinchet, Katarzyna Czarnocka, Said Faiq, Ana Gregorio Cano, Rovena Troqe and Giulia Magazzù for sharing resources relating to community translation. Even more special appreciation goes to Wei Teng for checking the Chinese text and to Alicia Rueda-Acedo for hosting me at the University of Texas at Arlington, sharing with me her teaching experience and resources, and facilitating meetings with her community translation students, alumni and partner organisation Proyecto Inmigrante.

I would like to thank all the students and alumni who have helped me in one way or another, including my own students at Western Sydney University and others at the University of Alcalá, the University of Texas at Arlington and Effat University.

I also extend thanks to those who provided industry insights relating to community translation, especially Rema Nazha and Linda Raynes from Multicultural NSW and Fatih Karakas and Ismail Akinci from All Graduates Translating and Interpreting, with whom I had productive discussions about current practices, quality standards and training gaps in community translation.

Finally, I would like to thank my Western Sydney University colleagues Masako Ogawa and Dae Young Kim for checking the Japanese and Korean texts respectively.

Introduction

Community translation (public service translation), as both a teaching and a research area, contributes to more equitable and sustainable communities by empowering minority groups such as migrants and refugees and people with language barriers in general. This area of translation studies has not received sufficient attention in terms of research publications and teaching and learning resources. There is a growing interest in the area, as demonstrated by recent publications, doctoral theses and courses such as the following:

- Edited volumes: *Translating for the Community* (Taibi, 2018), and *Community Translation: Research and Practice* (González, Stachowiak-Szymczak and Amanatidou, 2023).
- Doctoral dissertations: *Translators' Ethics: Case Studies of English–Japanese Translators in Community Translation* (Fukuno, 2023) and *Virtual Reality Training for Hajj Pilgrims as an Innovative Community Translation Dissemination Medium* (Munshi, 2022).
- Papers and book chapters: Linguistic diversity among Swahili-speakers: A challenge for translation in Australia (Burke, 2018), Translation policies and community translation: The U.S., a case study (Córdoba Serrano, 2016) and Translating child protection assessments for ELF users: Accommodation, accessibility, and accuracy (Määttä, 2020).
- New course: LANC404 Translating and Interpreting for the Community, as part of the Master of Applied Translation and Interpreting, at the University of Canterbury, New Zealand.

However, the only full-length book available so far is my co-authored book *Community Translation* (Bloomsbury, 2016). The book is a scholarly introduction to the nature, social function, challenges and approaches to community translation, but it was not specifically written as a textbook.

Community translation teachers and students face a lack of theoretical and pedagogical resources specifically addressing the community context and, consequently, often rely on generalist translation literature. With *Translation and Community*, which is published as part of the Routledge Introductions to Translation and Interpreting Series, I hope I have managed to offer you a self-contained teaching

DOI: 10.4324/9781003367741-1

2 *Translation and Community*

and learning resource that was missing in this area of translator education. The textbook has been structured and written in a manner that provides step-by-step guidance to students undertaking undergraduate or postgraduate (or further education) coursework in community translation, public service translation, translation as social action or translation as a social service in multilingual and multicultural societies. As I outline next, the textbook covers key topics and issues in community translation, with examples of different text types and suggested activities at the end of each chapter.

Chapter outline

Chapter 1: What is special about community translation?

The first chapter focuses on the distinctive features of community translation as a key facilitator of communication strategies between public services and people who do not share the language of those services. The chapter outlines and discusses some of the main issues in community translation as a professional activity and as a social service. The chapter covers the social role of community translation, the special agency and role of community translators, translation accessibility and plain language, dissemination methods and quality requirements, including, among other aspects, training, a functional understanding of translation and collaboration between translators and other stakeholders. Some of the points included in this chapter are discussed in more detail in other chapters (e.g., the role of community translators in Chapter 2; dissemination methods in Chapter 7).

Chapter 2: Your role as a community translator

This chapter opens with a general discussion of the role of translators as outlined in codes of ethics such as those of the American Translators Association and the Australian Institute of Interpreters and Translators. This is followed by a discussion of literature on the role of translators as intercultural mediators and as social agents. The specific and special role of community translators is subsequently discussed with a focus on their roles as members of their community and society, as members of the translation profession, as text processors, as communication facilitators, as intercultural mediators and as social agents. The chapter sets a boundary between activism and community translation as an enabling, context-sensitive and functional language service.

Chapter 3: Text types, translation brief and translation strategies

This chapter provides a brief overview of different translation approaches, especially reader-oriented and functional models, to identify the theoretical contributions most relevant to community translation. Based on key functionalist notions such as 'translation brief', 'text type' and 'text function', the chapter offers practical and illustrated advice for community translators in relation to translation strategies.

Among the works that I review to appraise relevance to community translation are Reiss and Vermeer's 2014 [1984] and Nord's (2018 [1997]). I also discuss the potential tensions between translation briefs and the social role of community language services. Lists of possible translation strategies are taken from Vinay and Darbelnet (1995 [1958]), Baker (2011 [1992]) and Molina Martínez (2022). The point I make in the chapter in relation to translation strategies is that their relevance and appropriateness can only be determined through a functionalist understanding of the communicative situation, the translation brief and how the two working languages compare.

Chapter 4: Translating public messaging

Following up on text types and translation strategies (Chapter 3), this chapter focuses on the practicalities of translating a broad category of texts called 'public messaging', which are generally informative and operative texts published by public institutions to raise awareness among the public about health, safety, social, environmental and other issues. I describe the main features of public messaging, especially in the health care sector, and provide step-by-step guidance to (future) community translators in relation to the identification of such texts, their functions within institutional communication strategies, appropriate translation strategies for them and the translator's communication and negotiation with other stakeholders to ensure translation transparency and appropriateness.

Chapter 5: Translating regulatory texts

This chapter focuses on how to translate 'regulatory texts', another broad category of texts handled by community translators. This class of texts usually adopts a more institutional perspective and tone and aims to regulate rights, services and relationships more than to inform citizens or residents. The nature of these texts makes it necessary to discuss the overlap between the translation of regulatory texts, institutional translation and legal translation. While translations of the texts covered in Chapter 4 are clearly communicative and reader oriented, those in Chapter 5 might better serve the official voice and power structures, which raises ethical questions for community translators (and other social agents) about translator role and loyalties (discussed in Chapter 2).

Chapter 6: Translating culturally sensitive texts

While I discuss issues relating to culture and cultural mediation in different parts of the textbook, Chapter 6 focuses on cultural mediation and cultural sensitivity in community translation. It includes a discussion of different communicative situations and sensitive contents that might require certain levels of mediation from the community translator. Case studies range from unimportant in-text references or examples that can easily be adapted to cater for the new readership to entire texts that address culturally sensitive issues such as sexual abuse, domestic violence,

4   *Translation and Community*

religion, offensive language and political correctness. I propose several parameters to assist translators in making decisions in relation to cultural adaptations, including awareness of cultural differences, the translation brief, ethical considerations, the nature and position of sensitive material in the source text and language resources and constraints.

Chapter 7: Translating for different dissemination media

Variation between communication channels, coupled with sociolinguistic variation in multilingual societies, poses serious challenges for both translation commissioners and translators. This chapter focuses on the differences between dissemination media and the adjustments community translators may have to make when translating from one medium to another. Adjustments include using different language varieties, varying register and style, simplifying sentence structures, editing for conciseness and changing address terms, among other aspects. The argument I present in the chapter is that based on an understanding of community translation as an integral part of an effective communication strategy, community translators can act as expert advisers in relation to the appropriateness of dissemination media for their target communities, and they need to be guided by the affordances of each medium when selecting language variants and translation strategies. With examples, especially relating to audiovisual and subtitled public messaging, I illustrate how community translators are guided by the communicative context and translation briefs to determine the most effective translation strategy.

Chapter 8: Translating personal official documents

This chapter is the only one to focus on translating personal official documents (civil registry certificates, driver's licence, academic qualifications, and so on). I include the translation of these documents in the textbook because they are part of the language services offered to speakers of non-dominant languages (e.g., migrants, refugees) to facilitate their integration into their host or mainstream societies. I outline the special nature, features and challenges of translating personal official documents and provide practical guidelines for professionals working in this area of translation practice. The key quality criteria covered in the chapter are accuracy, language appropriateness, document integrity and presentation.

Chapter 9: Locating and using resources

This part of the textbook provides practical advice to students on the translator resources they can use and how to use them. From traditional resources such as dictionaries, thesauri, glossaries and encyclopaedias to technologically advanced ones such as machine translation and artificial intelligence, I outline possible uses of these resources and the risks associated with each one of them. A recurrent theme is the need for students (and community translators) to be aware of the limitations of each resource. The discussion of machine translation and artificial intelligence

Introduction 5

in particular stresses the risks of over-reliance on technology, especially at early stages of translator education, and the need for careful postediting for quality assurance in community translation. This seamlessly links this chapter to the next one on translation revision.

Chapter 10: Revising your and another translator's work

Drawing mainly on Mossop (2020) and the AUSIT-FECCA (n.d.) *Revision Guidelines and Parameters for Community Translations*, this chapter offers a general introduction to translation revision—of another translator's work, not checking one's own drafts—followed by practical advice relating to revision in the context of community translation. Special emphasis is placed on language appropriateness, coherence, effective communication and information accessibility in the context of non-specialised translations for the community (e.g., general health care awareness, emergency response to health care crises such as COVID-19). Examples of translations and suggested revisions are provided in Arabic, Chinese, English and Spanish.

Chapter 11: Teamwork and community engagement

To conclude the textbook, Chapter 11 addresses the relationships of community translators and community translation trainees with their colleagues and respective language and cultural communities. The chapter underscores the importance of teamwork and interpersonal or soft skills for both students and translators. In relation to this, I discuss professional relationships and solidarity within a team of translators and revisers, as well as the translator's relationships with other professionals (e.g., interdisciplinary team). In terms of relationships with the community, I urge community translators and community translation students to engage with their communities, take part in community events and activities and establish and maintain connections with relevant cultural and language groups. This is part of the translator's language maintenance and ongoing professional development in terms of knowledge of the sociolinguistic and sociocultural profile of the communities they serve.

How to use this textbook

The textbook is written in a way that would allow readers, teachers and students to use each chapter separately, as a building block towards developing understanding of community translation and skills in this area of translation practice. Each chapter addresses one key topic in community translation, includes questions to consider or discuss, examples relevant to the topic at hand, suggested activities, further readings and a reference list. Chapters do not need to be read in the sequence in which they appear in the textbook, but it is advisable to start with the introductory ones, Chapters 1, 2 and 3 (and preferably 4 and 5 as well). Chapter 9 (on translator resources and tools) and Chapter 11 (on teamwork and community engagement)

6 *Translation and Community*

need not be left until the end of the semester or course, as they cover content that students must be aware of throughout their course of study (e.g., whether to use machine translation or not or the importance of interpersonal skills, situated learning and internships).

Each chapter opens with a box summarising the main points covered. Apart from Chapter 1, which provides a general (theoretical) introduction to community translation, chapters are written in a pedagogical style and include frequent examples and boxes to illustrate and discuss the question at hand. Each chapter concludes with a summary, a further reading list and suggested activities. Some of the readings are not specifically related to community translation, but they are useful for students to expand their knowledge of some of the issues or skills covered in each chapter.

The textbook can be used in different ways, depending on its position within the translator education program and the time and resources available. In those higher education providers where subjects are taught in a 12- or 13-week semester, it is easy to decide to cover one chapter per week, with two or three weeks, for instance, dedicated to the translation of personal official documents, which is a special area of translation practice requiring time to develop skills and familiarise oneself with the applicable conventions. Programs with more time available can also find in the textbook sufficient material to cover, not only in terms of the content included but also in terms of the questions and practical considerations each chapter raises.

Independent of the duration of the course, students must be provided with sufficient opportunities to practice community translation with authentic texts and in contexts as close to real-life professional practice as possible. At Western Sydney University, for example, Community Translation is taught by way of a one-hour lecture (common to all language streams) and a two-hour language-specific tutorial (practical class in Arabic–English, Chinese–English, Spanish–English, Korean–English and Vietnamese English). Before each tutorial, students are expected to submit two community translations, one from English and the other into English. Sample translations are used for classroom discussion and peer and tutor feedback. In addition to the weekly translation tasks, students have a final assignment consisting of revising a substandard community translation and a translation quality assessment essay. At the end of the semester, they sit a final examination including two translation tasks (one from English and the other into English) or one translation and a commentary on translation challenges and strategies.

To ensure student engagement with the textbook, teachers may consider different approaches, including integrating the reading and chapter summaries as part of the assessment or as mandatory activities before students attend the class. The questions suggested for discussion as well as the suggested activities at the end of each chapter can be used in different ways as well. They may be discussed in the classroom, either in small groups or as a class. Some of them can also be used for written assignments, reflections, portfolios or online discussions.

Teachers are encouraged to use the textbook creatively and take the chapters as starting points for engaging classroom and take-home activities. Chapter 9 (on translator resources and tools), for instance, may be used to implement a process-oriented approach to learning. Students can be asked to read the chapter and document their research and translation processes (which resources they decided to use, how they assessed their reliability and how they used them). Integrating discussions on the steps involved in comprehending the source text (e.g., through encyclopaedias and Internet searches) and locating terminological and translation solutions (e.g., through parallel texts) can assist students in reflecting critically on their learning experience and decision-making processes. Similarly, Chapter 11 (on teamwork and community engagement) can be used as a prompt for students (and tutors) to develop collaboration with relevant communities and organisations. One thing that (future) community translators need to do is to stop considering community members and organisations as end users only and start thinking of them as partners.

Mustapha Taibi
Sydney, 31 May 2024

1 What is special about community translation?[1]

> In this chapter, I outline and discuss some of the main issues that distinguish community translation as a professional activity and as a social service. The chapter covers the following:
>
> - The social role of community translation;
> - The special agency and role of community translators;
> - Translation accessibility and plain language;
> - Quality in community translation;
> - Community translation and dissemination methods.

1.1 Introduction

Community translation plays a key role in facilitating communication between public services and the public, particularly in situations where the two sides do not share the same language. On the one hand, community translation allows government departments, agencies and services (as well as the non-government sector) to reach out to all members of a society. On the other, it allows speakers of minority or minoritised languages access to public texts that would normally be inaccessible due to language barriers.

Community translation has attracted some research attention in the last two decades. The International Community Translation Research Group was founded towards the end of 2013. A year later, the First International Conference on Community Translation was organised at Western Sydney University. In 2019, the second conference was organised at RMIT University, Melbourne. A few publications have come out as well (e.g., Taibi, 2011; Lesch, 2012; Taibi and Ozolins, 2016; Córdoba Serrano, 2016; Tomozeiu, 2016; Kelly, 2018; García, 2018; Määttä, 2020); however, this is still a developing area of translation studies.

An indication of its early developmental stage is the conceptual and terminological variation surrounding it. Community translation is also known as 'public service translation'. It can also refer to professional public service translation

DOI: 10.4324/9781003367741-2

What is special about community translation? 9

(e.g., Taibi and Ozolins, 2016; Taibi, 2018) or volunteer (crowd sourced) translation for online communities (O'Hagan, 2011; García, 2018). This variation not only indicates the terminological diversity that characterises language and communication disciplines but also denotes different assumptions about professional standards. García (2018) suggests that the two notions and practices of community translation can work hand in hand by assigning high-stakes translation materials to professional translators and having non-critical ones undertaken by bilingual volunteers or amateurs.

In this book, the focus is on community translation as a professional service consisting of written translation intended to bridge the communication gap between public services and relevant organisations on the one hand and speakers of minority or minoritised languages on the other. 'Professional service' is understood as "a paid occupation which requires a formal qualification" (Schäffner, 2020: 64). Formal qualification can consist of a relevant educational degree, professional certification or any other adequate form of credentialing. In this sense, it contrasts with non-professional translation, which is offered by "individuals not only without formal training in linguistic mediation but also working for free" (Pérez González and Susam-Sarayeva, 2012: 151). However, while the focus is on community translation as a professional activity, reference is occasionally made to non-professional translation where relevant.

This chapter starts with theoretical considerations and a literature review covering recent contributions; then I discuss some of the most prominent issues in community translation (quality assurance, translation accessibility and dissemination methods).

1.2 Theoretical considerations

1.2.1 The social role of community translation

In previous work (Taibi, 2011; Taibi and Ozolins, 2016), I defined community translation as an area of translation with a social mission, that is, as a language service that empowers linguistically and socioeconomically disempowered communities. It has also been established that the work of community translators is constrained by power asymmetry between text producers and readers, imparity between source and target languages and sociolinguistic and educational diversity among audiences. Lesch (2018) agrees that community translation aims to enable and empower (minoritised) community members. He therefore argues that the social and linguistic needs of these people need to be prioritised.

Understandably, all translation is a social activity to some extent, and all translators have a social role and impact. As Wolf (2007: 1) puts it, "Any translation, as both an enactment and a product, is necessarily embedded within social contexts". Translators do their work having in mind benefits to humanity and a positive impact on society, or at least on their readership (Tymoczko, 2000: 26). This applies to news translation (Bielsa, 2016), audiovisual translation (Díaz-Cintas and Remael, 2007: 13) and even to literary translation (Cronin, 2003: 142), to mention just a few examples.

10 *Translation and Community*

What distinguishes community translation is that its social role is generally local and focused on minority or minoritised language communities within the same country or region. It usually covers texts about essential public services (health care, education, social services, environment, etc.), and caters to indigenous or migrant language groups in a particular country, state or municipality. Corsellis (2008: 32) notes that "Translation in the public service sector can also include an international dimension", as in the case of medical or social service reports travelling internationally. Ko (2018: 143, 145) also agrees that community translation can sometimes extend beyond national boundaries but acknowledges that it is usually "localised, context-specific and culture-specific", which requires translators to develop knowledge of the relevant local culture and institutions. In the case of general awareness campaigns such as those relating to human rights, the environment or preventive health care, for instance, community translation can clearly become an international exercise. Especially with the help of the Internet, resources translated locally can be used and have an impact internationally. However, community translation is generally guided by national or local policies and initiatives, and it aims to serve and empower national, regional or local communities.

1.2.2 *Translator agency*

Given the social mission of community translation and the social contexts where it is usually offered (or needed), translator agency is central to this area of translation practice. Translation in general is a social activity performed by social actors to fulfil certain social needs (Tyulenev, 2014: 126). As Way (2016: 1018) affirms, "translators are social agents who participate not only in the communication process but in society as a whole". Among other senses, the notion of agency is understood as "willingness and ability to act" (Kinnunen and Koskinen, 2010: 6), meaning that an agent has a disposition, consciousness and intentionality on the one hand and ability and power to choose and act on the other. Most important, "agency is about acting, that is, exerting an influence in the lifeworld" (Kinnunen and Koskinen, 2010: 7). In line with the latter, Jary and Jary (2000) define agency as "human action . . . which makes a difference to a human relationship or behaviour", and as such it applies more specifically to community translators. To empower communities, community translators, as a first step, take into consideration the sociolinguistic situation of their community, the often-asymmetrical relationships between social groups and between these and institutions, and particularly the relative social status of public service staff and the target readers of community translation. As a second step, they are expected to assume an active role in enabling access to information, literacy and, ultimately, societal and economic change (Taibi and Ozolins, 2016: 70–71).

In the last two decades or so, translator agency has been a major question in translation studies, probably "as a reaction to a more established tradition of studying norms and systems in translation" (Paloposki, 2007: 336) but most importantly as part of growing interest in the social role of translators, and the political, ideological and intercultural consequences of their work. Translator agency is the translator's ability and power to produce change in societies through the texts they

What is special about community translation? 11

choose to translate and how they translate them (Tymoczko, 2007: 200–216). It can also be associated with activism when it relates to international conflicts and ideological struggles (see e.g., Baker, 2006; Fernández and Evans, 2018).

In the case of community translation, translator agency is not about activism but rather about taking a translation approach that enhances the social role of community translation. Community translators as discussed here are not activists in the sense outlined, for instance, by Baker (2013): a group of (volunteer) translators who put their language and translation skills at the service of social or political movements. Instead, community translators are (ideally) adequately trained professionals who offer a language service for a fee or a salary and, while doing so, exercise agency by taking an active, functional and culturally sensitive approach to translation that aims to inform, educate and empower linguistically disempowered communities. Their agency does not consist of direct advocacy, lobbying or resistance but manifests itself in the impact of their translations and translation approach on society or certain groups within it.

Translator agency implies translator power: that translators have the necessary power and influence to trigger or contribute to change (Paloposki, 2007: 337; Marais, 2011: 192). Marais (2011: 198) notes that the debate on translator agency and power has focused mostly on literary translation, which raises questions about the applicability of statements about agency and power to the translation of pragmatic texts. In the case of community translators, one can hardly speak of power as it is generally understood: the capacity to influence individuals or groups and affect their behaviours by actually or potentially offering them or depriving them from desiderata (Dye, 1990: 4).

Firstly, community translators (as well as interpreters) do not generally enjoy a high status in society. Secondly, they do not choose what texts to translate or what languages to translate them into; this is usually the decision of authorities, public services and, in some cases, non-governmental organisations. The decision is political and is often in line with immigration policies, language policies and attitudes towards multilingualism and minority languages (Córdoba Serrano, 2016).

However, community translators do have a role and a degree of power in terms of the approach they take when translating for local communities. Their power lies in the extent to which they, consciously or unconsciously, enable access to information and education, not through tokenistic language transfer but through effective communication of contents and mediation between public services and community members. Thus, community translators may not have a say in relation to translation policy, funding available for community translation or production and selection of public service texts, but they can exercise agency in their translation choices by making them consistent with the needs of disempowered audiences.

1.2.3 Translation approach

The sense of agency that I have just described goes hand in hand with a full understanding of the role of community translation in society and of the translation approach required in each social and translational context. Referring to the translation

12 *Translation and Community*

of administrative documents, Way (2006: 581) stresses the role of community translators as intercultural mediators and advocates for "a more active role for the translator" as one who actively strives to mediate between cultures and overcome the issues surrounding this mediation. Community translation is offered (or needed) in local contexts that are characterised by linguistic and cultural diversity not only in terms of different ethnic, religious or cultural groups but also in the sense of differences between the cultural assumptions and (specialist) discourse practices of institutions on the one hand and those of (lay) community translation users on the other.

In line with the active mediation required of the community translator in such diversity, Lesch (2018) conceives of quality in community translation as a matter of adaptation, appropriateness and accessibility for the target readership. Taking as a starting point the work of generalist translation scholars such as Chesterman and Toury, he suggests a set of functional translation principles that revolve around the idea that effective communication through community translation requires plain or simplified language, explication strategies when necessary and accessible text organisation (see Section 1.3.2 on accessibility). Taibi and Ozolins (2016: 70) also suggest that "functionalist approaches to translation would be the most attractively suitable for community translators in their capacity as active social agents". Framed within a sociological understanding of the community translator's work, a functionalist approach 1) empowers translators by bringing their status closer to that of authors (in terms of text production, not socioeconomic standing); 2) places the intended function of the text/translation as the paramount criterion to guide the translator's decisions; 3) acknowledges differences between text types and the translation strategies appropriate for each and 4) allows "for a wide range of renderings and translatorial actions", such as adaptations, transcreations (creative rewriting or recreating) and summary translations depending on the translation context and needs (Taibi and Ozolins, 2016: 70).

Tomozeiu (2016) draws on Suojanen et al.'s (2015) *User-Centered Translation* to propose three methods to assist community translators in visualising the target audience needs and making informed decisions in the translation process. These are 'personas', 'implied readers' and 'audience design'. Personas are typical user profiles within the target community which a community translator can outline based on their knowledge of and experience with the community (Tomozeiu, 2016: 197, 202). One risk in the creation of personas, Tomozeiu (2016: 198) points out, is that they may be centred on some stereotypical elements and features of the target community and leave out others, thus undermining the inclusiveness aim of community translation. Implied readers are "the audience based on the analysis of the text" rather than previous knowledge of the target group (Tomozeiu, 2016: 199). In other words, while reading the source text, the translator infers the characteristics of its target audience, which they can subsequently compare with those of community translation user personas. Finally, audience design serves to identify not only primary readers (addressees) but also secondary ones (auditors, overhearers, eavesdroppers and referees). Once identified, the community translator will be in a position to make translation choices that address these different audiences and, where necessary, prioritise the needs of some of them (Tomozeiu, 2016: 200–201).

What is special about community translation? 13

1.2.4 Community translator's training and socialisation

The social roles of community translation, translator agency and a reader-oriented mediational translation that I just outlined require that community translators be adequately trained for the task and be socialised in the values associated with community translation as an empowering language service. In some cases, community translation knowledge, skills and role awareness may develop through apprenticeship opportunities in some public services and non-governmental organisations. However, like any other professional language service, community translation requires adequate training and socialisation, which can then be complemented by a supervised internship or practicum.

Kelly (2018) argues that it is possible to cater for community translation education within generalist translation programs; generalist courses would need to be accompanied with specialised community translation modules, and curricular design would need to be based on rigorous analysis and alignment of societal needs, professional expectations and the socioeconomic and institutional context of the planned translation program. In line with Kelly's (2018: 39) "meaningful curricular design", Rueda-Acedo (2018) shows how collaboration between universities and other relevant societal stakeholders (e.g., public services and NGOs) can contribute to meaningful, context-sensitive and effective community translation training. She stresses the benefits of service–learning partnerships for both trainee translators and members of the community.

However, as Kelly (2018) acknowledges, community translation is not highly recognised or catered to in education initiatives (see also Taibi, 2011; Taibi and Ozolins, 2016). This, together with public service policies and inexistent or inadequate funding, often leaves community translation in the hands of volunteers or bilingual staff with no demonstrated translation qualifications. Some authors (e.g., Susam-Sarayeva and Pérez González, 2012; Antonini et al., 2017) acknowledge the role of non-professional translators (and interpreters) as actors in society and the complexity of their role. As an existing phenomenon, non-professional translation for public services is worth investigating and acknowledging. However, the phenomenon raises two concerns at least: 1) about the extent to which non-professional translators (without adequate language skills and translation training) can translate competently and effectively for public services and minoritised communities and 2) about the political and ethical positions of governments and public instrumentalities who leave community translation (and interpreting) to the mercy of ad hoc solutions.

1.2.5 Professional vs. non-professional community translation

Within the context of what is desirable vs. what is available, García (2018) identifies areas where non-professional, crowd-sourced translation can coexist with and complement professional community translation. His argument is as follows: 1) Both community translation and grassroot volunteer translation, available mainly on Internet platforms, share the social inclusion ethos; 2) not all content that needs

14 *Translation and Community*

translation has the same value (e.g., some texts are "critical and enduring", while others are "inconsequential and ephemeral"; 2018: 105); 3) therefore, in critical situations (translations involving high risk) community translation needs to be assigned to professional translators, while low-risk translations can be done by non-professionals. A non-critical task is translating "peer-to-peer support pages" for newly arrived migrants (2018: 103), whereas high-risk translations would include instances such as official information about social security, health care or administrative procedures.

Pym (2021: 26) takes up this argument with reference to both translation and interpreting: "The basic argument . . . is that, when and where mistakes can be costly, it is worth paying for highly trained professional translators and interpreters so that error can be avoided". Pym (2021: 26) cites findings such as Canfora and Ottmann's (2018) on damages (partly) attributable to translation errors and concludes, "From one or two disasters, it certainly does not follow that all mistranslations are costly. Some are high-stakes, most are low-stakes, and the difference is important". While it is evident that in translation, as in life, there are high-stakes and low-stakes situations, García's and Pym's points raise several questions:

1) Given that 'high stakes' and 'low stakes' are relative and blurry, who would be entitled to make decisions in relation to classifying translation needs, areas and situations?
2) What types of cost or damage will be quantified and how? Production, dissemination and social costs can arise as a result of inexistent or inadequate community translation; there are also risks relating to the reputation and legal responsibilities of public service organisations and risks relating to the lives, livelihoods and welfare of community translation users; there is individual damage and collective damage, and there are quantifiable and unquantifiable costs and damages.
3) Inadequate community translation is not only about translation errors, which may lead to physical damage or safety incidents; it is also about inadequacies such as complete lack of community translation in all or some local languages, insufficient community translations in some key sectors such as health care or employment, or less effective community translations as a result of inappropriate translation approaches or dissemination strategies.

While notions of 'non-critical', 'low stakes' or 'low risk' may be operationally useful for reducing costs or prioritising certain needs in a public service context of limited resources, the notions themselves are controversial and fraught with risks, given the potential impacts of their operationalisation on the interests and welfare of minoritised groups.

1.3   Critical issues in community translation

As I believe I have emphasised, community translation stands out as a translation activity with a social mission and impact. It "is a means to an end, namely, to equip the community with the necessary information and other means to develop skills for themselves" (Lesch, 1999: 93). Given the pragmatic, functional

What is special about community translation? 15

and impact-driven nature of community translation, this section focuses on three interrelated critical issues: quality, accessibility and dissemination media. Community translation can only achieve its intended impact on society if it complies with quality standards, is accessible to its target users and is made available through appropriate and effective media.

1.3.1 Quality

For community translation to achieve its social aims, it needs to meet quality requirements. The first requirement is professional qualifications. However, in the case of community translation (and translation in general), translator qualifications are only one step towards ensuring quality; others rely on the role of other stakeholders. In an earlier work, I outlined a multilayered quality assurance framework with four main levels: 1) societal obligations (what the society in question needs to do to ensure quality in multilingual public messaging), 2) interprofessional collaboration (how professionals from different relevant fields can contribute to translation quality before translation takes place), 3) the translation stage and translator's role (what the translator needs to do and how they need to do it to ensure that their translations are appropriate and effective) and 4) posttranslation quality assurance (what needs to happen after a translation has been submitted: rigorous checking and end-user feedback) (Taibi, 2018). These levels should be taken as conditions for community translation to be at optimal quality standards. Naturally, only the translation stage applies to translators; the other levels show where other stakeholders or actors can contribute.

Level 1—Societal

This level of quality assurance relates to the responsibility of the society (or rather, nation-state and regional authorities) to recognise the need and lay the groundwork for quality communication for all. It has two complementary aspects.

1) Policymaking: developing and implementing favourable policies in relation to human rights, language rights, social justice and equal access to public services, including access to information;
2) Training: providing adequate education opportunities for future translators, preferably specific to community translation and the relevant languages, or generalist translation training where the former is not possible.

Level 2—Inter-professional

This level refers to collaboration between translators and other professionals involved in the production of public service texts, such as public servants, language service managers and translation agencies. This level includes three steps:

1) Select translators: recruit trained and/or certified translators where available and establish clear alternative selection criteria in other cases;

16 *Translation and Community*

2) Prepare source texts: carefully prepare and edit original texts with a linguistically and culturally diverse readership in mind;
3) Brief translators: inform translators about the purpose of the translation and the expectations of the key stakeholders, especially in relation to accuracy and effective communication of messages.

Level 3—Translation

1) The translator's awareness of the overarching mission of community translation (empowerment): An essential and distinctive aspect of quality in community translation is the extent to which a translation serves the purpose of target community empowerment. This criterion relates to the nature of community translation and to the translator's role as a social agent. As Tyulenev (2014: 126) points out, "understanding translation as an activity meeting certain social needs underlies all theorisation of translation. No discussion of translation would be possible if translation were not (seen) as a social activity playing its distinct role in society". However, what is special about the role community translation plays in society is that it contributes to social equity by giving certain groups access to essential information. A translator within this context will be guided by the commissioner's specifications, text type, target language textual norms and conventions and so on but most importantly by their role as a social agent whose professional activity impacts people's access to information and participation in society. Arguably, in community translation more than any other field of translation, the translator would (be expected to) ask Tyulenev's question (2014: 127): "What does translation do for society?"
2) A functionalist approach to community translation: Functionalist approaches to translation are now widely accepted all over the world and in different text genres (Nord, 2014: 120, 124). They treat texts and translations "as communicative occurrences whose form is determined by the situation in which they occur and by the persons who use them as well as by cultural norms and conventions" (Nord, 2014: 127). Skopos theory, a functionalist approach par excellence, considers translation a new culturally situated "offer of information" based on an offer of information in the source text (Reiss and Vermeer, 2014 [1984]). Thus, a key criterion of translation quality is the extent to which the translation is fit for purpose and suitable for the target readership. In the case of community translation in particular, a functionalist understanding of translation allows translators to make informed decisions about the form of translation and level of register to use, as well as about the level of intervention on the original text.
3) Language appropriateness: This criterion is closely related to functionalism in translation and to empowerment and accessibility in community translation specifically. Language appropriateness in the case of community translation may, of course, be guided by text type and institutional requirements, but it will often consist of catering to the target reader as the main stakeholder: determining and using the language variant, register and lexical choices that are most appropriate for the specific target community in light of available information

on the average literacy level, age group, national and cultural background and so on.

4) Consultation with the community: To ensure suitable translations, community translators sometimes need to check with members of the target community before or while undertaking the translation assignment. Consultation may relate to any relevant issue, but it tends to particularly focus on cultural sensitivities, appropriate language varieties and lexical choices. Naturally, this process is essential at other stages of content development as well (e.g., drafting original texts or posttranslation feedback, which I discuss shortly).

5) Translation checking: At this stage, translation checking consists of the translator's own revision, editing and proofreading to ensure content accuracy, textual coherence, language consistency and stylistic appropriateness.

Level 4—Posttranslation

1) Translation checking: At the posttranslation stage, checking consists of external revision (e.g., peer revision within the same translation team, external revision arranged by translation agencies or public services). This step provides a safety net to detect oversights that might have slipped through the cracks at the translation and typesetting phases.

2) Seeking community feedback: Community translation has real-life impacts on people's lives, both positive and negative. It is therefore important to seek the feedback of target communities on the quality and suitability of translated resources and to determine the extent to which these translations serve their purpose and make a difference in society. Understandably, this will only be possible in some cases, such as large translation projects and awareness campaigns run by government agencies. For these translation commissioners, regular quality checks and impact assessments (e.g., through surveys or focus groups but also through available public service user data) are important in terms of not only communication strategy but also cost-effectiveness. Cost is often used as an argument against providing language services (Taibi and Ozolins, 2016: 19; Pym, 2021), but by checking impact and seeking community feedback, commissioners (and funders) can find out which translation efforts and approaches reduce cost (by effectively addressing social, educational, environmental or health issues) and those that only end up producing ineffective parallel texts in minority languages.

1.3.2 Accessibility

Community translation cannot achieve its social mission unless it is accessible. 'Accessibility' is a general term used in different fields to refer to easy access, ability to function in a given environment, and ability to use a product, process or system. Suojanen et al. (2015: 49) define accessibility as "efforts making products and services available to all people, regardless of their individual abilities or backgrounds".

18 *Translation and Community*

In the context of communication, accessibility includes "intralingual subtitles for the hard of hearing, Braille translations, simplified texts and the use of plain language for those with cognitive challenges or limited language skills, and so on" (Suojanen et al., 2015: 57). In the particular context of community translation, it refers to translation strategies and adaptations intended to make multilingual resources readable, comprehensible and effective. These often consist of accommodations such as simplifying specialised terms, using verbs instead of nominalisations and active rather than passive voice, breaking down complex sentences and avoiding archaic language and constructions (Cornelius, 2010; Määttä, 2020).

Accessibility is crucial for translations, "particularly user-centered translation where the central purpose is to direct texts to their specified user groups and the needs of these groups" (Suojanen et al., 2015: 57). At the same time, making texts accessible depends on several variables, including the norms and conventions of the source and target languages, literacy levels in the target community of readers and the extent to which institutional discourse in a given country or organisation favours clarity and access to information or institutional power and prestige (Katan and Taibi, 2021: 296–324). Translators with the mindset of 'translation as a public service', 'translation as a social mission', or 'translation as empowerment' work within the possibilities and constraints of their working languages, the socioeducational levels of their readerships and the requirements or expectations of the institutions and organisations generating content and commissioning translations.

Firstly, in terms of language, while certain textual features may enhance readability and accessibility across languages (e.g., absence of specialised terms, shorter sentences, clear links between ideas), languages also vary in their tolerance for complex structures (e.g., embedded and conjoined clauses) and in their internal hierarchy of formality. A good example is diglossic languages such as Arabic (Taibi and Ozolins, 2016: 48–49), where the gap between spoken (colloquial) and written (Modern Standard Arabic) language is far greater than in non-diglossic languages. The implication is that changing the mode of communication from spoken to written significantly reduces the accessibility of the information. This applies to other languages as well, but the case of diglossic languages is more noticeable.

Some languages also have additional sources of complexity and therefore require adjustable readability metrics. To take Arabic as an example again, there are types of "linguistic complexity that would not be captured by currently available automated readability analysis" (Malik et al., 2019: 171). One such source of complexity is the absence of diacritics (El-Haj and Rayson, 2016; Malik et al., 2019). Although diacritics are not usually used in texts for highly literate adults, they can improve readability significantly, especially in the case of homographs and potential ambiguity (Malik et al., 2019).

In terms of literacy level, it is well known that literacy rates vary internationally and that lower socioeconomic groups tend to have lower literacy (Reardon et al., 2013; Lesch, 2018). Minoritised language groups have historically had less access to education than dominant groups (e.g., Lesch, 2012, 2018). Migrants and refugees may come from different socioeconomic backgrounds, but at least some

What is special about community translation? 19

of them face literacy challenges in their own mother tongue (or official language of their home country).

Syrian nationals, for example, have traditionally had high literacy levels (at least prior to the 2011 civil war), but although Syrian refugee statistics in Europe confirm this in comparison with some other nationalities, they also show that approximately a third of these refugees arrive with low literacy. German data, for example, show that "24% attended only primary school and 11% had not attended school at all" (OECD, 2015: 8). What this shows is that while aiming for comprehensible translation, community translators need to have updated knowledge of the sociolinguistic and literacy backgrounds of their readers. It also means that alternative dissemination media (e.g., video in colloquial language) could be considered (see Section 1.3.3 and Chapter 7).

As for the relationship between institutional discourse and public service users, the functions of institutional language and discourse vary: Texts are sometimes used to communicate (see e.g., Chapter 4) and other times to regulate and maintain institutional status and control (see Chapter 5). Accessibility of information is not always the focus of institutional communication; an organisation may produce texts to inform the public, to comply with legal requirements or, as Barron (2012: 50) notes, "to increase the status of this organisation". Public messaging usually consists of one-way communication from more powerful institutional agents to less powerful masses (Barron, 2012: 66–67), and the power differential is often reflected in language. The information in public messages is usually based on legal or institutional regulations. These are often expressed in complex language and specialised terms (Loiacono, 2013: 11).

Accessibility, then, needs to be addressed at the source (when drafting public service texts intended for the public). This was recognised as early as the 1970s, and especially in the 1990s, with the Plain Language Movement in countries such as Australia, New Zealand, the United States (Adler, 2012: 69), South Africa (Cornelius, 2010) and the European Union (*Fight the Fog*). This movement has later spread to other countries as well, including Japan and China (Adler, 2012: 69). The movement advocates presenting public information in plain and precise language and accessible design to minimise the receiver's effort and maximise their understanding (Adler, 2012: 68). In health care, for instance, Schipper et al.'s (2016) systematic review shows that preparing lay versions of health care information enables patients to understand it better. When such lay versions are unavailable, community translators have a major role in providing accessible multilingual information. The extent to which this is possible will naturally depend not only on their agency and knowledge but also on institutional practices and expectations.

1.3.3 Dissemination media

Dissemination methods are closely linked to accessibility. As Burke (2018) points out, sociolinguistic variation in situations where community translation is needed poses serious challenges for both translation commissioners and translators. As I have mentioned, community translation is written translation: Writing in many

20 *Translation and Community*

language communities is inseparably linked to the standard variety of the language, which is only accessible to certain socioeducational layers. This calls for community translation hand in hand with an effective communication strategy. Public services, translators and researchers need to determine the dissemination media that are most appropriate and effective for each audience (age group, regional language varieties, literacy level, etc.). Taibi et al. (2019: 147), for example, found that older Arabic speakers in Australia had different preferences: Some preferred reading health awareness materials because they can be referred to whenever needed, while others preferred audiovisual media because of literacy and eyesight challenges, among other reasons.

Suojanen et al.'s (2015: 93–110) "user-centred translation" calls for empirical studies with real translation users to determine their preferences. The authors note that usability can be tested using questionnaires, focus group discussions, interviews, think-aloud protocols or eye tracking. Usability testing can generate a wealth of data that would assist in better catering to users' needs. However, while usability can be separately tested for individual dissemination media (print translation, video, website, etc.), proactive research is needed to determine user preferences before actual production of (translated) dissemination material. Here, questionnaires, focus groups and interviews can also be useful. This, naturally, is the remit of public services and researchers, not translators.

Public services have much to learn from health care dissemination research and practice. The (Australian) National Health and Medical Research Council's (2019) *Guidelines for Guidelines: Dissemination and Communication*, for example, includes advice on assessing communication needs among the target audience or segment of society, message design and dissemination methods as well as assessing effectiveness. The guidelines also cite literature pointing out that leaflet or brochure campaigns are less effective than active dissemination methods such as face-to-face education campaigns and workshops. However, the fact that one dissemination medium is found to be more preferred or impactful than others does not mean that it should be used exclusively. As Schipper et al.'s (2016) systematic review shows, a combination of different approaches can enhance the effectiveness of messaging among target audiences.

Summary

Community translation is socially oriented translatorial action that aims to serve minority and minoritised language groups by enabling them to access public service contents. As such, this area of translation practice offers an interesting field for educators, researchers and other social actors, not only those interested in mediation between languages and cultural systems but also those concerned with language policies, social equity, democracy and community participation, mass communication and public service messaging. In this translation context, 'translation as empowerment', 'translator agency', 'accessibility', 'translation quality', 'effective dissemination' and 'social impact' emerge as central notions.

Translation, by nature, requires the collaboration of different stakeholders (author, commissioner, translator, translation checker/copyeditor, publisher, etc.). Because of its social mission and the pragmatic nature of its texts, community translation requires interventions by various social agents from the government level (language policy, access to information, funding) to the level of the translation team (translator, checker, team/service manager) going through other professionals, professional bodies and public services (translator certification, selection of translators, briefing translators, writing for multilingual and multicultural audiences).

Given the nature of community translation, translation practices and products within it cannot be studied in terms of language transfer and cross-linguistic text analysis alone: They also need to be researched in terms of their relevance to the lives and interests of community translation audiences and their social impacts on those audiences. In other words, both production and reception studies are needed. Community translation practices and products also need to be studied and understood as part of a broader public service communication strategy rather than as isolated instances of communication between author and reader through translator.

Suggested activities

1) In pairs or small groups, discuss similarities and differences between the social roles of different types of translation (e.g. community translation, literary translation, audiovisual translation for entertainment purposes, news translation).
2) Think about your local or national context. How often can you see translated materials that can be described as community translations? What type of texts are translated? What social and/or language groups are not catered to? What does this tell you about language policies in your local area/national context?
3) Group discussion: Do you agree that "community translation cannot achieve its social mission unless it is accessible"? Is this consistent with the expectation that translators only translate the source text without additions, omissions or distortions? (This discussion will pave the way for Chapter 2).

Further reading

- Chapter 1 (Community translation: Definitions, characteristics and status quo) in Taibi, Mustapha and Ozolins, Uldis (2016). *Community translation*. London, Bloomsbury.

22 *Translation and Community*

This book provides an introduction to community translation as a socially oriented translation activity. It discusses different aspects of this niche area, including its empowering role, the sociocultural issues facing translators, translation approaches and quality assurance. As its title suggests, Chapter 1 discusses definitions and distinctive features of community translation and provides an overview of the situation of this area of translation practice in terms of research, training and service provision.

- Córdoba Serrano, María Sierra (2016). Translation policies and community translation: The U.S., a case study. *New Voices in Translation Studies* 14: 122–163.

The author of this paper addresses the connection between translation policies and community translation, taking the situation in the USA as an illustrative case. The paper shows how language and translation policies lead to different levels and standards of community translation provision.

Note

1 This chapter is a slightly modified version of Taibi, Mustapha (2023). Public service translation. In Wadensjö, Cecilia and Gavioli, Laura (Eds), *The Routledge handbook of public service interpreting*. London and New York: Routledge. 106–122.

References

Adler, Mark (2012). The plain language movement. In Tiersma, Peter and Solan, Lawrence (Eds.), *The Oxford handbook of language and law*. Oxford: Oxford University Press: 67–86.
Antonini, Rachele; Cirillo, Letizia; Rossato, Linda and Torresi, Ira (2017). *Non-professional interpreting and translation: State of the art and future of an emerging field of research*. Amsterdam and Philadelphia: John Benjamins.
Baker, Mona (2006). *Translation and conflict: A narrative account*. London: Routledge.
Baker, Mona (2013). Translation as an alternative space for political action. *Social Movement Studies*, 12(1): 23–47.
Barron, Anne (2012). *Public information messages: A contrastive genre analysis of state-citizen communication*. Amsterdam and Philadelphia: John Benjamins.
Bielsa, Esperanza (2016). News translation: Global or cosmopolitan connections? *Media, Culture & Society*, 38(2): 196–211.
Burke, Jean (2018). Linguistic diversity among Swahili-speakers: A challenge for translation in Australia. In Taibi, Mustapha (Ed.), *Translating for the community*. Bristol: Multilingual Matters: 156–173.
Canfora, Carmen and Ottmann, Angelika (2018). Of ostriches, pyramids, and Swiss cheese: Risks in safety-critical translations. *Translation Spaces*, 7(2): 167–201.
Córdoba Serrano, Sierra María (2016). Translation policies and community translation: The U.S., a case study. *New Voices in Translation Studies*, 14: 122–163.
Cornelius, Eleanor (2010). Plain language as alternative textualization. *Southern African Linguistics and Applied Language Studies*, 28(2): 171–183.
Corsellis, Ann (2008). *Public service interpreting: The first steps*. Basingstoke: Palgrave Macmillan.
Cronin, Michael (2003). *Translation and globalization*. London: Routledge.

What is special about community translation? 23

Dye, Thomas (1990). *Power and society: An introduction to the social sciences.* California: Brooks and Cole Publishing Company.

El-Haj, Mahmoud and Rayson, Paul (2016). OSMAN: A novel Arabic readability metric. In Calzolari, N.; Choukri, K.; Declerck, T.; Grobelnik, M.; Maegaard, B.; Mariani, J. . . . Piperidis, S. (Eds.), *Proceedings of the language resources and evaluation conference 2016*: 250–255. www.lancaster.ac.uk/staff/elhaj/docs/elhajlrec2016Arabic.pdf.

Elrha (n.d.). *When translation saves lives.* www.elrha.org/project-blog/when-translation-saves-lives.

Fernández, Fruela and Evans, Jonathan (Eds.) (2018). *The Routledge handbook of translation and politics.* Abingdon: Routledge.

García, Ignacio (2018). Volunteers and public service translation. In Taibi, Mustapha (Ed.), *Translating for the community.* Bristol: Multilingual Matters: 98–109.

Jary, David and Jary, Julia (Eds.) (2000). *Collins dictionary of sociology* (3rd Edition). Glasgow: HarperCollins.

Katan, David and Taibi, Mustapha (2021). *Translating cultures: An introduction for translators, interpreters and mediators* (3rd Edition). London and New York: Routledge.

Kelly, Dorothy (2018). Education for community translation: Thirteen key ideas. In Taibi, Mustapha (Ed.), *Translating for the community.* Bristol: Multilingual Matters: 26–41.

Kinnunen, Tuija and Koskinen, Kaisa (2010). Introduction. In Kinnunen, Tuija and Koskinen, Kaisa (Eds.), *Translators' agency.* Tampere University Press: 4–10.

Ko, Leong (2018). Community translation in the Australian context. In Taibi, Mustapha (Ed.), *Translating for the community.* Bristol: Multilingual Matters: 138–155.

Lesch, Harold (1999). Community translation: Right or privilege? In Erasmus, Mabel (Ed.), *Liaison interpreting in the community.* Pretoria: Van Schaik: 90–98.

Lesch, Harold (2012). *Gemeenskapsvertaling in Suid-Afrika: Die konteks van die ontvanger as normeringsbeginsel.* Stellenbosch: Sunmedia.

Lesch, Harold (2018). From practice to theory: Societal factors as a norm governing principle for community translation. In Taibi, Mustapha (Ed.), *Translating for the community.* Bristol: Multilingual Matters: 69–95.

Loiacono, Rocco (2013). *Legal terms as proper names: The translation of culturally specific legal terms in bilateral agreements between Australia and Italy.* PhD thesis, University of Western Australia.

Määttä, Simo K. (2020). Translating child protection assessments for ELF users: Accommodation, accessibility, and accuracy. *Journal of English as a Lingua Franca*, 9(2): 287–307.

Malik, Abdulaziz; El-Haj, Mahmoud and Paasche-Orlow, Michael K. (2019). Readability of patient educational materials in English versus Arabic. *Health Literacy Research and Practice*, 3(3): e170–e173.

Marais, Kobus (2011). The representation of agents of translation in (South) Africa: Encountering Gentzler and Madonella. *Translation and Interpreting Studies*, 6(2): 189–206.

National Health and Medical Research Council (2019). *Guidelines for guidelines: Dissemination and communication.* www.nhmrc.gov.au/guidelinesforguidelines/implement/dissemination-and-communication.

Nord, Christiane (2014). Functionalist approaches. In Gambier, Yves and van Doorslaer, Luc (Eds.), *Handbook of translation studies.* Amsterdam and Philadelphia: John Benjamins: 120–128.

OECD (2015). Is this humanitarian migration crisis different? *Migration Policy Debates* 7. www.oecd.org/migration/Is-this-refugee-crisis different.pdf

O'Hagan, Minako (2011). Introduction: Community translation: Translation as a social activity and its possible consequences in the advent of Web 2.0 and beyond. In O'Hagan, Minako (Ed.), *Linguistica Antverpiensia: Special Issue on Translation as a Social Activity*, 10: 11–23.

Paloposki, Outi (2007). Translators' agency in 19th-century Finland. In Gambier, Yves et al. (Eds.), *Doubts and directions in translation studies: Selected contributions from the EST Congress, Lisbon 2004.* Amsterdam and Philadelphia: John Benjamins: 335–345.

24 Translation and Community

Pérez González, Luis and Susam-Sarayeva, Sebnem (2012). Non-professionals translating and interpreting: Participatory and engaged perspectives. *The Translator*, 18(2): 149–165.

Pym, Anthony (2021). Translation and language learning as policy options: Questions of costs and literacy development. *Translation & Interpreting: The International Journal of Translation and Interpreting Research*, 13(2): 24–37.

Reardon, Sean F.; Valentino, Rachel A.; Kalogrides, Demetra; Shores, Kenneth A. and Greenberg, Erica H. (2013). *Patterns and trends in racial academic achievement gaps among states, 1999–2011.* https://cepa.stanford.edu/content/patterns-and-trends-racial-academic-achievement-gaps-among-states-1999-2011.

Reiss, Katharina and Vermeer, Hans (2014 [1984]). *Towards a general theory of translational action: Skopos theory explained.* Translated by Christiane Nord. London and New York: Routledge.

Rueda-Acedo, Alicia (2018). From the classroom to the job market: Integrating service-learning and community translation in a legal translation course. In Taibi, Mustapha (Ed.), *Translating for the community.* Bristol: Multilingual Matters: 42–68.

Schäffner, Christina (2020). Translators' roles and responsibilities. In Angelone, Erik; Ehrensberger-Dow, Maureen and Massey, Gary (Eds.), *The Bloomsbury companion to language industry studies.* London: Bloomsbury: 63–90.

Schipper, Karen; Bakker, Minne; de Wit, Maarten P. T.; Ket, Johannes and Abma, Tineke A. (2016). Strategies for disseminating recommendations or guidelines to patients: A systematic review. *Implementation Science*, 11: 82.

Suojanen, Tytti; Koskinen, Kaisa and Tuominen, Tiina (2015). *User-centered translation.* London: Routledge.

Susam-Sarayeva, Sebnem and Pérez González, Luis (Eds.) (2012). *Non-professionals translating and interpreting: Participatory and engaged perspectives. Special Issue of the Translator*, 18(2).

Taibi, Mustapha (2011). Public service translation. In Malmkjaer, Kirsten and Windle, Kevin (Eds.), *The Oxford handbook of translation studies.* Oxford: Oxford University Press: 214–227.

Taibi, Mustapha (2018). Quality assurance in community translation. In Taibi, Mustapha (Ed.), *Translating for the community.* Bristol: Multilingual Matters: 7–25.

Taibi, Mustapha and Ozolins, Uldis (2016). *Community translation.* London and New York: Bloomsbury.

Taibi, Mustapha; Liamputtong, Pranee and Polonsky, Michael (2019). Impact of translated health information on CALD older people's health literacy: A pilot study. In Ji, Meng; Taibi, Mustapha and Crezee, Ineke (Eds.), *Multicultural health translation, interpreting and communication.* London: Routledge: 138–158.

Tomozeiu, Daniel (2016). Defining 'community' for community translation. *New Voices in Translation Studies*, 14: 190–209.

Tymoczko, Maria (2000). Translation and political engagement. *The Translator*, 6(1): 23–47.

Tymoczko, Maria (2007). *Enlarging translation, empowering translators.* St. Jerome.

Tyulenev, Sergey (2014). *Translation and society.* London and New York: Routledge.

Way, Catherine (2006). Translating for the authorities: The role of the translator. In Benelli, Graciano and Tonini, Giampaolo (Eds.), *Studi in Ricordo di Carmen Sánchez Montero.* Universitá degli Studi di Trieste: 579–588.

Way, Catherine (2016). The challenges and opportunities of legal translation and translator training in the 21st century. *International Journal of Communication*, 10: 1009–1029.

Wolf, Michaela (2007). Introduction: The emergence of a sociology of translation. In Wolf, Michaela and Fukari, Alexandra (Eds.), *Constructing a sociology of translation.* Amsterdam and Philadelphia: John Benjamins: 1–3.

2 Your role as a community translator

This chapter presents a general discussion of the role of translators as stipulated in codes of ethics (especially the notions of impartiality and accuracy), followed by a discussion of translators as intercultural mediators and as social agents, as reflected in existing translation studies literature. This is followed by a discussion of the specific and special role of community translators within their local or national context. The main points covered are:

- Community translators as members of their (smaller) community and (larger) society;
- Community translators as members of a profession;
- Community translators as text processors;
- Community translators as communication facilitators;
- Community translators as intercultural mediators;
- Community translators as (proactive) social agents.

2.1 The role of translators

The role of translators has traditionally been perceived, theorised and codified as that of detached and impartial professionals whose job consists of accurately transferring meanings from one language to another. This role entails that the translator is responsible not for the contents of the source text but for faithfully rendering what is in the source text without any evaluation, addition or omission. Although there is no consensus worldwide (McDonough Dolmaya, 2011; Feng, 2014), codes of ethics for translators and interpreters would often tell you that the role of translators and interpreters is "to convey meaning between people and cultures faithfully, accurately, and impartially" (American Translators Association (ATA), n.d.: 1), for instance this one from the Australian Institute of Interpreters and Translators (AUSIT):

> Interpreters and translators play an important role in facilitating parties who do not share a common language to communicate effectively with each other.

DOI: 10.4324/9781003367741-3

26   *Translation and Community*

They aim to ensure that the full intent of the communication is conveyed. Interpreters and translators are not responsible for what the parties communicate, only for complete and accurate transfer of the message. They do not allow bias to influence their performance; likewise, they do not soften, strengthen or alter the messages being conveyed.

(AUSIT, 2012: 5)

The American Translators Association Code of Ethics and Professional Practice refers to the role of translators using the term "linguistic integrity":

Linguistic integrity is at the core of what translators and interpreters do. Faithful, accurate and impartial translation or interpretation conveys the message as the author or speaker intended with the same emotional impact on the audience. Linguistic integrity is not achieved when the target language is rendered word-for-word from the source language. Linguistic integrity implies that nothing is added or omitted in the target message.

(ATA, n.d.: 1)

Along the same lines, AUSIT's code of ethics stresses the expectation that translators must provide an accurate, optimal and complete rendition of content and intent:

5.1 Interpreters and translators provide accurate renditions of the source utterance or text in the target language. Accurate is defined for this purpose as optimal and complete, without distortion or omission and preserving the content and intent of the source message or text. Interpreters and translators are able to provide an accurate and complete rendition of the source message using the skills and understanding they have acquired through their training and education.
5.2 Interpreters and translators do not alter, add to, or omit anything from the content and intent of the source message.

(AUSIT, 2012: 10)

Based on such statements in ethics codes, translators are expected to do the following:

1) Identify (the intended) meaning (in source texts, the texts to be translated);
2) Convey meaning accurately from one language to another, including not only the content of a text but also its tone ("they do not soften, strengthen or alter the messages being conveyed");
3) Facilitate communication between parties who speak/read different languages;
4) Convey meaning impartially (i.e., without taking the writer's or the reader's side).

Identifying the intended meanings in a text requires mindful reading and textual analysis, including awareness of the type of text being processed. Conveying

Your role as a community translator 27

meaning from one language to another requires knowledge of the two language systems. Facilitating communication between parties requires a good understanding of the communicative situation and of the backgrounds of those parties (cultural contexts, previous experience with the materials at hand, level of knowledge, etc.). Impartial transfer of meanings from one language to another requires a good understanding of the translator's position and role and of the potential implications of any translation choice.

At face value, the principles of accuracy, completeness, faithfulness and impartiality may appear straightforward and commonsensical. After all, translators work on what other people (authors) have written: They are not the intended readers of the texts they work with, and they are therefore expected to present the content and intent of the texts to the intended readers in the same way the original authors wanted them to be presented, without any omission, addition or alteration. However, this oversimplifies a number of issues and processes involved in translation and communication and overlooks many complexities, subtleties and dilemmas relating to notions such as 'intended meaning', 'accurate rendition' and 'facilitating communication'.

A couple of examples will illustrate that translation is a matter of context, and so is the role of translators (see Box 2.1).

Box 2.1   Context-sensitive translator role

Example 1: A translator is given a French novel to translate into Chinese. The commissioner (the person or agency requesting this translation) advises the translator that the description of characters and places in the original novel might be too detailed for Chinese readers and therefore recommends reducing such descriptions as much as possible. The translator is also aware that the main purpose of the novel is aesthetic, not informative: the readers of the translation expect to find the translated novel enjoyable as a piece of literature; they are not expecting a report about the French culture or an accurate rendition of every detail in the novel whether important or not.

Example 2: While translating a journalistic text from Persian into English, a translator comes across a statement saying (literally): "We swear by the blood of our pious martyrs and the honour of our mothers, spouses and daughters that we will remain loyal to the cause". Judging that the flowery language would not be suitable in the English translation, the translator opts for the following: "We vow to remain loyal to the cause".

Example 3: A translator is translating an official certificate from Arabic into English and finds an incomplete sentence that would be translated as follows: "Based on information received from the *Moqaddam* of Al-Nassim

28 *Translation and Community*

> District, the undersigned certifies that the person above is currently unem-
> ployed and has two". To explain the meaning of *moqaddam*, the translator
> adds the following footnote: "* Low ranking municipal officer in Mo-
> rocco, appointed to represent and inform about a district". The translator
> also adds [sic] at the end of the sentence to indicate that it is incomplete
> in the source text, not because of an oversight on the part of the translator
> (see Chapter 8 on the translation of personal official documents).

These examples show that translators proceed differently in different contexts:
Sometimes, it is appropriate to reduce or leave out content (Examples 1 and 2);
adapt to the stylistic norms of the target language, culture or dissemination medium
(Example 2) or provide additional information in the form of footnotes or in-text
clarification (Example 3). This suggests that although ethics codes may outline the
general principles and expectations relating to the role of translators, these must
not be taken literally and cannot be applied across the board regardless of the translation context and the text type. References to facilitating communication (in ethics codes and translation studies literature, e.g., O'hagan and Ashworth, 2002: 94;
Samuelsson-Brown, 2010: 41; Mundt, 2019) also raise several questions about the
nature and limits of this facilitating role, as well as about potential clashes between
this facilitation and impartial and accurate meaning transfer. They also lead to a
discussion of the role of translators as cultural mediators (Section 2.2 in this chapter) and as social agents (Section 2.3).

2.2 Translators as cultural mediators

As I have highlighted, to facilitate communication between people (i.e., between
the source text writer and the target text user), translators need to have, among
other things, a good understanding of the cultural backgrounds of those parties.
Texts are written in one language and translated into another and, because language
and culture are inextricably intertwined, both text comprehension (the translator's
reading) and text production (translator's meaning transfer in a new text) require
knowledge of and mediation between the relevant languages and cultures. As Hatim and Mason note:

> The translator stands at the centre of this dynamic process of communication,
> as a mediator between the producer of a source text and whoever are its TL
> [target language] receivers. The translator is first and foremost a mediator
> between two parties for whom mutual communication might otherwise be
> problematic and this is true of the translator of patents, contracts, verse or
> fiction.
>
> (2013 [1990]: 223)

Your role as a community translator 29

Translators' footnotes such as the one about *moqaddam* are just one example of cultural mediation in translation: The translator explicitly tells the translation reader what this culture-specific term means, thereby mediating between the cultural context of the source text writer and that of the target text reader.

However, cultural mediation in translation is not always this explicit: It can be seamlessly integrated into the translation without explicitly telling the reader about the cultural explanation, elaboration or adaptation that has taken place. In the example in Box 2.2, the French translator of a Spanish tourist information text understands *Comunitat Valenciana* in its cultural context and translates it as *Région de València* (Valencia Region). The translator neither translates the term *comunitat* literally as *communauté* ('community') nor unnecessarily explains that the term refers to a territorial, political and administrative division in Spain. After all, the text offers tourist information with the intent to appeal to prospective tourists, not to instruct them about the political system or territorial divisions of Spain.

Box 2.2   Translation from Spanish to French

Spanish

Te ayudamos a escoger entre un buen número de experiencias de todo tipo en la **Comunitat Valenciana** *para que tu visita tenga muchos recuerdos imborrables. ¡Y lo hacemos muy fácil con la ayuda de un sencillo buscador!*

French

Nous vous aidons à choisir parmi un large éventail d'expériences de toutes sortes dans la **Région de València** *pour que votre visite soit riche en souvenirs inoubliables. Laissez-vous guider par notre moteur de recherche simple et intuitif!*

Whether they do so explicitly or implicitly, translators need to deal with cultural differences at a range of levels. The most typical level consists of culture-specific terms relating to areas such as clothing (e.g., *Hanfu* and *cheongsam* in Chinese; *burnous* and *jilbab* in Arabic), food (e.g., hot dog, schnitzel, sandwich, wrapper, high tea), religion (e.g., altar, christening, circumambulation, penitence) or customs and traditions (e.g., wedding reception, *la Tomatina* in Spanish or *Tanz in den Mai* in German). These can be transferred unmediated, following the strategy of foreignisation (keeping the culture-specific term as it is—foreign and unfamiliar) or mediated through domestication (adapting the culture-specific term to the cultural context of the target text and readers, e.g., by replacing it with a more

30   *Translation and Community*

generic and culturally familiar term). (See Venuti, 2018 [1995] on the concepts of 'foreignization' and 'domestication'.) However, culture-specific terms are just the tip of the cultural iceberg: While customs, rituals, food, dress and so on are visible cultural signs, the most significant features of cultural identity and difference are value orientations, which are usually not as visible (Brake et al., 1995: 34–39).

Among the cultural orientations and conventions that are closely relevant to the work of translators—yet less often noted or discussed—are writing style and textual conventions, which may vary from one culture or language to another. Katan and Taibi (2021: 297–310) explain that certain cultures have a preference for KILCy (keep it long and complete) texts, while others tend to use a KISSy (keep it short and simple) style and text organisation. Among other things, KILC is characterised by a high information load, complex information and sentence structures, a high level of detail and a rich use of rhetorical language. A KISS-oriented culture or subculture, on the other hand, would prioritise clarity, simplicity, a reader-friendly tone and a focus on the main points or facts to be communicated. Translators processing texts between the two extremes often need to mediate between the two orientations to make their translations acceptable.

Another example of the need for translators' mediation between cultural orientations and conventions is the case of business correspondence. As Zhu (2005), for example, demonstrates, genres such as official communication or sales invitations as well as text functions such as persuasion vary from one culture to another. The author shows that while a logical approach (*logos*) may be the standard persuasive strategy in Western cultures, an emotional approach (*qing* in Chinese/*pathos* in classical Greek philosophy) has an important place in Chinese business contexts and culture in general.

Zhu (2005) also shows that managers' views on what constitutes an appropriate persuasive strategy vary depending on their cultural background. The notion of power is also crucial: Although power relationships exist in business contexts across cultures, they manifest themselves more saliently in some cultural contexts than in others. Zhu notes, for instance, that official letters in Chinese are categorized into *shangxing* (when the writer has less power than the addressee), *pingxing* (writing from equal to equal) and *xiaxing* (more powerful party writing to their subordinate). In terms of genres, conventions and rhetorical strategies, translators working with international business communication would understandably be required to mediate between writers and audiences who are culturally distant. In terms of power relationships, translators are also expected to be aware of cultural differences and nuances, as well as the power connotations and implications of each translation decision and choice.

In these and any other translation contexts, the translator is positioned as a cultural mediator between the reader and writer because they are the only person able to rewrite the source text for a culturally and linguistically different readership that does not have the same knowledge, assumptions and expectations (Bedeker and Feinauer, 2006; Liddicoat, 2016; Katan and Taibi, 2021). As Liddicoat (2016:

Your role as a community translator 31

356) puts it, "the translator is the sole true intercultural communicator in this communication process and mediates a text that was not designed for this intercultural communication for an audience that does not necessarily see it as intercultural communication". The translator, therefore, is bound not only by the principles of professional codes of ethics and practice but also by their role as someone who is able to understand meanings and texts in their source language and cultural context and is expected to communicate them across the linguistic and cultural divide. The translator as a cultural mediator is "a practitioner in diversity, in which acts of interpretation and meaning making are fundamental to communication" (Liddicoat, 2016: 355). The type and extent of mediation will, of course, be determined by the text type and the translation context (please see further discussion in Chapters 3–8).

2.3 Translators as social agents

I showed in Chapter 1 that one essential distinctive feature of community translation is that it has a social function in a local or national context in the sense that it addresses the communication needs of minority or minoritised language groups. I also pointed out that in exercising their role as communication facilitators, community translators contribute to ensuring more equitable access to public service information, thus acting as social agents. Quoting Jary and Jary's (2000) definition of agency again, we can affirm that community translators engage in "human action . . . which makes a difference to a human relationship or behaviour". Translators, in general, (can) act as social agents, and (may) have the ability to trigger change in societies, through the works they choose or accept to translate and the manner in which they translate them (Tymoczko, 2014: 189–216). In this book, I am more interested in the translator's social agency in terms of translation approach.

It is now widely accepted that the work of translators takes place in and is shaped by their social contexts (Wolf, 2007, 2010, 2011; Wolf and Fukari, 2007; Tyulenev, 2014; Berneking, 2016). As future professionals, translation trainees develop translation skills and knowledge about translation within social contexts (e.g., university program, further education course, practicum, mentorship, relationships with peers, teachers and mentors). As professionals, translators undertake their work within a sociocultural context as well: an international order (where some countries are more powerful than others and some languages are more dominant than others), a national political system (where there are more or less human rights or more or less freedom and democratic engagement), industrial relationships (with employers, clients, translation agencies, revisers, and so on), as well as professional norms and reference groups (professional associations, accreditation bodies, established professionals, etc.). In turn, translation as a product is produced and received in a social context: It is valued—or not—as an essential medium to access knowledge, it is widely used or restricted to certain social circles and it is in or out of line with the dominant social identity and ideology.

32 *Translation and Community*

As a social agent, the translator consciously or unconsciously plays a significant role through the translations they produce. It goes without saying that they facilitate access to information, knowledge and entertainment which would not be accessible without translation. More importantly, translators exercise social agency in the translation approaches they choose. Paloposki (2010: 104), for example, notes that although all translation work involves some degree of translator voice, the use of translator footnotes may more visibly add "an extra voice, a resisting opinion, a formative comment". The use of footnotes (as well as other strategies) depends on the genre and type of text being translated, the dominant translation norms and role expectations and the extent to which a translator is willing to enact individual agency.

The translator's agency does not need to be—and often is not—as explicitly displayed as in the case of footnotes. Hatim and Mason (1997: 147) noted decades ago that translators may intervene in the transfer process and feed their own knowledge, beliefs and ideology into the translation process and product. Note, however, that the use of "may" in the previous sentence is not an endorsement of departures away from the professional role outlined in codes of ethics, as explained earlier in this chapter. Rather, the point is that for one reason or another, some translators either consciously and explicitly choose to intervene ideologically in their representations of source texts (Farahzad, 2003; Valdeón, 2014; Pan and Huang, 2021; Leonardi, 2020) or unconsciously influence the ideological tone of the texts they translate as a result of their translation choices, language resources and repertoire limitations (Munday, 2007).

Leonardi (2020: 101–110) provides several examples of how translators (and publishers) adapt and manipulate children's literature to serve ideological purposes or adjust to the dominant social, cultural or political norms. One of these examples is the British and American translations of the Italian children's fantasy novel *Pinocchio*, by Mary Alice Murray and Walter Cramp respectively. Leonardi shows how Murray's translation follows the Italian source text quite closely and retains the violence depicted or suggested in the original, while Cramp's translation/adaptation tends to soften or leave out instances of violence. To illustrate the difference in approach, Leonardi (2020: 105) provides a comparison of the following two excerpts, taken from Murray's and Cramp's translations, respectively (emphasis added), which shows that Cramp makes the scene less dramatic by softening the violence and leaving out reference to the cricket's suffering:

> **Murray:** At these last words Pinocchio jumped up in a rage, and snatching a wooden hammer from the bench he threw it at the Talking-cricket. Perhaps he never meant to hit him; **but unfortunately it struck him exactly on the head, so that the poor Cricket had scarcely breath to cry cri-cri-cri and then remained dried up and flattened against the wall.**

> **Cramp:** At these words Pinocchio jumped up enraged, and taking a hammer from a bench flung it at the Talking Cricket. Perhaps he did not intend to do such a thing; **but unfortunately the hammer struck the poor little Cricket in the head and killed him.**

2.4 The role of community translators

As I indicated in Chapter 1 as well as in other publications (Taibi, 2011; Taibi and Ozolins, 2016; Taibi, 2022), community translators have an empowering role in society: Through their work, they enable readers of minority languages to access public service information, to make informed decisions in their lives and to engage more actively in their society. As Cluver (1992) and Lesch (1999, 2004) observed decades ago, in societies characterised by unequal power and uneven levels of access, community translators are expected not only to transfer meanings from one language to another, which AUSIT (2012) states, but also to address the needs of the intended readers and ensure that the information is accessible to them. However, community translators do not serve members of minority or disempowered groups only; they also work for and are often paid by government departments and agencies that insist that their public messaging should be translated accurately in terms of both content and form (Taibi and Ozolins, 2016: 66); for instance, in some cases, they expect key terms and institutional names to be kept in the original language.

In a doctoral study with Japanese translators based in Japan and Australia, Fukuno observed that community translators often face a dilemma between being impartial and being advocates, or in other terms between professional and moral considerations and obligations:

> Professional translators involved in community translation and therefore grappling with the ethical principle of impartiality and the professional mission for 'community empowerment'. . . may be in an even more acute dilemma regarding their ethical roles as translators.
>
> (Fukuno, 2023a: 15)

Fukuno (2023a) based her study on 71 questionnaires, 15 semi-structured interviews and three case studies. Her aims consisted of exploring how translators perceive and experience their roles and ethical positions; how they negotiate between their own moral values and professional ethics; how these perceptions, interpretations and negotiations are reflected in translation decisions; and the factors that may influence such perceptions and negotiations. Among other findings, the study reveals that while the code of ethics is recognised as an external authority aiming to ensure consistency of approach among all translators, "some translators are in empathetic and caring dialogues with TT [target text] readers and bring in their personal experiences, individual senses of conscience and understandings of social conscience" (Fukuno, 2023a: 195). In doing so, translators construct images of their audience based on the translation context and engage in a reflection about the social relationships and moral duties involved.

To understand the position of community translators and the dilemma they may (and often do) face regarding their role, we need to consider the complex nature of their work and the complexity of their network of identities and memberships: First, community translators are members of a profession; second, they are text

34   *Translation and Community*

processors; third, they are communication facilitators; fourth, they are intercultural mediators and finally, they are (proactive) social agents.

As translators who are affiliated with a professional body, either through formal membership or through their identification with the profession at large, community translators are bound by the applicable code of ethics, where there is one, or at least the main principles of accuracy and impartiality where no formal code of ethics has been adopted in the national or regional context. This is a key expectation to ensure that clients and intermediaries, including both individuals and organisations using and/or offering language services, trust the profession, the professional and the translation product (Abdallah and Koskinen, 2007; Chesterman, 2016; Pym, 2020). As Chesterman (2016: 179) notes, "Translators, in order to survive as translators, must be trusted by all parties involved, both as a profession and individually. They must therefore work in such a way as to create and maintain this trust. . . . Without this trust, the profession would collapse, and so would its practice".

As text processors, community translators are both readers (of a source text) and writers (of a translation). As readers, they engage with the source text to understand its genre, type, content and intent. If they are experienced and qualified translators, they will start at the highest level, first getting a sense of the genre, type and function of the text. If they are less experienced or not qualified, they may be bogged down in the meanings of single words and sentences. Generally speaking, a translator who is struggling with meaning at this level is less likely to engage with broader translation issues and ethical concerns such as the translator's role in society. Their understanding of the code of ethics will also tend to be literal, consisting mainly of faithfully and linearly reflecting the words and sentences of the source text in a new language and document. The different levels of understanding and competence also manifest themselves at the writing stage: Although this might not be always the case (especially due to the translator's target language proficiency), a translator who processes texts as texts, taking into consideration their type and communicative function, is more likely to produce a coherent and fit-for-purpose translation, one that not only conveys the communicative intent of the source text but also conforms to the norms and conventions of the target language.

In relation to this point, community translators serving as communication facilitators is an essential part of their identity and role. As I have shown, even some ethics codes stress the facilitating role of translators, that is, that they facilitate communication between parties who do not share the same language. In their book titled *The Translator as Communicator*, Hatim and Mason (1997) argue that the act of translating consists of, and should be viewed as, an act of communicating. This means that the translator needs to consider the source text as a record of a past act of communication and their translation as a new act of communication. It also means that the focus of attention is the pragmatics of language use rather than language per se (i.e., what is intended by the entire text and in each of its components based on what we know about how language is conventionally and creatively used in a real-life context). Another essential implication of this understanding of translation is that the participants in the communication act must be kept in mind,

Your role as a community translator   35

with reference to both the source text and, most important, the target text, as the new readership may have different needs and expectations. However, in terms of translator role, even when there is agreement that translation consists of a communication act, the question remains as to how much should or can be communicated beyond what is explicitly said in the source text (how to address the needs of the new readers without violating the ethics code).

Hatim and Mason (1997: 1) also add that translation is *"an act of communication which attempts to relay, across cultural and linguistic boundaries, another act of communication (which may have been intended for different purposes and different readers/hearers)"* (italics in the original). What adds to the complexity of the translator's role, especially in the context of community translation, is that they are intercultural mediators. As they exercise their profession and strive to be fair to all relevant stakeholders; as they read, process and rewrite texts and as they engage in converting one communicative act into another in a different language, they are aware that there are considerable cultural differences and issues that need to be addressed. They may, for example, realise that without further explication, certain cultural notions may remain unclear or unappreciated or that without adaptation and domestication, some culture-specific ways of structuring texts, reasoning or appealing to the reader might not work for the new readership. Again, we may agree about the principle that community translators are cultural mediators but not reach consensus about the extent to which they may intervene to bridge the cultural gaps.

At the same time, community translators are members of their society and their (smaller) community (e.g., ethnic, religious, political, etc.). "We do not cease being members of society with responsibility to it when we exercise our profession, least of all in translation", as Drugan (2017: 137) rightly acknowledges. The same applies to membership in smaller communities within the larger society. Looking back at what I said earlier about trust in the work of translators and in their profession, as well as the requirements of ethics codes, one would expect community translators to remain impartial and not manipulate texts in order to serve the interests of the people they identify with, either in the national context or internationally. However, what I pointed out in relation to social agency might suggest that it is acceptable, or even commendable, for community translators to exercise agency through their translations to achieve social change, promote human rights, resist dominant discourses and so on.

In cases such as South Africa, where there has been a long history of racial discrimination and social inequity, it might be justifiable for black translators (and other translators who share their political and ideological position) to perceive their role as involving a duty to advocate for the disadvantaged layers of their society. Similarly, in contexts where community translation is provided mainly to migrants and refugees (Australia, the USA, Canada, Spain, etc.), community translators are often migrants or children of migrants (Campbell, 2005: 31). While professional accreditation puts translators in a position of "double agency" between mainstream institutions and the periphery (disempowered ethnic communities), as Campbell

36 *Translation and Community*

(2005: 31) puts it, some may identify more with their disadvantaged group and assume an activist role. However, a clear line must be drawn between translator activism and community translation. Volunteer translators or those who work for activist organisations may engage in resistance, activism, lobbying and so on (see e.g., Gould and Tahmasebian, 2020). For community translators, social agency is not synonymous with activism; rather, it consists of doing translations, facilitating communication and mediating between people, organisations and cultures through a translation approach that empowers communities but at the same time remains within the principles of professionalism.

Fukuno (2023a: 180) argues that the community translator's responsibility revolves round accuracy of meaning transfer and ensuring readability for the target readership. "Such responsibility reflects two aspects of the translators' agency", the author continues: 1) mentally constructing reader profiles and 2) making judgments about how accuracy is to be interpreted in each context and how to balance accuracy and readability. She concludes, "In community translation settings, readability causes no conflict with the accuracy of the pragmatic meaning, but it is a necessary quality for the accuracy of the pragmatic meaning transfer" (180). Fukuno's participants revealed that they had both impartiality and advocacy (moral agency in society and a sense of duty towards target readers) as central dimensions in their role perceptions (2023a: 193).

As pointed out in Chapter 1, Taibi and Ozolins (2016: 70–71) had earlier explained that a functionalist approach to translation (see Chapter 3), coupled with continued mindfulness of the overarching function of community translation and its distinctive features, provides answers to many questions surrounding the role of community translators:

1) A functionalist approach is consistent with the role of community translators as active social agents, as functionalism empowers translators by "elevating them to equal status with authors, editors, and clients, entrusting them to make appropriate, rational decisions that best realize the intended cross-cultural communication" (Gentzler, 2001: 71);
2) The function of the translation is taken as the most important criterion to determine translation approach and decisions;
3) A translator adopting a functionalist approach always keeps in mind the distinction between text types (e.g., informative, operative, expressive) and the procedures appropriate for each one of them (see Chapters 3–8);
4) Functionalist translation theorists recognise the legitimacy of different types of translation and levels of intervention, including summary translations, adapted versions, transcreations and multimodal translation (using different modes of communication), which may be required in community contexts depending on existing needs and preferences.

A functional understanding of and approach to community translation can ensure the coexistence of, rather than a clash between, the different dimensions I described of the translator's identity and role (professional ethics, processing texts, facilitating communication, cultural mediation and social agency).

Firstly, functionalism can resolve many issues relating to the dilemma of accuracy (faithfulness to the source text) vs. appropriateness (the extent to which the translation is appropriate for the purpose, occasion or audience), as the translation brief and context are taken into consideration. Secondly, it allows a role expansion for community translators to communicate with commissioners or their intermediaries (e.g., public services, translation agencies) and advise when there are issues with the source text (e.g., clarity issues or culturally inappropriate content) or with the dissemination medium (e.g., when audiovisual translation is more appropriate and effective than written materials). This connects the dimensions of professionalism, text processing, communication facilitation, cultural mediation and social agency without violating ethics principles or falling into advocacy in the sense of activism.

As Abdallah (2010: 42) and Fukuno (2023a, 2023b) note, the translator will always face situations where they will need to independently solve the conflict between their moral values and professional norms, as well as the requirements of the working context. However, while a functionalist approach does not provide readily available answers for every question and situation, it offers a useful framework for the translator's assessment of translation tasks, communicative situations and relationships between parties and communities and for their informed decisions.

Summary

When considering your role as a (community) translator, you will most probably find scholarly and professional publications stating that translators are expected to be impartial professionals who accurately transfer meaning from one language to another. Translators are often referred to as language specialists who faithfully render the content of source texts without any additions or omissions. This is important for the translation profession to be trusted by clients and other stakeholders. At the same time, you will be aware that your community translation work will be bound by professional standards and involve engagement with an existing source text, a relationship with the local community (sharing the same language, ethnicity, culture, socioeconomic status, religion, etc.) and a need to facilitate communication and intercultural understanding between two parties. It might also trigger a need to act as a responsible citizen and community member promoting well-being and social justice, especially in situations where there is discrimination, marginalisation and social inequity.

If you read about manipulation in translation, translation and ideology or translation and activism, you will certainly find many cases where translators, journalists, publishers and other agents fail to comply with the principles of accuracy and impartiality. Some do so to serve the interests of

38 *Translation and Community*

powerful regimes, organisations and individuals; others do it to resist dominant discourses, or to advocate for powerless or oppressed groups. However, community translation is not about activism; rather, it is a professional language service that aims to ensure access to information and participation for linguistically disadvantaged groups. As a citizen or community member, you will have appropriate channels, venues and ways to advocate for social change, social equity or human rights, but as a community translator, this does not fall within your role or job description.

As a community translator, you are a social agent, but your social agency is not the same as activism: It is agency that is exercised through a professional service that grants people access to information and enables public services to communicate with all the layers of society. Your agency lies in applying a translation approach that takes into consideration the needs of the target audience and, by doing so, empowering communities. It can also include professional communication with other stakeholders (e.g., source text producers, translation agencies) to ensure that source texts are free from language or logical inconsistencies, to seek further information about the intended audience or to discuss translation choices when necessary. An appropriate translation approach will usually consist of a functional understanding of the source and target texts, which includes awareness of the communicative purpose of the translation and the sociocultural profiles and needs of the target readers.

Suggested activities

1) Search for two or three ethics codes for translators (in your own country and internationally) and compare their principles and requirements with the role of community translators as outlined in this chapter.
2) Think of five examples of situations or topics where a community translator would need to mediate between cultures. Write a 500-word discussion of the type of mediation that would be professionally acceptable.

Further reading

- Chapter 2 (Sociocultural issues in community translation) in Taibi, Mustapha and Ozolins, Uldis (2016). *Community translation*. London, Bloomsbury.

This chapter deals with culture and sociocultural challenges in community translation, which also relate to the role of community translators.

- Fukuno, Maho (2023b). Translators' ethics in community translation: A case study of English–Japanese translators in the Australian system. In González,

Erika; Stachowiak-Szymczak, Katarzyna and Amanatidou, Despina (Eds), *Community translation: Research and practice*. London: Routledge: 42–67.

This chapter is based on Fukuno's doctoral study; in it, she explores the perceptions of English–Japanese translators of their professional role.

References

Abdallah, Kristiina (2010). Translators' agency in production networks. In Kinnunen, Tuija and Koskinen, Kaisa (Eds.), *Translators' agency*. Tampere: Tampere University Press: 11–46.

Abdallah, Kristiina and Koskinen, Kaisa (2007). Managing trust: Translating and the network economy. *Meta*, 52(4): 673–687. DOI: 10.7202/017692ar.

ATA [American Translators Association] (n.d.). *American Translators Association code of ethics and professional practice*. https://atanet.org/wp-content/uploads/2020/06/code_of_ethics_commentary.pdf.

AUSIT (2012). *AUSIT code of ethics and code of conduct*. https://ausit.org/wp-content/uploads/2020/02/Code_Of_Ethics_Full.pdf.

Bedeker, Laetitia and Feinauer, Ilse (2006). The translator as cultural mediator. *Southern African Linguistics and Applied Language Studies*, 24(2): 133–141. DOI: 10.2989/1607361 0609486412.

Berneking, Steve (2016). A sociology of translation and the central role of the translator. *The Bible Translator*, 67(3): 265–281. DOI: 10.1177/205167701667023.

Brake, Terence; Medina-Walker, Danielle and Walker, Thomas (1995). *Doing business internationally: The guide to cross-cultural success*. Burr Ridge, IL: Irwin.

Campbell, Stuart (2005). English translation and linguistic hegemony in the global era. In Anderman, Gunilla M. and Rogers, Margaret (Eds.), *In and out of English: For better, for worse?* Clevedon, Buffalo and Toronto: Multilingual Matters: 27–38.

Chesterman, Andrew (2016). *Memes of translation: The spread of ideas in translation theory (Revised edition)*. Amsterdam and Philadelphia: John Benjamins.

Cluver, A. (1992). Trends in the changes of translating domains: An overview. In Kruger, Alet (Ed.), *Changes in translating domains*. Pretoria: University of South Africa: 195–216.

Drugan, Joanna (2017). Ethics and social responsibility in practice: Interpreters and translators engaging with and beyond the professions. *The Translator*, 23(2): 126–142. DOI: 10.1080/13556509.2017.1281204.

Farahzad, Farzaneh (2003). Manipulation in translation. *Perspectives*, 11(4): 269–281. DOI: 10.1080/0907676X.2003.9961480.

Feng, Man (2014). Cross-cultural comparison on codes of ethics for interpreters. *US-China Foreign Language*, 12(1): 83–92.

Fukuno, Maho (2023a). *Translators' ethics: Case studies of English–Japanese translators in community translation*. PhD thesis, Australian National University.

Fukuno, Maho (2023b). Translators' ethics in community translation: A case study of English-Japanese translators in the Australian system. In González, Erika; Stachowiak-Szymczak, Katarzyna and Amanatidou, Despina (Eds.), *Community translation: Research and practice*. London: Routledge: 42–67.

Gentzler, Edwin (2001). *Contemporary translation theories*. Clevedon, Buffalo, Toronto and Sydney: Multilingual Matters.

Gould, Rebecca and Tahmasebian, Kayvan (2020). *The Routledge handbook of translation and activism*. Abingdon and New York: Routledge.

Hatim, Basil and Mason, Ian (2013 [1990]). *Discourse and the translator*. London and New York: Routledge.

Hatim, Basil and Mason, Ian (1997). *The translator as communicator*. London and New York: Routledge.

40 *Translation and Community*

Jary, David and Jary, Julia (Eds.) (2000). *Collins dictionary of sociology* (3rd Edition). Glasgow: HarperCollins.

Katan, David and Taibi, Mustapha (2021). *Translating cultures: An introduction for translators, interpreters and mediators* (3rd Edition). London and New York: Routledge.

Leonardi, Vanessa (2020). *Ideological manipulation of children's literature through translation and rewriting: Travelling across times and places*. Cham: Palgrave Macmillan.

Lesch, Harold M. (1999). Community translation: Right or privilege? In Erasmus, Mabel (Ed.), *Liaison interpreting in the community*. Pretoria: Van Schaik: 90–98.

Lesch, Harold M. (2004). Societal factors and translation practice. *Perspectives: Studies in Translatology*, 12(4): 256–269. DOI: 10.1080/0907676X.2004.9961506.

Liddicoat, Anthony J. (2016). Intercultural mediation, intercultural communication and translation. *Perspectives: Studies in Translatology*, 24(3): 354–364. DOI: 10.1080/090767 6X.2014.980279.

McDonoughDolmaya, Julie (2011). Moral ambiguity: Some shortcomings of professional codes of ethics for translators. *The Journal of Specialised Translation*, 15: 28–49. www. jostrans.org/issue15/art_mcdonough.pdf.

Munday, Jeremy (2007). Translation and ideology. *The Translator*, 13(2): 195–217. DOI: 10.1080/13556509.2007.10799238.

Mundt, Klaus (2019). Against the 'Un-' in untranslatability: On the obsession with problems, negativity and uncertainty. In Large, Duncan; Akashi, Motoko; Józwikowska, Wanda and Rose, Emily (Eds.), *Untranslatability: Interdisciplinary perspectives*. London and New York: Routledge: 64–79.

O'hagan, Minako and Ashworth, David (2002). *Translation-mediated communication: Facing the challenges of globalization and localization*. Clevedon, Buffalo, Toronto and Sydney: Multilingual Matters.

Paloposki, Outi (2010). The translator's footprints. In Kinnunen, Tuija and Koskinen, Kaisa (Eds.), *Translators' agency*. Tampere: Tampere University Press: 86–107.

Pan, Li and Huang, Chuxin (2021). Stance mediation in media translation of political speeches: An analytical model of appraisal and framing in news discourse. In Wang, Binhua and Munday, Jeremy (Eds.), *Advances in discourse analysis of translation and interpreting: Linking linguistic approaches with socio-cultural interpretation*. London and New York: Routledge: 131–149.

Pym, Anthony (2020). Trust-based translation history. *Chronotopos—A Journal of Translation History*, 2(1&2): 146–160. DOI: 10.25365/cts-2020-2-1-6.

Samuelsson-Brown, Geoffrey (2010). *A practical guide for translators*. Bristol, Buffalo and Toronto: Multilingual Matters.

Taibi, Mustapha (2011). Public service translation. In Malmkjaer, Kirsten and Windle, Kevin (Eds.), *The Oxford handbook of translation studies*. Oxford: Oxford University Press: 214–227.

Taibi, Mustapha (2022). Community translation. In *ENTI (Encyclopedia of Translation and Interpreting)*. DOI: 10.5281/zenodo.6366194.

Taibi, Mustapha and Ozolins, Uldis (2016). *Community translation*. London and New York: Bloomsbury.

Tymoczko, M. (2014). *Enlarging translation, empowering translators*. London and New York: Routledge.

Tyulenev, Sergey (2014). *Translation and society*. London and New York: Routledge.

Valdeón, Roberto (2014). From adaptation to appropriation: Framing the world through news translation. *Linguaculture*, 1: 51–62. DOI: 10.1515/lincu-2015-0019.

Venuti, Lawrence (2018 [1995]). *The translator's invisibility: A history of translation*. London and New York: Routledge.

Wolf, Michaela (2007). Introduction: The emergence of a sociology of translation. In Wolf, Michaela and Fukari, Alexandra (Eds.), *Constructing a sociology of translation*. Amsterdam and Philadelphia: John Benjamins: 1–3.

Wolf, Michaela (2010). Sociology of translation. In Gambier, Yves and Van Doorslaer, Luc (Eds.), *Handbook of translation studies*. Amsterdam and Philadelphia: John Benjamins: 337–343.

Wolf, Michaela (2011). Mapping the field: Sociological perspectives on translation. *International Journal of the Sociology of Language*, 207: 1–28. DOI: 10.1515/ijsl.2011.001.

Wolf, Michaela and Fukari, Alexandra (Eds.) (2007). *Constructing a sociology of translation*. Amsterdam and Philadelphia: John Benjamins.

Zhu, Yunxia (2005). *Written communication across cultures: A sociocognitive perspective on business genres*. Amsterdam and Philadelphia: John Benjamins.

3 Text types, translation brief and translation strategies

> This chapter provides an overview of the functionalist model of translation
> to identify the theoretical contributions within this framework that are most
> relevant to community translation. Based on the notions of genre, text type
> and translation brief, I offer theory-based guidelines for community transla-
> tors. The chapter covers the following:
>
> - Skopos theory (Reiss and Vermeer, 2014 [1984]);
> - Nord's (2014, 2018) position on functionalism;
> - Text types;
> - Translation briefs;
> - Tensions between translation brief and audience expectations;
> - Possible translation strategies.

In the previous two chapters, I pointed out that a functionalist approach to transla
tion, together with awareness of the overarching mission of community translation
(empowering communities), is the most appropriate and effective way to facilitate
communication in this context. In this chapter, I explain what is meant by a functionalist approach and illustrate how it works better for translation in general and
community translation in particular.

Unfortunately, even today, after decades of scholarly publications and translator
training, we often come across translations that are quite literal. This is sometimes
the result of low language proficiency and limited target language resources; in
other cases, it is the result of a deeply rooted literalist conception of translation. Basically, a functionalist approach to translation is based on an understanding of texts
as communicative instruments with functions and a belief that translation strategies
and choices are determined based on the purpose or function of the translation.

3.1 Functionalist approach

There are several functionalist approaches to translation, but I use the singular form
here to keep things simple. Functionalist approaches are based on *Skopostheorie*

DOI: 10.4324/9781003367741-4

Text types, translation brief and translation strategies 43

(Skopos theory), put forward by the German scholar Hans Vermeer in the late 1970s and early 1980s (Nord, 2014: 120). Skopos theory "regards translation as a purposeful activity intended to mediate between members of different culture communities. *Skopos* is the Greek word for "purpose", and purpose, in the sense of intended communicative function, is the central concept of this theory (Nord, 2014: 120). For Vermeer (1989: 20), each text, including each translation, is produced for a purpose. Therefore, translation needs to be done in a manner that enables the final product to serve the purpose in the communicative context it is intended for (Vermeer, 1989: 20; Nord, 2014: 121).

In Skopos theory, translation is a particular form of action, an intentional behaviour with a goal or skopos. This goal is given priority when the translator needs to determine the most appropriate strategy or strategies for their target text and audience. Nord (2005: 53) distinguishes between *intention* and *function*, with the former determined from the viewpoint of the sender or source text writer and the latter from the perspective of the translation audience. This distinction is particularly necessary in situations where the source text writer and the translation audience are culturally different or distant and therefore have different expectations in terms of text type, textual features and writing norms and conventions (Nord, 2014: 122). As Kussmaul (1995: 149) notes,

[t]he function of a translation depends on the knowledge, expectations, values and norms of the target readers, who are again influenced by the situation they are in and by the culture. These factors determine whether the function of the source text or passages in the source text can be preserved or have to be modified or even changed.

(149)

Accordingly, before a translator decides how to approach a given translation assignment, it is essential for them to have a good understanding of the sociocultural background, knowledge, expectations and needs of the audience (Reiss and Vermeer, 2014 [1984]: 91, 92, 114).

In line with the argument that translation is a purposeful activity, the source text is considered a mere "offer of information" in its source language and culture, and the target text is a new offer of information in another language and culture (Reiss and Vermeer, 2014 [1984]: 94). A translation does not need to be an imitation of the source text but may consist of rewriting (in a new language) in a manner that is consistent with the function of the translation. Moreover, Skopos theory does not take translation as a purely linguistic exercise consisting of identifying and using equivalent linguistic forms to render meaning from one language to another. Rather, it considers translation a situated communicative action, taking into consideration the expectations of the new audience and using not only appropriate linguistic resources but also visual elements such as document design, illustrations and other visual aspects of text production.

In this functionalist theory, the focus is no longer on the source text and equivalence at word or sentence level but on the target text's functionality and adequacy.

44 *Translation and Community*

Reiss and Vermeer (2014 [1984]: 127) use 'adequacy' in the sense of an appropriate relationship between a target text and a source text once the purpose of the translation has been factored in: "*With regard to the translation of a source text (or any of its elements), adequacy shall refer to the relationship between a source text and a target text, where consistent attention is paid to the purpose (skopos) of the translation process*" (italics in the source). The two authors still refer to equivalence, but only when the translation and its source text have the same function: "*Equivalence is the relationship between a target text and a source text which (can) achieve the same communicative function at the same level in the two cultures involved*" (Reiss and Vermeer, 2014 [1984]: 127).

That is to say, equivalence is a particular case of adequacy that only applies when the source and the translation share the same purpose and function, while adequacy refers to the purpose of the translation process, which may be different from the function of the original text. For Reiss and Vermeer (2014 [1984]: 92), translation is fundamentally different from source text writing and, therefore, "a translational action may serve different purposes"; their functionalist approach gives legitimacy to a range of possible renderings of a source text, including summary translation, free translation and adaptation. It allows the translator a margin for decision-making and choosing from a range of possibilities between a formally faithful and a free translation approach depending on the context and the communicative purpose of the translation (Nord, 2018 [1997]: 28).

Skopos theory has attracted criticism in scholarly literature, among other things because of the conceptual ambiguity in relation to equivalence and adequacy and the ethical concerns arising from determining that the end justifies the means and the fact that the commissioner or client can determine the purpose of translation. Koller (1992 [1979]: 212), for instance, suggests that the "the end justifies the means" principle might give rise to arbitrariness in translator decisions and might depart away from the values of truth and fidelity in translation. Pym (1996: 338) went as far as to say that this functionalist approach might turn translators into "mercenary experts, able to fight under the flag of any purpose able to pay them".

However, this functionalist approach is still useful, especially in the context of community translation, for the following reasons, some of which have already been mentioned in Chapters 1 and 2; the ethical concerns can be easily overruled (see Section 3.3):

- Functionalism focuses on language and texts as means of communication (Reiss and Vermeer, 2014 [1984]: 135) and gives the intended function of the translation priority in guiding translator decisions.
- Functionalism places the target readers at the centre of the translational action. As Kussmaul (1995: 149) notes,

> [t]he function of a translation depends on the knowledge, expectations, values and norms of the target readers, who are again influenced by the situation they are in and by the culture. These factors determine whether

Text types, translation brief and translation strategies 45

the function of the source text or passages in the source text can be preserved or have to be modified or even changed.

Accordingly, before a translator decides how to approach a given translation assignment, it is essential for them to have a good understanding of the socio-cultural background, knowledge, expectations and needs of the audience (Reiss and Vermeer, 2014 [1984]: 91, 92, 114).

- "It [functionalism] recognizes that the translator works in a professional situation, with complex obligations to people, as well as to texts" (Pym, 2010: 56). This means that within a functionalist framework, the translator has obligations not only towards the source text but also towards stakeholders, including senders/original authors, commissioners/clients and translation receivers (Nord, 2018 [1997]: 113–117).
- It recognizes translators' expertise and elevates their status in terms of text production (Taibi and Ozolins, 2016: 70).
- It allows for a wide range of forms and levels of translation such as adaptations, transcreations and summary translations depending on context and needs (Taibi and Ozolins, 2016: 70). It also leaves the door open for multimodal forms of translation, which are extremely useful in community translation contexts where audience constraints or preferences require public messaging through audiovisual or other media (see e.g., Hajek et al., 2022).
- It raises translators' awareness of the differences between text types and the translation strategies appropriate for each (Taibi and Ozolins, 2016: 70). This is what I turn to in the next section.

3.2 Genres and text types

Writers and readers in general, and translators in particular, process texts as members of certain classes or types rather than as unique, one-off acts of communication. Texts are composed, read and interpreted as instances of the categories to which they belong. This is the same as the generalisation and classification processes people engage in to make sense of the world around us: We mentally create categories of objects, people, places, relationships and so on so that next time we come across or experience instances of them, we make sense of them based on background information about the class or group. Identifying the linguistic and textual features of categories of texts facilitates the task of making sense of them (Bell, 1991: 171; Neubert and Shreve, 1992: 48; Colina, 2015: 159).

Two useful notions to consider in categorising texts are 'genre' and 'text type'. Based on the definition provided by Lux (1981: 273), Reiss and Vermeer define genres as "supra-individual types of speech and writing acts associated with recurring communicative activities in which repeated occurrence has led to the development of characteristic patterns of language use and text composition" (2014 [1984]: 159–160). They add that genres and their associated conventions play an important role in the translator's comprehension of texts and their translation

46 *Translation and Community*

decisions (Reiss and Vermeer (2014 [1984]: 183). Hatim and Mason (2013 [1990]: 69) define genres as " 'conventionalised forms of texts' which reflect the functions and goals involved in a particular social occasion as well as the purposes of the participants in them", and regarding text type, they refer to it as "a conceptual framework which enables us to classify texts in terms of communicative intentions serving an overall rhetorical purpose" (140). Thus, for example, an argumentative text serves the purpose of persuading the reader to accept a point of view or course of action, while an expository text is used to expose facts and provide information about someone of something.

A classic contribution to translation theory is Reiss's (2000 [1971]) classification of text types for translation, which was based on Bühler's (2011 [1934]) language functions. Bühler identified three communicative functions: representative, expressive and appellative (appealing) (35); Reiss (2000 [1971]) refers to these functions and text types respectively as informative, expressive and operative (persuasive). Informative texts are information oriented, and their focus is on the referential or factual content (e.g., report, encyclopaedia entry, factsheet, etc.). Expressive texts are focused on the aesthetic value of language, "[t]he communication of artistically organised content" (Reiss, 1981: 124), as in novels, short stories and poems. Operative texts are oriented towards beliefs, values and behaviour, and they purport to elicit a certain response or action. Reiss and Vermeer (2014 [1984) point out that

> these three types are "encoded" at different levels. The informative type is encoded at the level of content; the expressive type is encoded at the level of content and aesthetic organization; the operative type is encoded at the level of content and persuasion (to which the level of aesthetic organization is occasionally added).
>
> (182)

They suggest that before writing a text, authors normally choose one of these basic communicative forms and that these types are probably universal (common to all cultures).

The basic assumption in relation to text types is that they represent different author intentions or rhetorical purposes and, accordingly, different text functions. Reiss's text typology would ideally serve as a set of guidelines for translators in the sense that it suggests a translation method for each text type. For instance, if the text is informative, the focus will be on referential or semantic equivalence, while aesthetic values and connotative meanings are considered secondary (Hatim and Munday, 2004: 281). If the text falls under the expressive category, priority in the translation process will be given to the aesthetic effect, while the referential or propositional content is relegated to a secondary position. If the text is operative, the translator needs to successfully render the text in a manner that is likely to achieve the desired response (e.g., persuading the reader of the writer's argument or persuading them to take action), "even if this has to be undertaken at the expense of both **form** and **content**" (Hatim and Munday, 2004: 281, emphasis in the source).

Text types, translation brief and translation strategies 47

However, these text types do not always appear in a pure and exclusive form (Reiss and Vermeer (2014 [1984]: 183). Echoing Lux (1981), Reiss and Vermeer (2014 [1984]: 162) note that genres too can be complex (one genre embedded in another, such as a personal or business letter embedded within a novel). Hatim and Mason (2013 [1990]: 146–148) also note the hybrid nature of texts and that one function is generally dominant. The translator therefore needs to identify the predominant function in the source text, as "an important yardstick in assessing the **text type** 'identity'" (Hatim and Munday, 2004: 74, emphasis in the source) and choose translation method based on that.

Hatim and Munday (2004: 285–286) point out that the feasibility and usefulness of the classification of texts has been controversial, not only because of text type hybridity inside the same text but also because the concept of text type is so broad that we can find a wide range of text forms classified under the same category (e.g., Acts of Parliament, technical instructions, political speeches, sermons and advertisements all falling under the category 'instructive' or 'operative'). Still, as Nord (2018 [1997]: 37) argues, "Text-type classifications sharpen the translator's awareness of linguistic markers of communicative function and functional translation units". While genre and text-type classification will not automatically lead the translator into easy and ready-made translation choices, awareness of both notions will contextualise both their comprehension and translation strategies.

3.3   Translation brief

To assist the translator in making the right decisions and producing an appropriate translation, the commissioner needs to provide as much information as possible about the context of how the translation is going to be used, including of course the intended audience: This information is referred to as the 'translation brief' (see example in Box 3.1). If the brief is insufficient, the translator may have to supplement it with additional information (Nord, 2014: 122). In the case of community translations, this additional information may be inferred from the text type and text content and/or from extralinguistic knowledge about the relevant commissioning organisation and speakers of the target language in the local or national context.

Box 3.1   Translation brief

The following is a press release from the Mayor of London. Please translate it into Arabic/Chinese/Hindi/Spanish/Urdu, etc. Please note that the translations of the press release will be published on social media. The target readers are residents in the City of London who do not have a high literacy level in English. Please feel free to adapt the style if necessary. For "London Policing Board" and "Metropolitan Police Service", please translate and insert the English names

48 *Translation and Community*

> *between parentheses the first time they appear in the press release. For further information, please email…*

Mayor to establish London Policing Board to oversee and scrutinise reform of the Metropolitan Police Service

The Mayor of London, Sadiq Khan, has today announced that he is setting up a London Policing Board to oversee and scrutinise the urgent reform of the Met.

Londoners with diverse lived experiences and backgrounds and a wide range of professional and personal skills are invited to apply and help drive forward the changes and improvements needed to make London a safe city for all.

Establishing a London Policing Board chaired by the Mayor was a recommendation in Baroness Louise Casey's review of culture and standards in the Met, which the Mayor requested to increase the transparency and accountability of the Met to all the diverse communities it serves.

This action is part of the Mayor's commitment to turning the recommendations of the Baroness Casey review into long-lasting and meaningful change to improve the service the Met provides to Londoners and foster a more open, fair and responsive culture within the force.

In line with Baroness Casey's recommendation, the new board will drive forward the changes needed, based on the transparent approach to accountability now used by Transport for London, with meetings held in public and a membership representing a range of skills and lived experiences. Arrangements will reflect the different legal structures in place for policing, including the oversight powers of the Mayor and the operational independence of the Commissioner.

Members of the board will provide specialist advice to assist the Mayor in holding the Met to account in delivering the reforms needed to rebuild confidence and trust in the police.

The new London Policing Board is part of a package of measures by the Mayor to accelerate the root and branch reforms of the Met's performance and culture so that every community in London can feel protected and served.

Source: www.london.gov.uk/media-centre/mayors-press-release/Mayor-to-establish-London-Policing-Board-to-oversee-and-scrutinise-reform-of-the-Metropolitan-Police-Service

Taibi and Ozolins (2016: 66, 72) note that the commissioner's translation brief might not be in line with the expectations and needs of the target audience. For example, the brief provided by the relevant organisation may insist on a literal translation or, as Chesterman (2016) notes, they may be intentionally unclear in their messages, while the target community is likely to expect clear communication

Text types, translation brief and translation strategies 49

and reader-oriented adaptations. Taibi and Ozolins (2016) explain that even with a functional approach to translation, community translators will inevitably find themselves in ethical dilemmas regarding the extent to which they should be guided by the commissioner's translation brief or by what they know about the social function of community translation in general and the expectations and needs of their specific target readership, that is, whose perspective to take to determine the function of translation.

In relation to this, Nord (2018 [1997]: 108) points out that among the reasons why Skopos theory has been criticised is that within the theory, the translation brief determines the translation purpose: The initiator or commissioner "tells the translator how to translate". In response to this criticism, Nord explains that a distinction should be made between the translation Skopos or aim and the actual strategies the translator uses to attain this aim:

> The Skopos is indeed determined by the initiator's needs and wishes with regard to the communicative action they intend to realize by means of the target text, whereas the actual procedures are entirely up to the translator as a competent expert in translation.
>
> (Nord, 2018 [1997]: 108)

As the same author notes, clients may have misconceptions about translation (e.g., as mechanical or literal transfer from one language to another), may boast of knowledge of the target language or may give instructions to the translator on how to translate.

However, the client's translation brief is not to be understood as a final verdict on translation procedures. In line with the source text as a mere "offer of information", one may add that the translation brief needs to be taken as a mere statement contextualising the translation assignment and specifying the commissioner's intentions, preferences and wishes. The community translator, as an expert in languages, translation and intercultural communication, can seek further guidance in the text, the community context and their own knowledge of the sociolinguistic and cultural profile of the target audience. If necessary, the translation brief can be a starting point for further discussion with the client, especially in the case of major public messaging campaigns and translation assignments.

Nord (2018 [1997]: 29) agrees that this discussion or negotiation between the client and the translator is often necessary, "especially when the client has only a vague or even incorrect idea of what kind of text is needed for the situation in question". If the client and the translator do not agree on the best approach to serve the intended purpose, "the translator may either refuse the assignment (and starve) or refuse any responsibility for the function of the target text and simply do what the client asks for" (29). As Taibi and Ozolins (2016: 72) note, if the translator's decision is based on remuneration only, they will end up serving the interests of the client who pays their salary or fees, which would raise concerns about their professional ethics.

50 *Translation and Community*

Nord (2014: 122) also argues that the notion of translation is culture specific and varies over time and from one cultural context to another. Some audiences might expect translations that are quite literal, while others might expect translations to convey the writer's intended messages without close attention to the words and expressions they use. Some communities might value translations that are stylistically elegant, while others might prefer practical, comprehensible and easily readable translations. The translator therefore needs to act as a responsible mediator between the parties involved in the communication act (Nord, 2014: 122). This, however, does not mean that translators must always follow the instructions or expectations of others. Rather, it means "that the translator has to anticipate any misunderstanding or communicative conflict that may occur due to discrepant translational concepts and find a way to avoid or solve them" (Nord, 2014: 122).

Nord's (2018 [1997]: 116–117) notion of 'loyalty' suggests that translators need to be loyal and committed to all the parties involved in a translation assignment, on both the source and target text sides (text producers, commissioners and translation users). The principle of bilateral loyalty makes it necessary for translators to discuss and negotiate translation assignments with their clients. If there are any discrepancies between the interests and expectations of the stakeholders, the translator needs to mediate and seek the understanding of all the relevant parties (Nord, 2018 [1997]: 116–117).

In the case of community translations, translators may receive a translation brief from public services (either through an agency acting as an intermediary or not), but may have no direct contact with the target communities of their translations. Still, as Abdallah (2010) rightly points out, "translators often feel a great sense of responsibility towards the reader, not only towards the party paying for their work . . . translators, by way of their professional ethics, feel that the reader has delegated authority to them to represent their interests in production networks" (17). This is especially applicable to community translators, who often provide their services in a context characterised by social disadvantage and are aware that for their translations to be useful, they must consider the needs and expectations of their audience. Again, the commissioner's translation brief is useful, but it should be the basis for further discussion with the relevant parties to determine the best translation approach and strategies. Sometimes, this negotiation between the commissioner's instructions and the (presumed) community preferences and needs takes place only in the translator's mind.

3.4 Translation strategies

In the early part of this chapter, I referred to a functionalist approach. This is the overall translation approach or method that (community) translators need to adopt to produce meaningful, fit-for-purpose translations. However, to operationalise this overall approach, the translator needs to process localised translation units and deal with micro elements of the text being translated, be they sentences, clauses, expressions or single lexical items.

Text types, translation brief and translation strategies 51

The way the translator proceeds at this level is referred to as translation procedures (Vinay and Darbelnet (1995 [1958]), techniques (e.g., Molina Martínez, 2022) or strategies (e.g., Baker, 2011 [1992]). Molina Martínez (2022) notes the inconsistency and confusion of these terms and distinguishes between strategy and technique:

> In that distinction, the term strategy refers to the procedures (whether conscious or unconscious, verbal or non-verbal) translators use to solve the problems that arise when carrying out a translation process with a specific objective in mind. Translators use strategies for comprehension (e.g., distinguishing between main and secondary ideas, establishing conceptual relationships, searching for information) and for reformulation (e.g., paraphrasing, retranslating, speaking out loud, avoiding words very similar to those of the ST [source text]). Strategies pave the way for an adequate solution to a translation unit, but the solution is actually found through the use of a particular technique.

Although I am aware of the terminological inconsistencies and the distinctions made between one concept and another, I use the term strategies here to refer the procedural options available to (community) translators to render textual components from one language to another. Within a functionalist approach to translation, of course, the choice of one option rather than another will be guided by the translation brief (the client's instructions, the purpose of the translation, intended audience), the text genre and type (informative leaflet, informative media release, operative council advertisement, expressive speech at a ceremonial act, etc.), the resources and constraints of the target language, the sociolinguistic and sociocultural profile of the target language community and so on.

Vinay and Darbelnet (1995 [1958]: 31–39) propose seven procedures or strategies:

1) **Borrowing:** The simplest strategy consists of taking a lexical item from a source language and using it as it is in the target text. This can be used when the translator faces a technical or culture-specific term that is not available in the target language, or when they prefer to maintain a flavour of the source language and culture, for instance with technical terms such as 'online'/'offline' as well as culture-specific terms such as the examples I mentioned in Chapter 2 (*Hanfu, cheongsam, burnous, jilbab*, hot dog, etc.).

2) **Calque:** A special kind of borrowing where a source language expression is taken as it is, but instead of using the same term or expression, the translator literally reflects its components in the target language. The French *Thérapie occupationnelle* for the English 'occupational therapy', which Vinay and Darbelnet (1995 [1958]: 33) considered an awkward calque, is now commonly used. As the authors note, both borrowings and calques can end up being accepted as integral parts of a given language.

52 *Translation and Community*

3) **Literal translation:** Direct, word-for-word transfer of the source text into similar grammatical structures in the target text provided that the resulting structure is idiomatically appropriate. This is possible in cases where there is a degree of linguistic and cultural convergence (e.g., translation between languages of the same family).

4) **Transposition:** A strategy involving replacing one word class or phrase type (e.g., noun phrase) with another (e.g., verbal phrase) without changing the message. In the following example from Sharkas (2024), the English verb 'ask' is translated using the nominalisation option in Arabic:

   Source Text: **Ask** your doctor or pharmacist for advice before taking any medicine.
   Target Text: **عليك استشارة** طبيبك أو الصيدلي قبل استعمال أي دواء
   Back translation: **On-you consultation** of your doctor or the pharmacist before using any medicine.

5) **Modulation:** "Modulation is a variation of the form of the message, obtained by a change in the point of view" (Vinay and Darbelnet (1995 [1958]: 33). According to the same authors, this strategy is justified when a literal or transposed translation results in a grammatical but awkward or unidiomatic utterance. Modulation goes a step further and makes the rendition more natural in the target language. An example is the translation of the French *le dernier étage* (literally, "the last floor") with "the top floor".

6) **Equivalence:** The use of entirely different structural and stylistic options to produce an equivalent translation or text that is appropriate in the communicative situation. Vinay and Darbelnet (1995 [1958]: 36) refer to idioms, clichés and proverbs as good examples of the usefulness of equivalence. One such example is the translation of the French *comme un chien dans un jeu de quilles* (literally, "like a dog in a game of bowling") as "like a bull in a china shop".

7) **Adaptation:** A special case of equivalence and an extreme limit of translation (Vinay and Darbelnet (1995 [1958]). The translator faces a situation that is unfamiliar in the target culture, and therefore, they need to create a new situation that can be considered equivalent. An example Vinay and Darbelnet (1995 [1958]: 39) provide is, "He kissed his daughter on the mouth", culturally adapted into French as *Il serra tendrement sa fille dans ses bras* ("He hugged his daughter tenderly").

Similarly, Baker (2011 [1992]) suggests eight strategies to deal with non-equivalence at word level and lexical gaps between languages:

1) **Translation using a more general word:** Translating a more specific concept in the source text with a more general word (superordinate) in the target language. If the target language, for instance, does not have a specific verb for "shampooing hair", the use of a more general verb such as "washing" could be an appropriate solution.

2) **Translation using a more neutral/less expressive word:** The use of a less expressive lexical item because the target language lacks an exact equivalent or because the closest equivalent does not have the same connotative meaning and

Text types, translation brief and translation strategies 53

expressive strength. Baker (2011 [1992]) gives the example of 'mumble', translated into Italian as *suggerisce* ("suggest") rather than *mugugnare* ("grumble, protest").

3) **Translation using cultural substitution:** Replacing a culture-specific word or expression with a target language lexical item or expression which ensures a comparable impact on the target reader. This is similar to Vinay and Darbelnet's (1995 [1958]) adaptation in that both make translations read more naturally and sound more culturally understandable and acceptable.

4) **Translation using a loan word or loan word plus explanation:** This is the same strategy as Vinay and Darbelnet's (1995 [1958]) borrowing used with or without explanation when the source text contains culture-specific items, technical concepts or buzz words.

5) **Translation by paraphrase using a related word:** Rewording or expressing the meaning of a source text segment using a related word, such as when the source text item has a lexical equivalent in the target language but the two are not lexicalised in the same form or are not used with the same frequency in their respective languages. For example, "This is a **lump sum payment** to help people who are unable to earn income due to a COVID-19 public health order" can be translated into Arabic as "وهو **مبلغ يدفع مرة واحدة** لمساعدةالأشخاص غير القادرين على الكسب بسبب أحد إجراءات الصحة العامة الخاصة بكوفيد ١٩" ("It is an amount paid only once to help people who are unable to earn due to one of COVID-19 public health measures"). "Lump sum payment" is lexicalised in Arabic as مبلغ إجمالي ("total amount") or دفعة واحدة ("one payment"), but neither of the two forms would be clear without the paraphrase strategy.

6) **Translation by paraphrase using unrelated words:** The same as 5) but using unrelated words to unpack a unit that is not lexicalised in the target language, especially if it is semantically complex. The Spanish *sobremesa*, for instance, does not have an equivalent in English, so paraphrase can usefully render the sentence "*Lo más importante es la sobremesa*" not as "The most important thing is the *sobremesa*" but as "The most important part of the meal is what comes after it, hanging out with family/friends, chatting and enjoying their company".

7) **Translation using omission:** In some contexts, it is appropriate to leave out a lexical item or expression if it is deemed not essential for the message or the development of the text. Translators may assess the impact of an omission like this and conclude that it is more appropriate to omit the expression in question than provide awkward or lengthy explanations.

8) **Translation using illustration:** In some contexts, when a source text item refers to a physical object and is difficult to translate without lengthy rephrasing and explanations, the object may be illustrated, through pictures for example.

Table 3.1 provides a more detailed list of strategies as described by Molina Martínez (2022); the definitions in the second column are from her work; the examples and comments in the third column are not.

54 *Translation and Community*

Table 3.1 Key translation strategies

Strategy	Molina Martinez's description	Examples and comparison with other authors
Adaptation	Making a shift in culture	As in Vinay and Darbelnet (1995 [1958])
Amplification	Adding clarifications (explicatory paraphrasing, footnotes, etc.)	Adding information or an explanation for instance when there is something implicit in the source text that needs to be made explicit (e.g., "louder than the 4th of July" translated into Japanese as 7月4日、独立記念日のお祝いより騒がしい, adding "Independence Day celebrations")
Borrowing	Incorporating a word or expression from another language into a TT	As in Vinay and Darbelnet (1995 [1958])
Calque	Giving a literal translation of a foreign syntagm that expresses a new concept or expression	As in Vinay and Darbelnet (1995 [1958])
Compensation	Including an element of information or a stylistic effect in a different place	Also mentioned by Baker (2011 [1992]: 86)
Description	Replacing a term or expression with a description of its form and/or function	Kilt: typical Scottish garment resembling a knee-length skirt
Discursive creation	Establishing a temporary equivalence that could never be anticipated out of context	Translating the film title "A Prayer for the Dying" into French as *L'Irlandais* ("The Irishman") because the film is about a former member of the Irish Republican Army
Established equivalent	Using a term or expression recognized (by a dictionary, through language use) as an equivalent	Similar to Vinay and Darbelnet's (1995 [1958]) equivalence
Generalization	Using a more general or neutral term	Covering both translation by a general word and translation by a more neutral/less expressive word (Baker, 2011 [1992])
Linguistic amplification	Adding words without a grammatical or normative need to do so	Translating "for any reason" into Arabic as لأي سبب من الأسباب ("for any reason from reasons), whereas لأي سبب would be sufficient
Linguistic compression	Summarizing words without a grammatical or normative need to do so	Especially where there are time or space constraints (e.g., audiovisual translation). For example, reducing "Failure to do so may result in your application not being accepted for filing" to "Otherwise, your application may not be accepted for filing"

(Continued)

Text types, translation brief and translation strategies 55

Table 3.1 (Continued)

Strategy	Molina Martinez's description	Examples and comparison with other authors
Literal translation	Giving a word-for-word translation of a syntagm or expression but not of a single word	As in Vinay and Darbelnet (1995 [1958])
Modulation	Changing the point of view, focus or cognitive category	As in Vinay and Darbelnet (1995 [1958])
Particularisation	Using a more precise or specific term	Translating 'health care provider' as 'doctor'
Pragmatic variation	Changing linguistic or paralinguistic elements that affect linguistic variation	Varying dialect or tone to achieve a special effect (more applicable to literary and film translation than to community translation)
Reduction	Suppressing an element of information	Related to Baker's (2011 [1992]) translation by omission. Reduction is the opposite of amplification; it is used when the information is assumed to be known/unnecessary.
Substitution (linguistic, paralinguistic)	Changing linguistic elements for paralinguistic elements or vice versa	Replacing non-verbal signs with expressions (more applicable to interpreting than translation)
Transposition	Changing a grammatical category	As in Vinay and Darbelnet (1995 [1958])

Taxonomies and strategies such as the ones listed in Table 3.1 have been criticised on the grounds that they tend to focus on the linguistic aspects of translation more than on its communicative function, and more on words, clauses and sentences than on the text as a whole unit (Snell-Hornby, 1995; Fawcett, 2014 [1997]). However, although translators need to be guided by the function of the text/translation as a whole, they have to deal with translation challenges at lower levels (e.g., lexical and syntactical levels). In addition, not all the strategies can be classified under the same category: Some are more communication focused than others (e.g., calque and literal translation vs. adaptation and translation by cultural substitution).

The functionalist approach I outlined in this chapter can be used as a guiding framework which will need to be implemented through concrete and localised translation strategies and choices. A list of possible translation techniques is not an endorsement that everything is legitimate: Whether a strategy is appropriate or not will depend on the text type and genre, the translation brief, the expectations and needs of the target audience and the characteristics and conventions of the source and target languages.

56 *Translation and Community*

Summary

A functionalist approach is probably the best for community translation because 1) it takes translation texts as means of communication and places the function at the top of considerations guiding the translator's decisions; 2) it considers the translation's audience, with their backgrounds and expectations including formal expectations relating to style and conventions; 3) it allows translators some leeway in assessing translation tasks and communicative situations to decide the most appropriate strategies and 4) it considers different translation and adaptation options and dissemination methods legitimate depending on context and needs.

Within a functional framework, the notions of genre, text type and translation brief are useful for the community translator's work. Awareness of the genre and text type the source text predominantly belongs to helps translators contextualise their comprehension and reformulation and apply the textual and stylistic adaptations required by the target language conventions relevant to the text type or genre. In addition, the translation brief provides further contextual information (purpose of the translation, intended audience, commissioner's preferences or guidelines, etc.) that will guide the translator and facilitate their decision making.

While functionalist theories provide a useful general framework, community translators still need to operationalise functionalist principles through concrete and localised translation strategies. In this chapter, I reviewed examples of strategies from Vinay and Darbelnet (1995 [1958]), Baker (2011 [1992]) and Molina Martínez (2022). Some of these strategies are more literal; others are more communicative and functional. The fact that they are listed as options does not mean that they can be used randomly or interchangeably. Rather, to determine which strategy is best in each case, you will need to take a functionalist stance as a starting point, considering the overall nature of the text, the translation brief and the similarities and differences between the source and target languages.

Suggested activities

1) Browse the website of a local council, government department or another organisation. Select three to five texts from different sections and classify them in terms of genre and text type. Write a list of linguistic and textual features that led you to this classification.
2) Choose a community translation that is publicly available (together with its source text) and identify 10 translation strategies from the lists presented in this chapter.
3) In pairs or small groups, discuss the relevance of functionalist translation theories to your local community translation context.

Text types, translation brief and translation strategies 57

Further reading

- Nord, Christiane (2014). Functionalist approaches. In Gambier, Yves and van Doorslaer, Luc (Eds), *Handbook of translation studies*. Amsterdam/Philadelphia: John Benjamins: 120–128.

This book chapter provides a brief overview of the development of Skopos theory and describes the basic concepts of the functionalist theory of translation.

- Molina Martínez, Lucía (2022). Techniques/strategies (of translation). *ENTI (Encyclopedia of Translation & Interpreting)*. AIETI. www.aieti.eu/enti/techniques_ENG/

This encyclopaedia entry provides a useful classification of translation strategies and explanation and illustration of each technique. While not all the strategies will be useful in the context of community translation, the entry will help you better understand some of the notions I covered.

References

Abdallah, Kristiina (2010). Translators' agency in production networks. In Kinnunen, Tuija and Koskinen, Kaisa (Eds.), *Translators' agency*. Tampere: Tampere University Press: 11–46.

Baker, Mona (2011 [1992]). *In other words: A coursebook on translation*. Abingdon: Routledge.

Bell, Roger T. (1991). *Translation and translating: Theory and practice*. London and New York: Longman.

Bühler, Karl (2011 [1934]). *Theory of language: The representational function of language*. Amsterdam and Philadelphia: John Benjamins.

Chesterman, Andrew (2016). *Memes of translation. The spread of ideas in translation theory (Revised edition)*. Amsterdam and Philadelphia: John Benjamins.

Colina, Sonia (2015). *Fundamentals of translation*. Cambridge: Cambridge University Press.

Fawcett, Peter (2014 [1997]). *Translation and language*. London and New York: Routledge.

Hajek, John; Karidakis, Maria; Amorati, Riccardo; Hao, Yu; Sengupta, Medha; Pym, Anthony and Woodward-Kron, Robyn (2022). *Understanding the experiences and communication needs of culturally and linguistically diverse communities during the COVID-19 pandemic*. https://rest.neptune-prod.its.unimelb.edu.au/server/api/core/bitstreams/d6b30546-ded4-56ce-8b2c-3625bf8d0215/content.

Hatim, Basil and Ian Mason (2013 [1990]). *Discourse and the translator*. London and New York: Routledge.

Hatim, Basil and Munday, Jeremy (2004). *Translation: An advanced resource book*. London and New York: Routledge.

Koller, Werner (1992 [1979]). *Einführung in die Übersetzungswissenschaft* (4th Edition Rev.). Quelle & Meyer.

Kussmaul, Paul (1995). *Training the translator*. Amsterdam and Philadelphia: John Benjamins.

Lux, Friedemann (1981). *Text, Situation, Textsorte. Probleme der Textsortenanalyse, dargestellt am Beispiel der britischen Registerlinguistik. Mit einem Ausblick auf eine adäquate Textsortentheorie. mit einem Ausblick auf eine adäquate Textsortentheorie*. Narr.

Molina Martínez, Lucía (2022). Techniques/strategies (of translation). *ENTI (Encyclopedia of translation & interpreting)*. AIETI. www.aieti.eu/enti/techniques_ENG/.

58 *Translation and Community*

Neubert, Albrecht and Shreve, Gregory M. (1992). *Translation as text*. Kent and Ohio: The Kent State University Press.

Nord, Christiane (2005). *Text analysis in translation: Theory, methodology, and didactic application of a model for translation-oriented text analysis*. Amsterdam and New York: Rodopi.

Nord, Christiane (2014). Functionalist approaches. In Gambier, Yves and Van Doorslaer, Luc (Eds.), *Handbook of translation studies*. Amsterdam and Philadelphia: John Benjamins: 120–128.

Nord, Christiane (2018 [1997]). *Translating as a purposeful activity: Functionalist approaches explained*. Abingdon: Routledge.

Pym, Anthony (1996). Material text transfer as a key to the purposes of translation. In Neubert, Albrecht; Shreve, Gregory and Gommlich, Klaus (Eds.), *Basic issues in translation studies: Proceedings of the fifth international conference Kent forum on translation studies II*. Kent and Ohio: Institute of Applied Linguistics: 337–346.

Pym, Anthony (2010). *Exploring translation theories*. London and New York: Routledge.

Reiss, Katharina (2000 [1971]). *Translation criticism: The potentials and limitations*. Manchester: St. Jerome.

Reiss, Katharina (1981). Type, kind and individuality of text: Decision making in translation. *Poetics Today*, 2(4): 121–131. DOI: 10.2307/1772491.

Reiss, Katharina and Vermeer, Hans (2014 [1984]). *Towards a general theory of translational action: Skopos theory explained*. Translated by Christiane Nord. London and New York: Routledge.

Sharkas, Hala (2024). Nominalization in Arabic translations of patient information leaflets. *Translation & Interpreting*, 16(1): 1–16. DOI: 10.12807/ti.116201.2024.a01.

Snell-Hornby, Mary (1995). *Translation studies: An integrated approach*. Amsterdam and Philadelphia: John Benjamins.

Taibi, Mustapha and Ozolins, Uldis (2016). *Community translation*. London and New York: Bloomsbury.

Vermeer, Hans (1989). *Skopos und Translationsauftrag—Aufsätze*. Heidelberg Universität.

Vinay, Jean Paul and Darbelnet, Jean (1995 [1958]). *Comparative stylistics of French and English: A methodology for translation*. Translated and edited by Juan Sager and M.-J. Hamel. Amsterdam and Philadelphia: John Benjamins.

4 Translating public messaging

> Building on the overview of text types and translation strategies provided in Chapter 3, Chapter 4 is the first one to deal with the practicalities of how community translators are expected to deal with different text types. Rather than classify texts into informative, expressive or operative only (Reiss, 2000 [1971]), in Chapters 4 and 5, I draw a distinction between two broad categories of 'community texts': 'public messaging' texts, which are usually informative and/or operative texts aiming to raise awareness, and 'regulatory texts', whose aim is to regulate rights, eligibility, services, relationships and so on. In this chapter, I cover the following:
>
> - Main features of public messaging, especially in the health care sector;
> - Translating public messaging as part of a communication strategy;
> - Common issues in translating public messaging;
> - Step-by-step guidance to future community translators in relation to translating public messaging (textual analysis, audience awareness, translation strategies, communication and negotiation with relevant stakeholders, etc.).

4.1 What is public messaging?

Public messaging generally refers to any public-interest communication released into the public domain. It is communication from governments, public services and non-governmental organisations to the community at large or to certain groups within the community. It is communication that is in the public interest, is aimed at the public and takes place in public space (Bonfadelli, 2022: 61). Barron (2012) uses the term 'public information messages', which is the title of her book, while others use terms such as 'social marketing' (e.g., McKenzie-Mohr, 2011; Saunders et al., 2015), 'social advertising', 'public sector marketing' (Barron, 2012: 52) or 'public communication campaigns' (Bonfadelli, 2022).

DOI: 10.4324/9781003367741-5

60 *Translation and Community*

Public messaging campaigns tend to be anonymous and impersonal in the sense that they are aimed at a mass audience, whether it is a whole society or a specific segment in that society, such as a specific age group (Barron, 2012: 53). They aim to raise awareness, educate, advise or change behaviours in a society or a social group. The contents relate to a variety of areas, including health, legal and political matters, welfare, education, industrial relations, and so on. As I noted in Chapter 1, organisations may disseminate contents not only to inform the public, but also to enhance their own status and image (Barron, 2012: 50). Bonfadelli (2022: 61), however, notes that public messaging must not be confused with "other types of communicative strategies like a) advertising and marketing for commercial products, and b) public relations for commercial or non-profit organizations as image-campaigns that intend to enhance the appearance of an organization". Still, it is possible to find in public communication campaigns a combination of explicit information sharing and awareness raising and implicit public relations and institutional image enhancement.

In terms of text type, public messaging is mostly informative and operative: It provides information to raise awareness and at the same time may—directly or indirectly—instruct the audience to act in a certain way. As Bonfadelli (2022: 61) notes, public communication campaigns are generally systematic and purposeful communication attempts which aim "to inform, persuade and/or motivate behavior changes" in a manner that is positive and socially desirable. In the examples in Box 4.1, taken from three English-speaking countries (the USA, the United Kingdom and Australia), the public service organisations inform the public about the risks of smoking, domestic and family violence and COVID-19 vaccines, respectively; in the process, they imply that the correct response is for the reader to quit smoking, call sexual and domestic violence counselling services about abuse or make arrangements for vaccination. Ultimately, these actions and behaviours are expected to improve the health and well-being of the readers; reduce the social and economic impact of undesirable behaviours such as smoking and domestic violence and improve the safety, well-being and cohesion of society at large.

Box 4.1   Excerpts from public messaging campaigns

1) Despite enormous progress in reducing smoking, tobacco use is still the leading cause of preventable death in the United States and imposes a terrible toll on families, businesses and government. Tobacco kills more than 480,000 people annually—more than AIDS, alcohol, car accidents, illegal drugs, murders and suicides combined. Tobacco costs the U.S. over $241 billion in health care expenditures and more than $365 billion in lost productivity each year (www.tobaccofreekids.org/problem/toll-us).

2) There are culturally sensitive services in Australia that can help.

1800RESPECT is Australia's national sexual assault, family and domestic violence counselling service. It provides free, confidential telephone and online counselling and information. Counsellors will listen to you, answer questions and can refer you to other support services in your local area.

Call 1800 737 732 or go to the 1800RESPECT website at www.1800RESPECT.org.au (www.dss.gov.au/women/publications-articles/reducing-violence/domestic-and-family-violence).

3) Who can get a COVID-19 vaccine? You may be able to get different doses of the vaccine depending on your age and if you're at increased risk from COVID-19.

This can include getting

- a 1st and 2nd dose of the COVID-19 vaccine
- an additional primary dose of the COVID-19 vaccine
- a booster dose of the COVID-19 vaccine

(www.nhs.uk/conditions/covid-19/covid-19-vaccination/about-covid-19-vaccination)

Public messaging can be considered a macro-genre, super genre or genre colony, defined as "a grouping of closely related genres which to a large extent share their individual communicative purposes although most of them will be different in a number of other respects" (Bhatia, 2014: 66). This broad category encompasses genres such as leaflets, fact sheets, announcements, social media posts, guides, awareness videos and so on, which all share the communicative purpose of informing, raising awareness and prompting citizen responses. However, these genres vary in terms of standard length, level of detail, tone, dissemination medium (print, website, television, community radio, etc.) and structural and stylistic conventions, among other respects.

Box 4.2   Questions to consider

1) What is your understanding of public messaging so far? How would you define it in your own words?
2) How does public messaging relate to the text types I presented in Chapter 3 (informative, expressive and operative)?
3) How does public messaging relate to the notion of genre (also covered in Chapter 3)?

62 *Translation and Community*

4.2 Translating public messaging as part of a communication strategy

Public messaging is the most common content that community translators process as part of their work. Public services in countries where the need for multilingual access to information is recognised are the main social agents generating public-interest texts for translation. A public service may commission the translation of a one-off text, but as I indicated, public messaging is usually systematic and purposeful (Bonfadelli, 2022: 61). As Bonfadelli (2022: 61) notes, information campaigns are often designed as part of a communication strategy for a well-defined audience, and they usually involve implementation steps, monitoring of progress and evaluation of the entire campaign. The translation of public messages, therefore, needs to be viewed and approached as part of a systematic communication strategy implemented by the relevant organisation.

Translation quality in this context lies in the communicative effectiveness of translations, that is, the extent to which they are fit for purpose and aligned with the translation brief and target user needs (Taibi and Ozolins, 2016; Taibi, 2018). Public service organisations produce texts to inform people and prompt them to act. Community translations should also be produced in a manner and style that ensures that the message is conveyed effectively and increases the likelihood of target audiences responding as expected.

I have described in previous chapters that community translation requires a functionalist approach to translation and awareness of the overarching mission of this language service—empowering communities—and this is probably nowhere more applicable than in the translation of public messaging. As I pointed out in Chapter 3, functionalist theories view translation as a purposeful activity and the intended communicative purpose or function as the most important factor in translation choices (Vermeer, 1989: 20; Nord, 2014: 120). Therefore, translation needs to be done in a manner that serves the purpose in the most appropriate and effective way to facilitate communication in this context.

One key requirement for communication through translation to be effective is accessibility: A message cannot be effective if the audience are unable to understand it. Public messaging in many countries has become increasingly accessible and user friendly, probably as a result of the Plain Language Movement I mentioned in Chapter 1. However, public messaging, as Barron (2012: 66–67) affirms, often involves one-way communication (from institutions to citizens and residents) characterised by a power differential, and this power asymmetry between public services and their audiences is often reflected in language. Especially in those countries where administrations have not been influenced by movements such as the Plain Language Movement, public messaging is still full of formal or specialised language, complex structures and inaccessible language that is intended to mark authority and power rather than an interest in communicating with the target audience. The two examples in Box 4.3 are both in English, but the first was published on the website of HealthDirect, an Australian government-funded service providing health information and advice, and the other was published on the website of the Saudi Ministry of Health.

Translating public messaging 63

Box 4.3   Different levels of accessibility

Example 1: Excerpt from awareness resources (Australia)

What is addiction?

Addiction is when you have a strong physical or psychological need or urge to do something or use something. It is a dependence on a substance or activity even if you know that it causes you harm. It can impact your daily life.

What is drug abuse?

Drug abuse is when a drug is used inappropriately. This can be when it is

- used for a different purpose than it is meant for
- taken in excessive amounts

Substances such as alcohol can be used in harmful ways. However, drug abuse usually refers to the use of illicit drugs (www.healthdirect.gov.au/substance-abuse).

Example 2: Excerpt from awareness resources (Saudi Arabia)

Addiction and drugs

Narcotics are addictive drugs that act as depressants upon the nervous system. The term (narcotic) refers to an agent that inhibits and suppresses the activity of one's intellect, due to chemical substances that cause drowsiness, sleeping or falling unconscious.

   Addiction—substance or drug abuse—may lead to dependence syndrome, which involves a cluster of physiological, behavioral, and cognitive phenomena in which the use of substances takes on a much higher priority for a given individual. This usually includes a strong desire or sense of compulsion to take the substance despite its harmful consequences, as well as a physiological withdrawal state.

(www.moh.gov.sa/en/HealthAwareness/EducationalContent/AddictionandDrugs/Pages

---

A quick comparison of the two examples shows that Example 1 is organised under headings/questions and written in the form of bullet points and short sentences, while Example 2 consists of larger and denser paragraphs. In terms of language, Example 2 uses specialised or less common terms more frequently (e.g., narcotics, depressants, inhibit, suppress, dependence syndrome, cluster of physiological/

64 *Translation and Community*

behavioural/cognitive phenomena, compulsion). This comparison is not intended to make any generalisations about the countries or institutions where such texts are produced but to point out that different people, organisations, languages and cultures have different ways of communicating information to the public.

Translating public messaging will require awareness of such differences and, most important, the communication strategy the translation is part of. Depending on the reason an organisation is publishing material and/or having it translated, the community translator may need to adapt text organisation, structural complexity and lexical or terminological choices. In addition to information received from the commissioner (client), this is also based on what the translator knows about the target audience, to which I turn in the next section.

4.3 Audience design and personas

Every writer, including translators, has an audience in mind. In the translation of public messaging, the source text writer might have in mind a monolingual and monocultural audience or might be aware that the source text is going to be used by other audiences and therefore translated to other languages, translated for the benefit of culturally and linguistically diverse communities, translated into minority languages or similar broad notions of community translation. The translator, however, will generally have a more specific audience in mind based on the translation brief, the text type and contents and their knowledge of the community or communities they usually translate for.

In Chapter 1, I discussed personas, translation user profiles within the target audience which assist the translator in visualizing the audience and their expectations and needs (Tomozeiu, 2016; Suojanen et al., 2015). Based on their knowledge about the target community and their previous experiences and interactions with them, the translator can sketch out common user profiles (Tomozeiu, 2016: 197, 202) that consist of brief sentences or bullet points focusing on information that is relevant to the translation task (e.g., ethnic/national/regional background, education/literacy level, dissemination medium preferences), as in the examples in Box 4.4.

Box 4.4 Examples of personas

Samar Labeeb: 40-year-old Lebanese woman; migrated to Scotland recently together with her partner; her partner speaks and reads English very well, but she is still learning the language; she left school when she was 15; at this stage, she prefers to read public service information in Arabic; finds Arabic texts relatively easy to understand, but quite challenging when the text contains complex structures or specialised terminology.

Oscar Herrero: 60-year-old man originally from Mexico; has been living in the USA since 1995; completed secondary school in Mexico; able to speak some English in everyday situations but finds reading English texts quite challenging; speaks only Spanish at home. Able to read and write in Spanish but finds administrative and legal language difficult to understand; often uses a Spanish monolingual dictionary.

Ruying Han: 30-year-old woman who migrated from China to Australia as a refugee; works in a Chinese restaurant in Sydney, high literacy in Chinese but limited English proficiency so far; finds English texts difficult to understand and often refers to Chinese social media and websites for information about health care.

Ravi Kumar: Originally from South India; been working in the United Arab Emirates for 10 years; able to read materials in English and Hindi but unable to read or speak Arabic; when reading materials in English, he is able to understand business-related texts more than health care or legal ones.

In Chapter 1, I also mentioned the notions of 'implied reader' and 'audience design'. Implied readers are the target readers as inferred from one's analysis of the source text (Suojanen et al., 2015: 57; Tomozeiu, 2016: 199); before translating the text, the translator can analyse it in terms of "an assumed addressee to whom the work is directed and whose linguistic codes, ideological norms, and aesthetic ideas must be taken account of if the work is to be understood" (Hühn et al., 2009: 170) or, to use Suojanen et al.'s (2015) words, "hypothetical readers to whom writers target their texts or whom a researcher can construct from the text through textual analysis" (63). The same analysis can later be undertaken in relation to the translation to see how the implied reader of the source text compares with that of the target text. "By identifying the characteristics of the ST readership in detail", Tomozeiu (2016: 199) advises, "the translator can compare and contrast them with those of the TT readership and make informed translation decisions".

Audience design refers to the overall context of reception with all the macro- and micro-levels of the communicative situation (Suojanen et al., 2015: 68). Bell (1984) uses the term to explain that speakers (and writers) accommodate their communication style to the people they are addressing and the general context of reception. Bell (1984: 159) distinguishes four audience roles:

- The addressee: The main person addressed by the speaker using the second person. They are known, ratified as participants in the communication and addressed by the speaker.
- Auditors: Third persons who are in the communication situation but are not directly addressed. They are known and ratified.
- Overhearers: "Third parties whom the speaker knows to be there, but who are not ratified participants".
- Eavesdroppers: Other parties who intentionally or unintentionally receive the communication but whose presence is unknown.

66 *Translation and Community*

Bell (1984: 161, 186) also refers to 'referee design' and 'referees': Reference groups who are not present in the communicative situation but exercise certain influence on the speaker's (or writer's) attitudes and language use. Another point Bell makes that is even more relevant to community translation is that unlike interpersonal communication, the audience design in mass communication (e.g., radio or TV broadcasting, written public messaging) is influenced more by the mental image the speaker/writer forms of their likely audience than by responses to the audience itself (177). This is the case because "the communicator cannot know exactly who is being addressed" (Hatim and Mason, 1997: 69). As Suojanen et al. (2015: 69) explain, audience design can potentially clarify who the target audience of the translation is, but translations are generally intended for mass readers rather than a specific reader who is known to the translator, and "the target audience can therefore easily become a murky, faceless entity". Suojanen and her co-authors continue to say that the audience design framework can at least assist translators in identifying their primary and intended readers so that they can then address their needs through translation options and solutions.

In the case of community translations, the addressees are generally members of the community who have difficulty accessing information in the official, mainstream or dominant language. They can be all the people who fall under this category and speak a given nondominant language or a specific group within this target community (e.g., Arabic-speaking young Syrian men and women who arrived recently in Berlin, Germany, as asylum seekers). In either case, the addressees would be known to the translator as personas, not as individual addressees as would be the case in community interpreting for example.

Auditors can include public service agents involved in the communication campaign (although institutional decision makers may not be able to understand translations, they may have bilingual assistants who are able to advise on translations). The group of auditors can also include community organisations and leaders interested in social equity, inclusiveness and the human rights of the target community. Overhearers and eavesdroppers are probably less important in this context, but other professional translators may be referees (a reference group) with significant influence: As a community translator drafts their translation, they will be thinking about the community profile and the persona profile, but at the same time, they may have in mind what other translators (or revisers) might have to say about their translation choices and language use.

Bell (1984) notes that in the case of a large target audience or mass communication (e.g., radio or TV interview), "mass auditors are likely to be more important to a communicator than the immediate addressees" (177). Similarly, in the case of translators (and interpreters) for large target audiences, the auditors (e.g., the public service commissioning the translation in our case) might be given more weight than the intended addressee (Hatim and Mason, 1997: 83). However, in the context of community translation, particularly the translation of public messaging, it is important to remember that the main stakeholder is the public being addressed. Consideration of the audience design helps in identifying the intended readers or users (primary addressees), as well as secondary ones (auditors, overhearers, eavesdroppers, and

Translating public messaging 67

referees). Once these roles have been identified, the community translator will be able to translate in a way that takes them into consideration and, where necessary, prioritise the needs and expectations of some audience roles over others (Tomozeiu, 2016: 200–201; Taibi, 2023). In translating public messaging (and community translation in general), the intended users should come first.

4.4 Common issues and aspects to consider

4.4.1 *Priorities: Accuracy or accessibility and appropriateness?*

I discussed the nature of community translation in Chapter 1, the role of community translators in Chapter 2 and the functional approach to translation and translation strategies in Chapter 3. One common issue that relates to community translation in general and to the translation of public messaging in particular is whether the translator should give priority to message accuracy or to accessibility and appropriateness from the perspective of the target audience.

As I pointed out in Chapter 3, there may be competing interests and expectations, with the commissioner of the translation, for example, asking for or expecting a quite literal translation or the relevant organisation being intentionally unclear in their public messaging (Chesterman, 2016) and the target audience, on the other hand, expecting clear and accessible translations that cater to their needs and literacy levels. This loyalty dilemma (whose needs to prioritise and whose perspective to take to determine the function of translation) will always be there, but as I noted in Chapter 3, the commissioner's brief can be taken as a statement of intentions and preferences, while the community translator as a professional stakeholder and language and cultural expert can both discuss the translation approach with the commissioner and use their knowledge about the community's sociolinguistic context to decide the most appropriate translation strategies.

In translating public messaging, accuracy vs. accessibility should not be a major dilemma. Firstly, the translation of public messaging is not the same as other types of translation, such as the translation of legal and official documents (see Chapter 8). Secondly, as I mentioned, translating public communication campaigns is generally intended to share information with communities and make positive and socially desirable impacts on them, which requires translation to be accessible and effective for the target audience. Accessibility, appropriateness and effectiveness are clearly key in community translation in general and in this area of translation particularly. Thirdly, accessibility and appropriateness are not incompatible with accuracy. Some might believe that accuracy is a close rendition of content and form, including order of information, sentence structure (whether complex or not), the register (level of language formality) and terminology. However, accuracy needs to be understood in a pragmatic sense, i.e., focusing on the message being conveyed.

For that message to be conveyed effectively, translators often need to make formal adjustments because messages are not communicated in the same way across languages, cultures and audiences. Making such adjustments and improving readability (e.g., adding or omitting lexical or syntactic elements to ensure clarity) are

68   *Translation and Community*

not considered translation errors in this context. As long as the message is not altered and the addition, deletion or stylistic variation is contextually justified, that is not a mistranslation.

4.4.2 *Cohesion and coherence*

Related to accessibility and appropriateness are cohesion and coherence. Cohesion, according to Halliday and Hasan (1976: 10), "refers to relations of meaning that exist within the text, and that define it as a text". These relationships can be grammatical (e.g., referring to something or someone with a pronoun after they were mentioned by name) or lexical (e.g., referring back to something mentioned earlier through repetition of the same lexical item or substitution with a synonym or a more general word).

Cohesion is a textual feature which ensures that parts of a text are grammatically and semantically connected and enables the interpretation of some elements with reference to others (Halliday and Hasan, 1976: 4). Coherence is the extent to which a text reads or sounds conceptually and logically connected and makes sense to the audience in a real-life or imagined context. Cohesion and coherence are related, may overlap and may even be confused, but as Tanskanen (2006: 7) states, it is generally accepted that "cohesion refers to the grammatical and lexical elements on the surface of a text which can form connections between parts of the text. Coherence, on the other hand, resides not in the text, but is rather the outcome of a dialogue between the text and its listener or reader".

To illustrate, consider the following example in Box 4.5.

Box 4.5   Cohesion and coherence

Physical activity and cancer prevention

We know that by maintaining a healthy body weight, being physically active every day and enjoying a healthy diet, you can lower your risk of developing cancer. We know that these factors account for at least 30 per cent of all cancers.

Before you continue reading, please consider the following questions:

1) "Physical activity" and "cancer prevention" are joined with the conjunction "and". Does that provide some kind of link between the two? Does it suggest any conceptual or logical relationship?
2) Both sentences start with the pronoun "we", while the first sentence refers to "you". Who do you think is being addressed or referred to here?

Translating public messaging 69

3) The second sentence refers to "these factors". Does this provide a link to the first sentence? If so, how can you locate what "these factors" refers to in the first sentence?
4) Overall, does this example read logically? Does it make sense to you?

The fact that "physical activity" and "cancer prevention" are joined with the conjunction 'and' shows that they are connected somehow. This connection may suggest something as simple as being together, as in, for instance, "I can see Alan and Rebecca on the sofa". It may also suggest a logical relation such as "physical activity" causing, leading to or contributing to "cancer prevention". "We know" may refer to a group of people attending a meeting, a group of experts who have specialist knowledge, or people in general, including both the writer/speaker and the audience. Similarly, "you" in English can refer to the addressee (singular or plural) or people in general (in the sense of "one/people can lower one's/their risk of developing cancer"). Our knowledge about health and the world we live in can help us to make sense of the sentence "We know that by maintaining a healthy body weight, being physically active every day and enjoying a healthy diet, you can lower your risk of developing cancer".

So far, we can take this statement as comprehensible, true or at least reasonably logical. An issue starts to arise in the second sentence: "We know that these factors account for at least 30 per cent of all cancers". In terms of cohesion, we can see that "these factors" (demonstrative pronoun + general word) provides a referential link to the first sentence. So while a cohesive tie is provided between the two sentences, at a logical level, the link suggests an odd relationship. If we replace "these factors" with the factors referred to in the first sentence, we obtain the following reading: "We know that maintaining a healthy body weight, being physically active every day and enjoying a healthy diet account for at least 30 per cent of all cancers". Our first reaction would be to find that the statement does not make sense, as it is inconsistent with what we know about good practices and lifestyles conducive to good health:

- "As one of society's most considerable public health problems, having an unhealthy body weight accounts for 4 million premature deaths globally each year" (Glosz, 2021).
- "Unhealthy diet accounts for more than 11 million deaths annually, with four million deaths due to obesity, the United Nations health agency said today" (UN News, 2016).
- "Globally the study estimated that an unhealthy diet accounts for about 30% of cases [of myocardial infarction]" (Hoekstra et al., 2009).
- "Physical inactivity accounts for more than 3 million deaths worldwide, and is implicated in causing 6% of coronary heart diseases, 7% of diabetes, and 10% of colon or breast cancer" (Gichu et al., 2018).

Most probably, the coherence issue in the "physical activity and cancer prevention" example was just an oversight. Readers are also likely to understand the point

70 *Translation and Community*

intended by the writer. However, this kind of coherence issue can affect people's understanding of public messaging and impact on the awareness campaign itself. Translators should therefore pay attention to such inconsistencies both in the source text and in their draft translations.

4.4.3 Language variety

As Taibi and Ozolins (2016: 15–16) point out, the diversity of users is one of the challenges in community translation. Both in cases of autochthonous multilingualism and in language diversity arising as a result of migration, the target audiences of community translations will usually show a great degree of diversity, including in terms of literacy levels and the language variants they speak or are able to understand. I also described in Chapter 1 that translation and writing in many language communities are closely associated with the standard variant of the community language, although this variant may only be accessible to some socioeducational levels within the community. This suggests that public services need to—and many already do—consider the dissemination of translated public messaging in other formats such as audiovisual materials (see Chapter 7), which are more appropriate and effective for the target audience.

As a general pragmatic rule, the choice of language variant needs to be based on 1) the dissemination medium (e.g., whether the translation is going to be published in print or as audiovisual subtitles); 2) the target group (whether the material is aimed at all the community that speaks a language or a specific group within it); and 3) the sociolinguistic demographics of the community in question (e.g., Arabic speakers in Spain or France are mostly from North Africa, while Arabic speakers in Australia are mainly from Lebanon, Iraq and Egypt), as well as; 4) the applicable sociolinguistic and cultural norms (e.g., for some communities, formal communication is more trustworthy for public messaging than colloquial or informal language). As I pointed out in Chapter 2, such questions can be discussed with the commissioner of the translation, and the translator may have a role to play in advising both about appropriate language varieties and dissemination channels (communication and negotiation between the translator and relevant stakeholders).

For example, Burke (2018) suggests that for the Swahili-speaking community in Australia, Standard Swahili is the most suitable for community translations because of its neutral status and because it is "a lingua franca for inter-ethnic communication as used in mass media, education and government in relevant African countries" (168). However, Burke also acknowledges that translations in Standard Swahili are not accessible to all speakers of the language. The same applies to Arabic: Standard Arabic is the language of writing and the language variant that can be understood in all Arab countries but only among those who have undertaken sufficient formal education in the language.

As Burke (2018) recommends, "Translators should be prepared to adapt their translations in order to communicate optimally", in line with the aim of public services "to achieve receptive understanding of their communications by a broadly targeted audience" (168). The aim in translating public messaging is to maximise the

Translating public messaging 71

audience's chances of understanding and acting upon the messages communicated. The language variant to be used, therefore, needs to be as neutral and inclusive as possible. In Australia, the USA and the UK, for instance, Spanish speakers come from different parts of the world, including Spain, Mexico and South America; the same can be said about Arabic-speaking migrants, who have their origins in over 20 countries.

In determining the language variant, therefore, neutral and inclusive linguistic choices (avoiding regionalisms and localisms in terms of syntax, lexical choices and idioms) are best for meeting everyone's needs, or at least most of the target community. For example, to translate "face mask" into Spanish, "the term '*barbijo*' might not be generally understood, whereas more people will be familiar with the term '*mascarilla*'" (AUSIT-FECCA (n.d.)). Where the audience is known to use a specific variant of the language in question, that variant should be used in the translation, subject of course to other considerations (e.g., whether the dissemination channel is written or oral/audiovisual). The AUSIT-FECCA (n.d.) *Style Guide for Community Translations into Spanish*, for example, recommends, "If the information is aimed at a particular Spanish-speaking community (e.g., Mexican), use the relevant regional dialect, or decline the assignment if unable to translate into that variant".

4.4.4 Language appropriateness and naturalness

Translations of public messaging need to be appropriate in terms of language and style. This means appropriateness at four levels at least: grammar, register and style, and appropriateness for the audience. Consistency with the grammatical rules of the target language is the most basic level, and it therefore tends to be taken for granted. However, errors and inconsistencies at this level can create major issues in terms of impact on meaning, user experience or both.

Register and style are the next level of language appropriateness. The fact that a translation is grammatically correct does not mean that it complies with the language appropriateness criterion. Translations must read naturally: They need to be idiomatic, using lexical choices, expressions, collocations and sentence structures that are typical of the target language and the text genre and type at hand. In addition, the register and style used in the translation need to be appropriate both to the public messaging text being translated and from the perspective of genre and text type norms and conventions applicable in the target language and culture. Finally, and in relation to the last point, language appropriateness including register appropriateness needs to be considered in relation to the audience design, especially the literacy level and expectations of the target users. As Burke (2018) suggested, translators are expected to make adaptations to ensure optimal and effective communication.

4.4.5 Cultural appropriateness

Like advertising, public messaging needs to be culturally appropriate to be effective: It needs to be relevant, relatable and culturally sensitive. While cultural

72 *Translation and Community*

appropriateness needs to be addressed by public services when they are still planning or developing source texts (e.g., Seale et al., 2022; Crezee and Wong Soon, 2023), translators can also have a role before or during the translation stage (Taibi and Ozolins, 2016; Taibi, 2018; Sengupta et al., 2024). As Sengupta et al. (2024: 138) recommend, "when there are features that require modifications beyond the constraints of accurate linguistic translation, translators should be encouraged to at least make proposals as to the kinds of transcreation required". Examples of modifications that translators can make to ensure the cultural appropriateness of their translations can include examples used in the source text (e.g. lifestyle, diet), figures of speech, culture-specific references, offensive language and so on (see Chapter 6). Features translators may be able to advise about (if the source text development stage failed to address them) include illustrations (cartoons, photographs, body images, etc.), taboo topics and other cultural sensitivities.

4.5   Practical example

4.5.1   Translation brief

The text in Box 4.6 is a part of English-language resources developed by the South African Police Service in relation to cyberbullying and other safety issues. The text provides information and tips about cyberbullying for children, teenagers and parents. The South African Police Service would like to publish translations into the other 10 official languages on its website. In addition, the same content will be published in the form of leaflets in languages including Arabic, Chinese (Mandarin), Hindi, Spanish, etc. Please translate the information below into your other working language. Please feel free to make the register more/less formal if that is appropriate for your target audience. If major adaptations are required, please discuss with us before you proceed.

Box 4.6   Dealing with cyberbullying

With the advent of technology, bullying is no longer limited to schoolyards or street corners. Cyberbullying can occur anywhere, even at home, through email, texts, cellular phones or social media websites. For those who suffer cyberbullying, the effects can be devastating, leaving you feeling hurt, humiliated, angry, depressed or even suicidal. However, no type of bullying should ever be tolerated. These tips can help you protect yourself online and deal with the growing problem of cyberbullying.

What is cyberbullying?

Cyberbullying occurs when a child or teen uses the Internet, emails, text messages, instant messaging, social media websites, online forums, chat rooms or other digital technology to harass, threaten or humiliate another child or teen. Cyberbullies come in all shapes and sizes. Almost anyone with an Internet connection or cellular phone can cyberbully someone else, often without having to reveal their true identity. Cyberbullies can torment their victims 24 hours a day, and the bullying can follow the victim anywhere, so that no place, not even home, ever feels safe, and with a few clicks, the humiliation can be witnessed by hundreds or even thousands of people online.

How cyberbullying harms people

The methods children and teens use to cyberbully can be as varied and imaginative as the technology they have access to. It ranges from sending threatening or taunting messages through email or text to breaking into your email account or stealing your online identity to hurt and humiliate you. Some cyberbullies may even create a website or social media page to target you.

Tips for children or teens dealing with cyberbullying

Do not respond. If someone bullies you, remember that your reaction is usually exactly what the bully wants. It gives him or her power over you.

Do not retaliate. Responding with similar threats reinforces the bully's behaviour. Help avoid a whole cycle of aggression.

Save the evidence. Online messages can usually be captured, saved and shown to someone who can help. Save evidence even if it is minor. Cyberbullying can escalate.

Block the bully. Use preferences or privacy tools to block the person. If it happens while you are chatting, leave the "room." Report any abusive comments to the social media website administrators.

Reach out for help. Talk to a friend or a trusted adult who can help.

Tips for parents and teachers to stop cyberbullying

No matter how much pain it causes, children are often reluctant to tell parents or teachers about cyberbullying.

Spot the warning signs of cyberbullying

Your child may be the victim of cyberbullying if he or she

- becomes sad, angry or distressed during or after using the Internet or a cellular phone.
- appears anxious when receiving a text or email or have been on social media websites.

74   *Translation and Community*

- avoids discussions or is secretive about computer or cellular phone activities.
- withdraws from family, friends and activities they previously enjoyed.
- refuses to go to school or to specific classes or avoids group activities.
- illustrates changes in mood, behaviour, sleep or appetite or shows signs of depression or anxiety.

Source: www.saps.gov.za/child_safety/teens/teens.php

4.5.2   Context

The translation brief in Box 4.6 provides part of the translation and communicative context: The commissioner is the South African Police Service; the purpose of the translation is to provide information and tips to children, teenagers and their parents in relation to cyberbullying; the target languages are both the official languages of the country and other community languages; the dissemination media consist of a website text (for official languages) or a leaflet text (for other languages) and the commissioner is happy for necessary adaptations to be made, although major ones need to be discussed with them first.

As a community translator, you will need to complement this information with insights from the source text (e.g., information about cyberbullying and typical behaviours and impact, the tone of the text and the extent to which the writer appears to be distant or close to the reader, etc.); your extralinguistic knowledge about Internet activities, bullying in general and cyberbullying in particular, and about children, teenagers and parents; your knowledge about the South African Police Service (or any other organisation that is relevant to the text); your knowledge about the South African society as a whole and the target community of your translation and most important, the linguistic, sociocultural and sociolinguistic elements that are likely to facilitate or impede translation into your target language (for the relevant local community). In relation to the latter, it is worth outlining a few community member personas as suggested in Section 4.3.

4.5.3   Comprehension

Comprehension ability and challenges will vary from one person to another depending, among other reasons, on familiarity with the topic and proficiency in the source language; in the case of the cyberbullying message, English. Generally speaking, the text is written in a language that is easy to understand; the syntactical structures are not too complex, and specialised terminology is not frequently used. However, there are some lexical items and expressions that might be challenging, not so much so at the comprehension phase but rather when you start rendering the text into your other language:

Cyberbullying: Bullying in general means to try to harm, intimidate or pressure someone, especially someone who is perceived as vulnerable. This is a definition

Translating public messaging   75

that you can find in a general monolingual English dictionary. Cyberbullying can be morphologically understood as bullying that takes place the cyberspace (the Internet). General dictionaries will also tell you that cyberbullying is the use of electronic communication to bully someone, for example by sending intimidating or threatening messages. Now that you have a clear understanding of the term, your main challenge will be identifying the available target language resources and acceptable and appropriate translation options for this context.

Advent: This is a quite formal word which means arrival or coming into existence, especially for an important person, event or invention. Whether you maintain the level of formality will depend on your analysis of the communicative situation and your target audience. However, you might want to note that the meaning of the sentence "With the advent of technology, bullying is no longer limited to schoolyards or street corners" will not change if you omit "the advent of". Remember we are translating messages, not words.

Taunting messages: Sarcastic or otherwise harmful messages or remarks that are intended to hurt, provoke, demoralise or anger someone. As a translator, you also need to consider how this term relates to other terms in the same text (e.g., *Abusive comments* in this section) and whether your target language has lexical options available to distinguish one from the others.

To target you: In this context, this means to aim an attack or cyberbullying campaign at the person in question.

Cycle of aggression: Aggression refers to physically or verbally attacking someone or showing hostility towards them; here, the text relates to cyber activities only. 'Cycle of aggression' refers to the perpetrator attacking and the victim responding in an endless and sometimes intensifying loop of bullying activities.

Escalate: In this case, to increase the seriousness, intensity or severity of cyberbullying activities.

Block the bully: As you most probably know, blocking in general means preventing someone from going or entering somewhere (e.g., by standing in front of them or parking your car in a way that prevents them from driving out). In the world of social media and electronic communication, blocking consists of not allowing someone to contact you or access your online content.

Preferences or privacy tools: Settings and options that allow a user to determine their level of privacy when using electronic communication and social media. Again, the challenge might not lie as much in comprehending the terms as in finding the right way to express them in the target language, especially in cases where the language has not developed robust technology and communications terminology.

Abusive comments: Offensive and insulting comments; see *Taunting messages.*

Website administrators: The technical professionals who are in charge of the websites or other platforms where cyberbullying can take place.

Reach out for help: This is one of those non-technical expressions that are easy to understand but at the same time might be challenging for some, especially non-native speakers. To literally 'reach out' means to stretch out your arm to reach something or someone, but it figuratively means to contact someone to

76 *Translation and Community*

offer or seek something, in this instance to request assistance with being bullied, which becomes clear in the sentence that follows: "Talk to a friend or a trusted adult who can help". Indeed, the source text itself often provides helpful context that explains terms and expressions that might initially be ambiguous or difficult to understand.

Sad, angry or distressed: Distress refers to suffering from extreme anxiety, sorrow or pain. While it is easy to distinguish between sadness and anger, it might be difficult in some languages to distinguish between sadness and distress or between anger and distress. Other languages might have more nuanced lexical items for more specific emotions.

Depression or anxiety: The difficulty with sadness versus distress also applies to this pair of lexical items: While general dictionaries and reference works will tell you the difference between depression and anxiety, you might find it challenging to express and distinguish between them in your target language.

4.5.4 *Translation stage*

You can go through the translation strategies covered in Chapter 3 and consider which would be the most appropriate; this, of course, will vary depending on the language you are translating into and the community you are translating for. Possible translation techniques could include establishing equivalents (if your target language already has a term or concept commonly recognised as equivalent to 'cyberbullying'), borrowing the English term and providing an explanation between parentheses (translation using a loan word plus explanation, as suggested by Baker, 2011 [1992]) or simply rephrasing the term. If you are not sure about the options available in your target language, a search in related texts will be helpful. For example, UNICEF (2023) has the text "Cyberbullying: What is it and how to stop it" available in four languages: Arabic, English, French and Spanish. It is interesting to note the different ways the concept is expressed in the four languages:

English: Cyberbullying
French: *L'intimidation en ligne* ("online intimidation")
Spanish: *Ciberacoso* ("cyberharassment"/"cyberbullying")
Arabic: التنمّر عبر الإنترنت ("bullying through the Internet")

In both English and Spanish, the term is created by blending 'cyber' (meaning) and 'bullying'. In French, the term 'bullying' is usually translated as *harcèlement* or *intimidation*, so 'cyberbullying' is translated through the analytical rephrasing strategy *intimidation en ligne* (intimidation or bullying that takes place online). Similarly, the Arabic version takes an established equivalent for 'bullying' and adds the qualifier 'through the Internet'.

As I said in Chapter 3, the fact that translation theories classify several translation strategies or techniques as possible options is not to be interpreted as suggesting that strategies are interchangeable. Rather, the appropriateness of each strategy

Translating public messaging 77

needs to be determined based on the language we are translating into, the type of text we are translating, the translation brief we have received from the client and so on. For example, it goes without saying that omission and generalisation would not be appropriate strategies in translating 'cyberbullying' in the message: The term cannot be omitted because it is the main topic of the text and is central to the entire message. Similarly, it cannot be replaced with a more general word such as 'bullying', 'intimidation', 'abuse' or 'misconduct' because these terms do not specifically denote that the harassment is taking place online. Translation, of course, is not just a matter of finding the right words or expressions in the target language that could be accepted as equivalent to those in the source text. It is also, and most importantly, about identifying logical and conceptual links between parts of the text and conveying ideas in the most natural, coherent and cohesive way possible (see Section 4.4).

4.5.5 *Translation revision*

An essential step in translation is revision or checking. This consists of comparing a draft translation with its source text to identify any accuracy issues such as mistranslations or unjustified omissions or additions. It also consists of reading the translation to ensure that it is free from language inconsistencies, coherence issues, style awkwardness or typographical oversights. I discuss translation revision in more detail in Chapter 10; in this section, I only include a brief note on self-revision (checking done by the translator) as a necessary step in translating the cyberbullying advisory. As Mossop (2007: 196) notes, self-revision can take place "over two phases: the drafting phase and the post-drafting phase". At the drafting phase, the translator will usually monitor their writing, think about the structures and lexical choices they are using and, if necessary, amend or rewrite segments. At the postdrafting phase, the translator will revise the entire draft for both content accuracy and language and textual appropriateness. The following questions will be useful when revising your draft:

*   Does the translation make sense? Is the message consistent?
*   Is the translation complete?
*   Is the translation accurate in comparison with the source text?
*   Does the translation flow smoothly and read easily?
*   Is the message easy to understand?
*   Is the language used (structure, words, expressions, etc.) correct?
*   Is the language used natural/acceptable?
*   Is the register appropriate?
*   Is the translation consistent with the translation brief?
*   Is the translation culturally appropriate and politically correct?
*   Is the layout appropriate and consistent (including display of your language script, spacing, margins, indentations, positioning of footnotes, relationship of text to graphics)?

78 *Translation and Community*

> **Summary**
>
> Public messaging is the backbone of community translation: Public-interest communication intended for the society in general or some social groups in particular constitutes the staple content for community translators. Public messaging campaigns aim to educate and raise awareness about social, health, environmental, political and other issues. As such, their communicative intent is not only informative but also outcome oriented; that is, they are expected to achieve certain effects or responses among the target audience such as changing their behaviours or practices. The quality of community translations in this area is therefore determined by the extent to which they are suitable, accessible, effective and impactful for the intended audience.
>
> To ensure that community translations meet these quality criteria, translators need to treat translation tasks as part of a public-service or public-interest communication strategy. Based on the translation brief and the source text itself, they need to identify the communicative functions of the text, the aims of the public messaging campaign and the priorities of the relevant public service. Taking into consideration their knowledge about the nature of community translation and the language-specific community they serve, translators can outline or visualise user profiles (e.g., personas, roles in an audience design) to produce translations that are not only accurate but also culturally, linguistically and stylistically appropriate; trustworthy and effective. In this regard, accuracy is understood in a pragmatic or communicative sense, and considerations such as cohesion, coherence, naturalness of expression and consistency with the genre and text type conventions of the target language/ culture are paramount.

Suggested activities

1) Look back at the text in "Dealing with cyberbullying". Imagine that this text was commissioned by your national or local police and think of your potential audience in your local or national context. Outline five personas that would represent different common profiles in your language community (potential users of your translation).
2) Translate the text into your other language. As you translate, write brief reflections on translation challenges and questions and your decision-making process (why you chose a specific word or expression, why you restructured or rephrased a sentence, why you simplified the language, etc.).
3) Give your translation to 1) a peer who is bilingual in English and the other language and 2) a speaker of the target language whose English literacy is not very high and ask both for feedback.

Further reading

- Tomozeiu, Daniel (2016). Defining 'community' for community translation, *New Voices in Translation Studies 14:* 190–209.

As I mentioned earlier, this paper relates to user profiles and how the community translator can visualise them to make informed decisions in their translation process. The author discusses the notions of persona, implied reader and audience design and illustrates the applicability of the concepts through a United Kingdom National Health Service text.

References

AUSIT-FECCA (n.d.). *Style guide for community translations into Spanish.* https://ausit. org/wp-content/uploads/2024/03/AUSIT-Style-Guide-for-Spanish-Community-Translations_042023.pdf.

Baker, Mona (2011 [1992]). *In other words: A coursebook on translation.* Abingdon: Routledge.

Barron, Anne (2012). *Public information messages: A contrastive genre analysis of state-citizen communication.* Amsterdam and Philadelphia: John Benjamins.

Bell, Allan (1984). Language style as audience design. *Language in Society,* 13: 145–204.

Bhatia, Vijay (2014). *Worlds of written discourse: A genre-based view.* London, New Delhi, New York and Sydney: Bloomsbury.

Bonfadelli, Heinz (2022). Theoretical approaches of health campaigns and practical applications to COVID-19 campaigns. *Science Journal of Public Health,* 10(1): 60–72. DOI: 10.11648/j.sjph.20221001.17.

Burke, Jean (2018). Linguistic diversity among Swahili-speakers: A challenge for translation in Australia. In Taibi, Mustapha (Ed.), *Translating for the community.* Bristol: Multilingual Matters: 156–173.

Chesterman, Andrew (2016). *Memes of translation. The spread of ideas in translation theory (Revised edition).* Amsterdam and Philadelphia: John Benjamins.

Crezee, Ineke and Wong Soon, Hoy Neng (2023). Speak my language! The important role of community translation in the promotion of health literacy. In González, Erika; Stachowiak-Szymczak, Katarzyna and Amanatidou, Despina (Eds.), *Community translation: Research and practice.* Abingdon and New York: Routledge: 101–141.

Gichu, Muthoni; Asiki, Gershim; Juma, Pamela et al. (2018). Prevalence and predictors of physical inactivity levels among Kenyan adults (18–69 years): An analysis of STEPS survey 2015. *BMC Public Health,* 18(Suppl 3): 1217. DOI: 10.1186/s12889-018-6059-4.

Glosz, Cambria (2021). *A new obesity drug on the block: Is this medication a game changer for weight loss?* https://au.prohealth.com/blogs/control-how-you-age/a-new-obesity-drug-on-the-block-is-this-medication-a-game-changer-for-weight-loss.

Halliday, Michael A. K. and Hasan, Ruqaya (1976). *Cohesion in English.* London: Longman.

Hatim, Basil and Mason, Ian (1997). *The translator as communicator.* London and New York: Routledge.

Hoekstra, Tiny; Beulens, Joline and van der Schouw, Yvonne (2009). Cardiovascular disease prevention in women: Impact of dietary interventions. *Maturitas,* 63(1): 20–27.

Hühn, Peter; Pier, John and Schmid, Wolf (2009). *Handbook of narratology—narratologia: Contributions to narrative theory.* Berlin: De Gruyter: 19.

McKenzie-Mohr, Doug (2011). *Fostering sustainable behavior: An introduction to community-based social marketing.* Gabriola Island: New Society Publishers.

Mossop, Brian (2007). *Revising and editing for translators.* Manchester: St. Jerome.

80 *Translation and Community*

Nord, Christiane (2014). Functionalist approaches. In Gambier, Yves and Van Doorslaer, Luc (Eds.), *Handbook of translation studies*. Amsterdam and Philadelphia: John Benjamins: 120–128.

Reiss, Katharina (2000 [1971]). *Translation criticism: The potentials and limitations*. Manchester: St. Jerome.

Saunders, Stephen G.; Barrington, Dani J. and Sridharan, Srinivas (2015). Redefining social marketing: Beyond behavioural change. *Journal of Social Marketing*, 5(2): 160–168.

Seale, Holly; Harris-Roxas, Ben; Heywood, Anita; Abdi, Ikram; Mahimbo, Abela; Chauhan, Achfaq and Woodland, Lisa (2022). Speaking COVID-19: Supporting COVID-19 communication and engagement efforts with people from culturally and linguistically diverse communities. *BMC Public Health*, 22(1): 1257. DOI: 10.1186/s12889-022-13680-1.

Sengupta, Medha; Pym, Anthony; Hao, Yu; Hajek, John et al. (2024). On the transcreation, format and actionability of healthcare translations. *Translation & Interpreting: The International Journal of Translation and Interpreting Research*, 16(1): 121–141. DOI: 10.12807/ti.116201.2024.a07.

Suojanen, Tytti; Koskinen, Kaisa and Tuominen, Tiina (2015). *User-centered translation*. London: Routledge.

Taibi, Mustapha (2018). Quality assurance in community translation. In Taibi, Mustapha (Ed.), *Translating for the community*. Bristol: Multilingual Matters: 7–25.

Taibi, Mustapha (2023). Public service translation. In Wadensjö, Cecilia and Gavioli, Laura (Eds.), *The Routledge handbook of public service interpreting*. London and New York: Routledge: 106–122.

Taibi, Mustapha and Ozolins, Uldis (2016). *Community translation*. London and New York: Bloomsbury.

Tanskanen, Sanna Kaisa (2006). *Collaborating towards coherence*. Amsterdam and Philadelphia: John Benjamins.

Tomozeiu, Daniel (2016). Defining 'community' for community translation. *New Voices in Translation Studies*, 14: 190–209.

UNICEF (2023). *Cyberbullying: What is it and how to stop it*. www.unicef.org/end-violence/how-to-stop-cyberbullying.

UNNews (2016). *Taxing sugary drinks can curb global epidemic of obesity and diabetes—UN health agency*. https://news.un.org/en/story/2016/10/542442.

Vermeer, Hans (1989). *Skopos und Translationsauftrag—Aufsätze*. Heidelberg Universität.

5 Translating regulatory texts

In this chapter, I focus on how to translate 'regulatory texts', that is, texts written from an institutional perspective to regulate rights, services and relationships between public services and citizens or residents. I do not cover specialised legal texts, contracts or agreements or other types of regulatory texts, but only legislative or institutional texts that are intended for the wider public (elections, social security benefits, school governance structures, etc.). The nature of these texts requires a discussion of the following:

- The overlapping relationships between regulatory, legal and institutional texts;
- Institutional translation and "government by translation" (Koskinen, 2014);
- Translation ethics in relation to regulatory texts (translator role and loyalties).

5.1 What are regulatory texts?

As the name suggests, regulatory texts relate to regulations, authoritative rules dealing with conditions, standards or procedures; these can be issued by governments, international organisations, professional bodies and so on. Examples include environmental regulations (e.g., waste management, industrial impact on the environment), employment regulations (e.g., employee rights, laws against child labour), product labelling regulations (e.g., product transparency, country of origin, nutrition information) or drug safety regulations (e.g., relating to naming, labelling and packaging medicines).

In this chapter and textbook, I use 'regulatory texts' to refer to texts written from an institutional perspective and serving to regulate rights, services and relationships between public services on the one hand and citizens and/or residents on the other. The focus is not on specialised legal texts (e.g., private contracts, international treaties or court sentences) but on legislative or institutional texts that are intended for the wider public (elections, social security benefits, school governance structures, etc.).

DOI: 10.4324/9781003367741-6

82   *Translation and Community*

While public messaging texts, covered in Chapter 4, are mainly informative and aim to educate the public and raise awareness among them, regulatory texts are informative as well but have the main purpose of defining institutional or procedural concepts, establishing terms and conditions and setting out rules for a given area. However, as I pointed out in Chapter 3, texts will not always fall under one type or genre only (Reiss and Vermeer (2014 [1984]: 183). Texts can be hybrid in terms of type and genre (Hatim and Mason (2013 [1990]: 146–148; Reiss and Vermeer (2014 [1984]: 183), with the features and functions of one text type usually being dominant. Thus, a public messaging text may include regulatory parts, and regulatory texts may contain public messaging, as the examples in Box 5.1 show.

Box 5.1   Regulatory text with public messaging

Making it official

Your relationship can be official in a few ways. Your relationship may be de facto, registered or married. You may need to confirm your relationship status with us.

If you have a partner, we consider you a member of a couple.

You'll need to let us know if you become partnered. This is so we can pay you the right amount.

If you or your partner are making a claim for a payment, you'll need to confirm your relationship status with us.

We assess relationship types as married, registered or de facto.

De facto relationship

A de facto relationship is where you and your partner meet all of these conditions:

- you're in a relationship similar to a married couple
- you're not married or in a registered relationship
- you're over the age of consent in the state or territory you live in
- you're not in a prohibited relationship under section 4(12) and section 4(13) of the *Social Security Act 1991*.

Being in a de facto relationship can have an effect on what payments you can get and your payment rate.

There's no minimum time period for a relationship to be de facto.

There are different relationship rules for ABSTUDY Living Allowance, Youth Allowance and Disability Support Pension.

When you tell us about your relationship change, it can help us determine if you're independent for these payments. This may affect your rate of payment.

If you get one of these payments and you're dependent, we don't consider you as a member of a couple. (www.servicesaustralia.gov.au/making-your-relationship-official?context=60029)

The text in Box 5.1 is from the website of Services Australia, an agency that delivers government payments and services and provides advice on several areas, including education, work, ageing, health and disability. *Making it official* relates to partner relationships (de facto, registered or married), how they are defined and how their status may impact entitlements and payments. It is not a legal text in the traditional sense of the term (see Section 5.2), but it does regulate a given area of life, which is marital status and different types of couple relationships. Although the text is not written in legal language (note, for instance, the use of contractions and personal pronouns such as "you" and "we"), it outlines conditions and makes reference to legislation, as in "not in a prohibited relationship under section 4(12) and section 4(13) of the *Social Security Act 1991*". At the same time, there are parts that can easily be described as general information or public messaging:

- Your relationship can be official in a few ways, as de facto, registered or married.
- Your relationship change can help us determine if you're independent for these payments, and this may affect your rate of payment.

Box 5.2   Public messaging with regulatory text

What is elective home education?

The government definition:

> 'Elective home education is a term used to describe a choice by parents to provide education for their children at home or in some other way they desire, instead of sending them to school full-time'.

You may wish to educate your child without any assistance from others. You may also wish to use

- private tutors
- tuition centres
- other adults or settings
- flexi-schooling (a mixture of school-based and home-based)
- part-time college (for Key Stage 4, those aged 14 to 16)

It's important to understand that schools may not always agree to flexi-schooling and college places have limited agreed criteria for enrolment. Other adults or settings may not be inspected and regulated in the same way that schools and learning providers are. Parents using other adults and settings need to be satisfied that their children are safe.

What does the law say?

You are responsible for making sure that your child is properly educated between the ages of 5 and 16 years old. This does not have to take place through attendance at school.

Section 7 of the Education Act 1996 says:

The parent of every child of compulsory school age shall cause them to receive efficient full-time education suitable

(a) to his age, ability and aptitude, and
(b) to any special educational needs he may have,

either by regular attendance at school or otherwise.

This means that if you choose to educate your child outside of a mainstream school through Elective Home Education, you are still meeting your legal requirements as a parent or carer. (www.barnsley.gov.uk/media/15952/parental-guidance-for-elective-home-education.pdf)

The text in Box 5.2 is from *Parental Guidance for Elective Home Education (EHE)*, published by the Barnsley Metropolitan Borough Council (United Kingdom). As the title of the publication states, it is a home education guide for parents; it provides guidance in relation to aspects to consider when deciding to provide home education to one's children (e.g., cost, space, social skills); the process to follow; definitions of suitable, efficient and full-time education and so on. The excerpt is mainly informative, explaining what elective home education consists of, but at the same time it includes regulatory parts such as the following:

- You are responsible for making sure that your child is properly educated between the ages of 5 and 16 years old.
- Section 7 of the Education Act 1996 says that

The parent of every child of compulsory school age shall cause them to receive efficient full-time education suitable

(a) to his age, ability and aptitude, and
(b) to any special educational needs he may have, either by regular attendance at school or otherwise.

As I said in Chapter 3 in the discussion of informative, expressive and operative (persuasive) text types, the translator needs to be aware that the same text may include more than one text type and needs to identify the text type based on its predominant function. Translation strategies and approaches will then be based on this predominant function. This awareness of how text types work and relate to one another can also guide the translator to vary translation approach locally: Within the same translation, different sections may be translated with slightly different approaches depending on the function and text type of the section in question. Thus, regulatory texts and regulatory parts in public messaging texts will normally require more attention to accuracy and language precision and consistency. This is not to say that these aspects are not important in other types of (community) translation; the point is that public messaging intended to inform, educate or guide users will usually allow the translator more leeway in terms of creativity and adaptation to the target audience, while regulatory texts will normally require more attention to conceptual, terminological and stylistic precision and accuracy. In this respect, they are quite similar to personal official documents (see Chapter 8).

5.2 Translating regulatory, legal and institutional texts

From the definition of regulatory texts that I give, it can be easily concluded that there might be—and there is—some overlap with other concepts and areas of translation practice, especially legal and institutional translation.

Legal translation is a well-known area of specialised translation which covers legal texts or any text that may be used for judicial purposes. Because of its legal implications, legal translation is usually more regulated than other areas of translation, such as literary or community translation. As Koskinen (2014: 487) points out, "Governance is centred around regulation and control, and legal translation is often among those fields that are well-organized and institutionalized". The texts that are common in this area are laws, international treaties, contracts, deeds, wills and court sentences.

Legal texts are characterised by notoriously complex (and sometimes archaic) structures, formal register, specialised terminology (e.g., 'apprehended violence order', 'representative proceeding', 'statement of claim', 'subpoena'), archaic or special phraseology (e.g., 'hereinafter', 'without prejudice to', 'at the motion of'), the use of couplets and triplets (e.g., 'no remorse or contrition', 'without let or hindrance', 'null and void'), and so on (Alcaraz Varó and Hughes, 2014). For translating such documents, the main requirements are accuracy (faithfully conveying the messages in the source texts) and register appropriateness (using a type and level of language that is suitable for the legal genre being translated). However, in addition to the difficulties I have already cited, legal translation presents challenges relating to cultural differences and differences between legal systems (Cao, 2010). Each legal system has its own deeply rooted culture and may be markedly different from others in terms of legal concepts, institutions, practices, conventions and language, which makes translation accuracy or equivalence a major challenge.

Institutional translation, in a broad sense, refers to "any translation that occurs in an institutional setting" (Schäffner et al., 2014: 493). In a more specific and useful definition, Schäffner et al. (2014) note that, in translation studies, "the label 'institutional translation' is generally used to refer to translating in or for a specific

86 *Translation and Community*

organisation. . . . Institutional translation is typically collective, anonymous and standardised" (493–494). Koskinen (2008: 22) offers an even more specific definition, although she includes a reference to individuals besides institutions, which might add to the confusion surrounding the concept of institutional translation:

> when an official body (government agency, multinational organization or a private company, etc.; also an individual person acting in an official status) uses translation as a means of 'speaking' to a particular audience. Thus, in institutional translation, the voice that is to be heard is that of the translating institution.
>
> (22)

Typical examples that are often cited in this context are translations for the UN, the European Commission or officially bilingual or multilingual countries such as Canada and Belgium. As Koskinen (2008: 22) points out, what distinguishes institutional translation from other types of translation is the expectation that the voice (i.e., public image, discourse, ideology and interests) of the relevant institution is to be prioritised. This is why organisations, especially large ones, have mechanisms and resources in place to ensure consistency and standardisation of translations (Schäffner et al., 2014: 494; Svoboda et al., 2017: 3). The standardisation of the terminological, structural and stylistic consistency of translations is often facilitated through "style guides and CAT tools, revision procedures, and mentoring and training arrangements" (Schäffner et al., 2014: 494).

What regulatory (as used in this chapter), legal and institutional texts have in common is that they are all related to regulation and governance. As Koskinen (2014: 488) argues, regulation is an essential activity in governing, and translation (legal, official and authorised translation, as the author puts it) is part of "the art of government by translation": "using translating as a technique for 'directing the conduct of the governed' in multilingual government" (Koskinen, 2014: 480). Typical text genres handled by translators in this area are juridical and administrative texts in addition to other (secondary) documents that are required as part of legal or administrative processes. Koskinen (2014) identifies four areas of text production and translation that are involved in government by translation:

- Maintenance: Foundational, documentary, administrative. This includes drafting the foundational documents of the governing institution and documenting and archiving its administrative processes to maintain its institutional legitimacy, accountability and functioning capacity. This is "the most introverted layer" (Koskinen, 2014: 488) in the sense that it is aimed at the institution or organisation itself rather than the public it governs or deals with.
- Regulative: Juridical, legal, official. Text production and translation in this area mainly cover legislation and other legal and administrative texts, but they may also include other text and translation types.
- Implementational: Informative, instructive. "Once the regulatory system with its related documentation is in place, the functioning of governance also requires

the **implementation** of regulations and norms, thus creating a need for various informative and instructive modes of communication" (Koskinen, 2014: 488; emphasis in the source).
- Communicative/image building: Symbolic, persuasive, political. This layer is at the opposite end of the spectrum from maintenance: It is the most extroverted (Koskinen, 2014: 488) in the sense that it is the most open to and focused on the public or governed populations. At this level, institutions, especially in democratic countries, seek to enhance their legitimacy and authority through the production (and, in many cases, translation) of texts that have a persuasive, political and/or symbolic nature. Such texts are labelled 'communicative' because they are aimed at the public and 'image-building' because they are often designed to convey and promote a specific image of the relevant institution.

The four layers are not necessarily all regulatory, at least not to the same extent. The implementational and communicative/image-building areas may be closer to the type of public messaging texts covered in Chapter 4, although implementational texts (informative and instructive) may be of both regulatory and public messaging types. Out of the four levels, implementational and communicative/image building are the most relevant to the work of community translators as they typically involve non-specialised texts aimed at the public. The regulative level may also involve communication with the public, especially in cases where legal frameworks, legislation and official texts are disseminated in abridged, more accessible or more user-friendly versions. In terms of the relationships between regulatory, legal and institutional texts (and the corresponding areas of translation), it should be noted that the three categories will always form overlapping circles, as illustrated in Figure 5.1.

Most legal texts are regulatory; this is the case for laws, treaties, contracts, wills and so on. However, as I have mentioned, a legal text can also consist of any text (e.g., personal correspondence, commercial receipt, invitation to an event, etc.) that is presented for legal purposes including those that are clearly not regulatory;

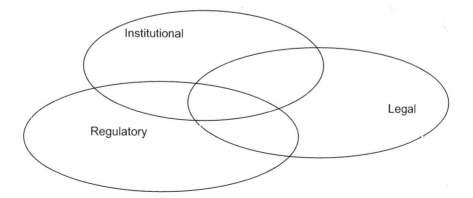

Figure 5.1 Relationships between institutional, regulatory and legal texts.

88 *Translation and Community*

likewise, some regulatory texts are legal, and others are not. The best example is the case of regulatory texts as discussed in this chapter: While they may regulate certain areas of life such as entitlement to services and procedures to follow, they can hardly be categorised as legal in the proper sense of the word. Finally, institutional texts may be legal, regulatory or neither. If we take Schäffner et al.'s (2014) and Koskinen's (2008) definitions of institutional translation, especially with reference to international institutions such as the UN, we will clearly realise that the body of texts falling under this category could include from conventions and treaties (legal and regulatory) to statements made by officials (neither legal nor regulatory). Box 5.3 offers some questions to consider at this point in the chapter.

Box 5.3   Questions to consider

1) So far, what is your understanding of regulatory texts?
2) How do regulatory texts compare with public messaging?
3) How do you say 'regulatory', 'legal' and 'institutional' in your other language(s)?
4) Do the terms in your other language(s) make it easy to distinguish between 'regulatory', 'legal' and 'institutional'?
5) What would be a good example of an institutional text having a communicative/image building function as described by Koskinen?

5.3   Translation approach

As is expected in every act of translation, the translator will need to refer to the translation brief and consider the type and function of the text at hand. As pointed out earlier, while public messaging is mainly communicative and reader oriented, regulatory texts may cater more to the official voice and power structures. Accordingly, a general guiding rule could be that the more communicative and informative a text is, the more leeway the translator will have to adapt to audience needs; the more regulatory a text is, the greater the need for accuracy, precision and maintenance of the institutional voice.

One aspect that demonstrates that institutions expect accuracy, precision and consistency is the control they exercise over lexical choice, particularly terminology (Mason, 2021). This often extends to control over tone and style. Schäffner (2018: 210) notes that for institutions in general, "consistency and standardisation are seen as essential and their achievement is supported by tools such as glossaries, style guides, and translation memory systems. Since all the language versions need to be equivalent to each other, terminology has to be consistent". In the case of large organisations, the texts are often previous

Translating regulatory texts 89

documents produced by the same organisation or relevant bodies (intertextuality), which requires interdocument consistency as well, that is, the exact translations of previous texts being used when text is quoted from those documents (Schäffner, 2018: 210).

Some organisations take the extreme position of requiring literal translation of their resources (Mossop, 1988) or asking translators to keep key terms in the source language. The rationale behind this translation policy is a belief that the translation of institutional and regulatory terms is synonymous with loss of control or that the target audience is expected to be familiar with the terms because they live in the same country or would have dealt with the organisation in question before. Translators' compliance with such instructions often results in translations that are partly in the source language and partly in the target language. Such practice is especially conspicuous when the source and target languages use different scripts, as is the case for English, Arabic and Chinese (see Box 5.4).

Box 5.4   Excerpt from the Arabic translation of "Balancing your family assistance payments" (Services Australia)

عندما نوازن مدفوعاتك

يمكننا فقط اجراء توازن Benefit Tax Family بعد أن سددنا آخر دفعة من Benefit Tax Family للسنة المالية وقمت بتأكيد دخلك. ستحصل عادةً على آخر دفعة بحلول منتصف شهر يوليو .
عندما نوازنBenefit Tax Family ، نتحقق مما إذا كان يجب دفع أي دفعة مكملة لك. وهذا يشمل الدفعة المكملة من Tax Family Single Income وجو Family Tax Benefit Part B supplement ، المكملة والدفعة، Benefit Family Supplement. Part A supplement.
نبدأ في إجراء توازن Subsidy Care Child في وقت متأخر عن .Benefit Tax Family قبل أن نتمكن من إجراء توازن Child Subsidy Care لك، نؤكد حضور طفلك أثناء السنة المالية. نحصل عليها مباشرة من خدمة رعاية الطفل الخاصة بك. نقتطع نسبة مئوية من Subsidy Care Child للمساعدة في تعويض أي مدفوعات زائدة محتملة. إذا لم ندفع لك مبالغ فائضة، فسوف ندفع لك أي مبلغ مقتطع مباشرة عندما نُجري توازن Subsidy Care Child.

https://www.servicesaustralia.gov.au/sites/default/files/2022-07/14638-2206ar.pdf

---

Multilingualism goes hand in hand with a relationship between government/governance and translation (Meylaerts, 2013; Koskinen, 2014). The translation approach required by each organisation or government body also reveals the extent of control that institution would like to have over its texts, especially the regulatory ones. Some institutions may find it both desirable and feasible to leave documents untranslated (monolingual policy; maximum level of control), but as Koskinen (2014: 488) warns, if there are no translated image-building and implementational materials, "the governing institution may find it difficult to reinforce its regulations and to maintain its legitimacy". Another dilemma institutions face is that lack of standardisation and institutionalisation of translations

90 *Translation and Community*

means that they lose "control over what gets communicated and how", while too much control, "especially if it stifles translation solutions", may lead to complaints about excessively official and inaccessible texts (Koskinen, 2014: 488).

As I said in Chapter 2, community translators also face a similar dilemma: "As communication mediators, community translators will often find themselves in a loyalty paradox whereby serving one party faithfully may have an impact on the other parties' trust" (Taibi and Ozolins, 2016: 72). In the case of regulatory texts, there will always be tension between institutional requirements for maximal accuracy and precision (sometimes unwittingly viewed as synonymous with literalism) and audience needs and expectations (the more readable and understandable translations, the better). Even when the community translator adopts a functional approach, they will still face the ethical dilemma of whose perspective to take to determine text function and whose expectations to prioritise. Still, given the nature of regulatory texts and the contexts in which they are translated, we can propose the following guiding principles:

1) There are differences between public messaging (intended to raise awareness and influence behaviours) and regulatory texts (intended to set and communicate regulations).
2) It is understandable that institutions and organisations will endeavour to keep their rules and regulations under control, including and perhaps most particularly when their documents are translated into other languages.
3) However, the legitimacy of institutional control does not make literal translation or non-translation (leaving parts of the text untranslated) legitimate, appropriate or effective.
4) Borrowing terms from the source text may be appropriate in some cases but not too frequently in the same text. Otherwise, there will be an impact on translation readability and reception.
5) Borrowing can also be used together with other translation solutions, for instance translation followed by the source term between parentheses to ensure more clarity and understanding.
6) Institutions may ensure consistency by developing institution-specific bilingual or multilingual glossaries for translators to consult and implement.
7) For translators, a key criterion is whether a text (or part of a text) falls under the category of public messaging (more communicative and informative), in which case they may have more leeway to address the needs of the readership, or under the category of regulatory texts, in which case they will need to attend more to institutional requirements in relation to accuracy and official or institutional voice.
8) In both cases, applying the norms and conventions of the target language is required (e.g., acceptable and natural structures, natural lexical choices and expressions, appropriate links between clauses and sentences).
9) Continuous communication and consultation between institutional commissioners, translation agencies and translators are key. Commissioners can provide insights and feedback about institutional expectations and priorities, while language service experts can advise on expectations, challenges, constraints

Translating regulatory texts 91

and resources relating to translation in general and to the languages and communities they work with in particular.

The same aspects I covered in Section 4.5 (translation brief, context, comprehension, translation stage, and revision) apply to regulatory texts such as the one in Box 5.5 as well. However, they will apply differently given the different nature of regulatory texts.

5.4 Practical example

There may be slight or significant differences between the aspects in Section 4.5 when dealing with public messaging and when translating regulatory texts. The translation brief, for example, is likely to stress the need for accuracy, consistency of institutional terminology and maintenance of the institutional tone and register.

Box 5.5 Practical example

Exceptions and accommodations

There are exceptions and modifications to the naturalization requirements that are available to those who qualify. USCIS also provides accommodations for individuals with disabilities.

Continuous residence exceptions

If you are engaged in certain kinds of overseas employment, you may be eligible for an exception to the continuous residence requirement. For more information, visit our Continuous Residence and Physical Presence Requirements for Naturalization page and the USCIS Policy Manual Citizenship and Naturalization Guidance.

Medical disability exceptions to English and civics

You may be eligible for an exception to the English and civics naturalization requirements if you are unable to comply with these requirements because of a physical or developmental disability or a mental impairment.

To request this exception, submit Form N-648, Medical Certification for Disability Exceptions. This form must be completed by a licensed medical or osteopathic doctor, or licensed clinical psychologist.

For more information, see the USCIS Policy Manual Citizenship and Naturalization Guidance.

(Source: www.uscis.gov/citizenship/exceptions-and-accommodations)

92 *Translation and Community*

The translation revision stage might not give priority to the same questions I listed in Chapter 4:

1) Does the translation make sense? Is the message consistent?
2) **Is the translation complete?**
3) **Is the translation accurate in comparison with the source text?**
4) Does the translation flow smoothly and read easily?
5) Is the message easy to understand?
6) Is the language used (structure, words, expressions, etc.) correct?
7) Is the language used natural/acceptable?
8) **Is the register appropriate?**
9) Is the translation consistent with the translation brief?
10) Is the translation culturally appropriate and politically correct?
11) Is the layout appropriate and consistent (including display of your language script, spacing, margins, indentations, positioning of footnotes, relationship of text to graphics)?

Questions 2 (translation completeness), 3 (accuracy) and 8 (register appropriateness) are likely to be given more priority (from the commissioner's perspective) than questions 4 (readability and smoothness), 5 (understandability) or 10 (cultural appropriateness), for instance. This does not mean, of course, that it is acceptable to produce translations that do not make sense, are not internally consistent or are offensive to certain cultural groups. It just means that in the case of regulatory texts, the commissioning organisations will probably give more weight to conceptual and content accuracy, consistency of institutional terms and maintenance of the institutional voice.

Rather than repeating the points from Section 4.5, I here focus on accuracy, terminology and register. In regulatory texts such as the one in Box 5.5, one of the most important (and challenging) aspects is terminological and conceptual accuracy. To translate the USCIS exceptions, the translator will need to ensure full understanding and accurate communication of the meanings of concepts such as exceptions, accommodations, naturalization requirements, qualify, eligible, disabilities, continuous residence, physical presence requirements, civics, developmental disability and mental impairment.

The term 'accommodations', for example, might be problematic and challenging. An inexperienced translator might understand it and translate it in the most common sense, as a place where people can live or stay. They might be further encouraged to settle for this solution when they read "USCIS also provides accommodations for individuals with disabilities", which might suggest a reasonable link between disability and accommodation in the sense of lodging. This reading, however, is not consistent with the preceding sentence "There are exceptions and modifications to the naturalization requirements that are available to those who qualify". 'Accommodations', therefore, needs to be understood in the context of

Translating regulatory texts   93

exceptions and modifications. A more cautious translator may look up the word in the dictionary and find the following:

- something supplied for convenience or to satisfy a need, such as lodging or transport;
- the act of accommodating someone or something, in the sense of providing them with something they need, giving consideration to them, or making adjustments for them, etc.

They may go further and search in a legal or business dictionary, which may refer to a different sense of the word: a favour done for an individual or company without any compensation, such as a signature to guarantee payment of a debt, also called an accommodation endorsement.

The translator is not only guided by the words used in the source text, the list of definitions provided in a monolingual dictionary or possible equivalents listed in a bilingual one. First and foremost, they need to rely on the context and use their critical skills to choose the most relevant definition or equivalent. In this case, the context shows that accommodations refer to adjustments to the rules or procedures or special arrangements for people with special needs or circumstances (e.g., people with a disability). Once this becomes clear, the other challenge is to find a term or expression in the target language that conveys the same meaning.

Some languages might have an equivalent term; others might have words or expressions that mean "special arrangements" or something similar. In choosing one or another, the translator needs to determine whether the source and target terms mean the same thing in the context of this translation, whether the target language term or expression may lead to confusion (e.g., because of multiplicity of meanings), whether the term or expression is commonly used in this context, whether it is consistent with relevant institutional glossaries (if applicable) and, if not, whether deviation from such glossaries is justifiable. Box 5.6 offers more questions to consider.

Box 5.6   Questions to consider

1) Of the following terms, which would be more challenging to translate into your other language: 'naturalization requirements', 'qualify', 'eligible', 'disabilities', 'continuous residence', 'physical presence requirements', 'civics', 'developmental disability' or 'mental impairment'?
2) Which are translatable with words you can find in a dictionary and which can only be translated by paraphrase (Chapter 3)?
3) What are the risks (for the commissioning organisation or for the community reader) that each option entails?

94 *Translation and Community*

Another aspect that requires attention for accuracy in translating regulatory texts is acronyms, for instance USCIS, which a quick Internet search would reveal that it refers to the United States Citizenship and Immigration Services. Depending on how well this or another acronym is known to the audience, and also on the target language, the translator may use the same acronym, translate the full name of the service or translate it and place the English acronym in parentheses.

Accuracy in regulatory texts is not limited to terminology and institutional names and acronyms. It extends to modality, which is a key linguistic and pragmatic element in such texts. In the excerpt in Box 5.5, we have the following: "This form **must** be completed by a licensed medical or osteopathic doctor, or licensed clinical psychologist". The modal verb 'must' is used in this case to express obligation or necessity. The target language may not have a modal verb with the same meaning, but the translator is expected to identify the most suitable expression to convey the idea that it is compulsory/a requirement that the form be completed by a licensed medical or osteopathic doctor or licensed clinical psychologist. A verb or expression that conveys modality at the level of optionality, recommendation, advice or suggestion, for example, would not be accurate.

Regulatory texts often contain intertextual references to other institutional or legislative documents, for instance the hyperlink to the "USCIS Policy Manual Citizenship and Naturalization Guidance". As I observed earlier in this chapter, organisations, especially large ones, strive to ensure consistency and standardisation in their translations. This particularly applies to regulatory texts. It follows that the translator will need to check whether the Policy Manual has been translated into their target language or whether it is included in an institution-specific glossary and if so, whether the existing translation is correct and appropriate. If previous translations or glossary entries are deemed incorrect, ambiguous or awkward, then the translator would need to read and research more institutional literature to determine (and advise on) a more appropriate translation. In the Exceptions text, the hyperlink to the Policy Manual takes the reader to a large amount of useful information and documents.

Exploring such resources is always helpful, as it provides the translator with more contextual and institutional knowledge, more information about the document(s) in question and, in some cases, opportunities to discover hidden versions or additional resources in one's target language. For instance, judging by its syntactical structure, the phrase "USCIS Policy Manual Citizenship and Naturalization Guidance" seems to be missing a preposition between "Manual" and "Citizenship" such as 'on' or 'about'. It may also suggest an unclear relationship between "Manual" and "Guidance". In English, this is often the case when there is a noun phrase with several premodifiers (nouns or adjectives describing or specifying the main noun). "USCIS Policy Manual Citizenship and Naturalization Guidance" may mean "USCIS Policy Manual on Citizenship and Naturalization", in which case "Guidance" would be superfluous, or "Citizenship and Naturalization Guidance in the USCIS Policy Manual". Further exploring the webpage shows that the Policy Manual features the headings "Guidance", "Resources", "Appendices", "Updates"

Translating regulatory texts 95

and "History" for each of its 12 volumes. For Volume 12, which is Citizenship and Naturalization, Guidance includes the following sections:

- Part A—Citizenship and Naturalization Policies and Procedures
- Part B—Naturalization Examination
- Part C—Accommodations
- Part D—General Naturalization Requirements
- Part E—English and Civics Testing and Exceptions
- Part F—Good Moral Character
- Part G—Spouses of U.S. Citizens
- Part H—Children of U.S. Citizens
- Part I—Military Members and their Families
- Part J—Oath of Allegiance
- Part K—Certificates of Citizenship and Naturalization
- Part L—Revocation of Naturalization

With this contextual information, it becomes easier to understand and accurately translate document titles (and other source text elements). The translator can then safely and justifiably use words or expressions equivalent to 'on', 'about', 'relating to', 'section', 'volume' or 'chapter' when necessary.

A final aspect that requires attention in translating regulatory texts is register. Register, according to Halliday (1978: 23) "is the set of meanings, the configuration of semantic patterns, that are typically drawn upon under the specific conditions, along with the words and structures that are used in the realization of these meanings". Simply put, it is the level of formality and style of language, which vary depending on the context of communication (e.g., formality of the situation, relationship between speaker/writer and audience).

Register analysis, maintenance or appropriateness is a key determinant of translation quality. This is recognised in scholarly literature (e.g., House, 1997, 2001, 2013; Hatim and Mason, 2013 [1990]) as well as in professional standards. For instance, the (Australian) National Accreditation Authority for Translators and Interpreters (NAATI) has "application of textual norms and conventions" as one of its certification assessment criteria, and under it comes register and style: "Application of textual norms and conventions: The skill to apply the knowledge of textual norms and conventions of the target language to the target text. This entails the use of register, style and text structure appropriate to the genre and context of the translation" (NAATI, n.d.).

In the case of regulatory texts, the expectation that the institutional voice and tone are to be conveyed as intended in the source text means that translation register and style need to be given special attention. Although not specialised and often written in a non-legalistic language (see Plain Language Movement in Chapter 1), regulatory texts tend to define legal and administrative concepts and processes and tend to do so with institution-specific terminology and precise language. Attention to accuracy and level of formality at the terminological level (e.g., accommodations, naturalization requirements, continuous residence, physical presence requirements,

96 *Translation and Community*

civics, developmental disability or mental impairment in the USCIS exceptions guidance text) will contribute to maintaining the register of the source text.

In addition, the translator needs to maintain register as reflected in other linguistic and textual aspects such as syntactical structures and formal presentation. However, this will also be subject to the textual norms and conventions in the target language: Variations in register may be appropriate if justified by common practice in the target language and culture. For example, the AUSIT-FECCA (n.d.: 8). *Style Guide for Community Translations into Chinese* recommends the following:

> For government documents, English often has a more friendly author–reader relationship than Chinese. This relationship is often conveyed by personal pronouns like 'you' and 'we'. However, these words can seem overly friendly in Chinese, softening the impact a source text attempts to have. Sometimes they even sound awkward in Chinese. In such cases, more imperative expressions will better serve the translation function.

Summary

In this chapter, I have discussed regulatory texts, a category of texts that are commonly translated by community translators. These texts are mostly written with an institutional tone to communicate regulations, policies and procedures to the wider public, not specialists. Although not specialised and often written in a non-legalistic language, regulatory texts tend to define legal and administrative concepts and processes and to do so with institution-specific terminology and precise language. The category is used in this chapter in contrast with what I called public messaging in Chapter 4.

While all community translations need to be communicative and meet the needs of the readership, in the case of regulatory texts, values such as accuracy, lexical precision and maintenance of the institutional voice and tone are generally given priority. Accuracy and language precision, however, do not mean literal translation. Although some organisations may unwittingly demand literal translation of their regulatory texts or ask translators to keep key terms in the source language, community translators need to consider all relevant contextual parameters: not only institutional expectations and the regulatory nature of such texts but also the risks relating to the readership (e.g., readability and presentation of the translation and consistency with the target language norms and conventions). Translators of regulatory texts need to keep in mind the desire of institutions to standardise translations and maintain control over how their regulations are communicated but at the same time be aware that too much control, "especially if it stifles translation solutions" may lead to excessively inaccessible translations (Koskinen, 2014: 488). To strike a balance, communication between key stakeholders (institutional commissioners, translation agencies and translators) is essential.

Suggested activities

1) How do regulatory texts in English and in your other language compare? Explore some regulatory texts in both languages and compare them in terms of tone and formality (register). Please focus on regulatory texts aimed at the wider public, not specialist audiences.
2) Based on the definitions and explanations provided in this chapter, please identify two texts in your other language, one that can be classified as mostly or exclusively regulatory and another which combines features of both public messaging and regulatory texts. Compare the features of both texts and write down key points in which the translator may need to treat them differently.
3) Translate the text in Box 5.5 into your other language. As you translate, write brief reflections on translation challenges and questions and your decision-making process (e.g., the terminological options available in the target language, the terms you decided to use, the reasoning behind stylistic and terminological choices).

Further reading

- Schäffner, Ch. (2018). Translation and institutions. In Fernández, Fruela and Evans, Jonathan (Eds), *The Routledge handbook of translation and politics*. Abingdon: Routledge: 204–220.

Schäffner's book chapter is about institutional translation, not regulatory texts as presented in this textbook (in the context of community translation). However, in the chapter, she discusses relevant issues such as the constraints imposed on translators in institutional settings and institutional efforts to standardise translations into different languages and to ensure terminological and stylistic consistency. Schäffner covers international and supranational institutions (e.g., the UN), national political institutions and non-governmental organisations (e.g., Amnesty International). Although community translators do not usually work with texts published by such organisations, the conceptual issues and research findings covered are likely to increase your understanding of institutional policies and practices relating to translation.

References

Alcaraz Varó, Enrique and Hughes, Brian (2014). *Legal translation explained*. London and New York: Routledge.

AUSIT-FECCA (n.d.). *Style guide for community translations into Chinese*. https://ausit.org/wp-content/uploads/2023/05/AUSIT-Style-Guide-for-Chinese-Community-Translations_CLEAN_042023.pdf.

Cao, Deborah (2010). Legal translation. In Gambier, Yves and Van Doorslaer, Luc (Eds.), *Handbook of translation studies*. Amsterdam and Philadelphia: John Benjamins: 191–195.

Halliday, M. A. K. (1978). *Language as social semiotic: The social interpretation of language and meaning*. London: Edward Arnold.

98 Translation and Community

Hatim, Basil and Mason, Ian (2013 [1990]). *Discourse and the translator*. London and New York: Routledge.

House, Juliane (1997). *Translation quality assessment: A model revisited*. Tübingen: Gunter Narr Verlag.

House, Juliane (2001). Translation quality assessment: Linguistic description versus social evaluation, *Meta*, 46(2): 243–257.

House, Juliane (2013). Quality in translation studies. In Millán, Carmen and Bartrina, Francesca (Eds.), *Routledge handbook of translation studies*. London and New York: Routledge: 534–547.

Koskinen, Kaisa (2008). *Translating institutions: An ethnographic study of EU translation*. Manchester: St. Jerome.

Koskinen, Kaisa (2014). Institutional translation: The art of government by translation. *Perspectives*, 22(4): 479–492.

Mason, Ian (2021). Text parameters in translation: Transitivity and institutional culture. In Venuti, L. (Ed.), *The translation studies reader* (4th Edition). London and New York: Routledge.

Meylaerts, Reine (2013). Multilingualism as a challenge for translation studies. In Millán, C. and Bartrina, F. (Eds.), *The Routledge handbook of translation studies*. Routledge: 519–533.

Mossop, Brian (1988). Translating institutions: A missing factor in translation theory. *TTR Traduction, Terminologie, Rédaction: Études sur le texte et ses transformations*, 1(2): 65–71.

NAATI (n.d.). *Certification glossary of terms*. www.naati.com.au/resources/certification-glossary/.

Reiss, Katharina and Vermeer, Hans (2014 [1984]). *Towards a general theory of translational action: Skopos theory explained*. Translated by Christiane Nord. London and New York: Routledge.

Schäffner, Christina (2018). Translation and institutions. In Fernández, Fruela and Evans, Jonathan (Eds.), *The Routledge handbook of translation and politics*. Abingdon: Routledge: 204–220.

Schäffner, Christina; Tcaciuc, Luciana Sabina and Tesseur, Wine (2014). Translation practices in political institutions: A comparison of national, supranational, and non-governmental organisations. *Perspectives: Studies in Translatology*, 22(4). 493–510. DOI: 10.1080/0907676X.2014.948890.

Svoboda, Tomáš; Biel, Łucja and Łoboda, Krzysztof (2017). Quality aspects in institutional translation: Introduction. In Svoboda, Tomáš; Biel, Łucja and Łoboda, Krzysztof (Eds.), *Quality aspects in institutional translation*. Berlin: Language Science Press: 1–13.

Taibi, Mustapha and Ozolins, Uldis (2016). *Community translation*. London and New York: Bloomsbury.

6 Translating culturally sensitive texts

> Cultural sensitivities and cultural mediation are mentioned in different parts of this textbook (e.g., Chapter 2), but this chapter provides a theoretical introduction to intercultural mediation in (community) translation, followed by a discussion of different scenarios and contents that might be culturally sensitive to translate in a multilingual society. The chapter covers the following points:
>
> - Cultural mediation in community translation;
> - Cultural assumptions in translated texts;
> - Different politeness norms in written texts;
> - Dealing with culturally sensitive contents in translation (e.g., sexuality, sexual abuse, domestic violence, religion, or offensive language).
>
> This chapter will trigger questions about the translator's professional ethics, role, ideology, and (professional, cultural and social) identity. I recommend that you refer to Chapter 2 before or while reading this chapter.

6.1 Cultural mediation in community translation

As I discussed in Section 2.2, translation requires and involves some level of cultural mediation. As Pym (2010 [1992]: 150) notes, "translators by definition have a greater awareness of foreign cultures than do those who need to read translations". Translators are expected to demonstrate understanding of the cultural backgrounds of both source and target texts and of both the writer of the original text and the intended audience of the corresponding translation. With this cultural understanding and knowledge, they are expected to bridge the cultural divide and rewrite the source text in a manner that suits a culturally and linguistically different audience (Bedeker and Feinauer, 2006; Liddicoat, 2016; Katan and Taibi, 2021).

Translation studies literature (e.g., Bassnett, 2002 [1980]; Vermeer, 1986; Snell-Hornby, 1995 [1988]; Pym, 2010 [1992], or Hatim and Mason, 2013 [1990]) abounds

DOI: 10.4324/9781003367741-7

100 *Translation and Community*

with references to culture, intercultural communication/mediation, intercultural skills and cultural transfer. Bassnett (2002 [1980]), for instance, clearly affirms,

> Language, then, is the heart within the body of culture, and it is the interaction between the two that results in the continuation of life-energy. In the same way that the surgeon, operating on the heart, cannot neglect the body that surrounds it, so the translator treats the text in isolation from the culture at his peril.
>
> (23)

Vermeer (1986) and Snell-Hornby (1995 [1988]) argue that translation does not consist of language transfer only but is primarily an operation of cultural transfer. Vermeer (1986), Snell-Hornby (1995 [1988]) and Hatim and Mason (2013 [1990]), among other scholars, believe that translators must be bicultural to be able to mediate between one cultural context and another. As Hatim and Mason (2013 [1990]: 223) put it, "the translator has not only a bilingual ability but also a bi-cultural vision. Translators mediate between cultures (including ideologies, moral systems and socio-political structures), seeking to overcome those incompatibilities which stand in the way of transfer of meaning".

Community translation, as Taibi and Ozolins (2016: 38–43) note, also requires and involves cultural mediation. In this area of translation practice as well, cultural knowledge and intercultural skills are required to grapple with the challenges of cross-cultural transfer, including culture-specific concepts, idioms and metaphors; differences in cultural backgrounds and assumptions and differences in terms of expectations, conventions and norms. However, my colleague and I point out some slight differences between the position of culture in community translation and other areas of translation.

Firstly, in community translation, cultural mediation usually takes place in a local context that is characterised by coexistence of the two relevant cultures and, therefore, varying degrees of cultural contact and acculturation. Secondly, cultural mediation is often required not only between two broader cultural contexts but also between an institutional subculture (e.g., health care providers or taxation administration) and a minority culture (e.g., ethnic group). Finally, although the material on which community translators work is mainly published by public services, texts to be translated may also come from community organisations, community leaders or individuals, which means a great level of diversity in cultural and educational backgrounds, discursive and textual practices and idiosyncrasies in rhetoric and writing style. Taibi and Ozolins (2016: 43) therefore recommend the following:

> When translating from and into (minority) community languages, community translators need to continuously assess the cultural differences between the original writer and the ultimate target reader. Texts must be analysed not only with regard to the broad cultural context wherein they are produced, but also in light of the institutional subculture and conventions of the organization or public service that originates the material or commissions its translation.

Translating culturally sensitive texts 101

Box 6.1   Culture-specific references requiring mediation

"A recent survey conducted with teenagers in the UK showed that social media platforms impacted their health and wellbeing. The survey results found that time spent on these platforms led to increased feelings of depression, anxiety, poor body image and loneliness. Parents are generally aware of the impact of social media on children. **As a parent, you most probably prefer to see your children watch David Attenborough rather than browse Snapchat, Facebook, Instagram or X.**"

The paragraph in Box 6.1 is about the impact of social media on teenagers. The last sentence refers to David Attenborough, the British broadcaster, biologist and natural historian, best known for his natural history documentary series. David Attenborough is not the focus of the text; his name is included as an example of informative and educational content, in contrast to social media. In fact, he may be entirely unknown for the readers of an Arabic, Chinese or Vietnamese translation, for example. When this is the case, the translator can replace this culture-specific reference with an example that is more known to the target audience. The example does not need to refer to a broadcaster or a documentary about nature. It just needs to convey the point of "something informative and educational".

Similarly, the last sentence refers to "Snapchat, Facebook, Instagram or X", but again, when the focus is not on these specific brands or platforms, the translator can act as a cultural mediator and replace with social media that are more popular among the target cultural group. A Chinese translator, for instance, might want to refer to Sina Weibo, WeChat or Xiaohongshu (小红书: Little Red Book). After all, the point that needs to be conveyed is the contrast between beneficial and harmful screen time for teenagers. Box 6.2 presents a list of questions you should consider before you proceed with this chapter.

Box 6.2   Questions to consider before reading the following sections

1) Given that community translations are aimed at local or national communities, when would cultural mediation be unnecessary?
2) You are translating a health care leaflet which contains examples of foods that are not relevant to the audience of the translation. Would you replace them with dietary options that are more relevant to the target community? Would you discuss this with the client?
3) The text you are translating for a language minority is about a sensitive topic (e.g., same-sex marriage, sexual relationships among teenagers,

102 *Translation and Community*

> sexual identity). You are aware that the content will be culturally shocking for the target group. Would you use euphemisms, circumlocutions, or other strategies to make the translation more culturally acceptable?
> 4) The source text is too direct for the audience of the translation (e.g., it consists of a list of straightforward dos and don'ts without any politeness expressions). Would you adjust the tone and use politeness markers if that is the expectation in the target culture? Would that depend on the text and context?
> 5) You are asked to translate a text about social cohesion which makes references and assumptions that are likely to be judgemental or offensive for the target community. Would you just translate the text as it is, or would you discuss with the commissioner first?

6.2 Areas for cultural mediation

Practically any culture-specific reference, practice or norm may be subject to cultural mediation in translation. Cases requiring mediation may range from unimportant in-text references or examples, which can easily be substituted or adapted to cater to the new readership, as in Box 6.1, to entire texts that address culturally sensitive issues (e.g., LGBT rights, sexual abuse, domestic violence, religious freedom, strong language in political discourse). In the following subsections, I focus on shared cultural assumptions, relevance to the target cultural group, politeness in texts, and political correctness. In Section 6.3, I focus on culturally sensitive content.

6.2.1 Cultural assumptions

The example in Box 6.1 referred to David Attenborough with the assumption that he is well known in the United Kingdom and probably in other English-speaking countries as well. Although knowledge about the British broadcaster can be considered general extra-textual knowledge (knowledge about a famous person), it is also a culture-specific reference because when you mention David Attenborough, you assume that the addressee or reader knows him and shares the same cultural context with you (what is popular in that context, what is an example of a serious program, what is a frivolous gossip or celebrity show, etc.). In community translation as well as other types of translation, cultural assumptions that can be inferred from the source text are not necessarily shared by translation users. As I said in Chapter 3, before a translator chooses a translation approach or strategy, they need to have a good understanding of the sociocultural background, knowledge, expectations and needs of the audience (Reiss and Vermeer, 2014 [1984]: 91, 92, 114).

When there is a cultural reference or assumption that the user of the translation is unlikely to understand or infer, the translator can use a number of translation strategies depending on the case. One of these strategies, as explained in

Translating culturally sensitive texts 103

Section 3.4, is amplification, adding information to clarify a concept or to make an implicit assumption explicit (Molina Martínez, 2022). Thus, the sentence "As a parent, you most probably prefer to see your children watch David Attenborough rather than browse Snapchat, Facebook, Instagram or X" can be rendered as "As a parent, you most probably prefer to see your children watch **an educational show such as David Attenborough's documentaries** rather than browse Snapchat, Facebook, Instagram or X".

Another strategy is adaptation (Vinay and Darbelnet, 1995 [1958]: 39) or "translation by cultural substitution" (Baker, 2011 [1992]), creating a new situation or reference that is deemed equivalent to the source text reference but that is more appropriate to the cultural context of the translation (see Section 3.4). This is the strategy proposed for translating Box 6.1, where I suggested replacing David Attenborough with a culture-appropriate reference to "something informative and educational", and replacing "Snapchat, Facebook, Instagram or X" with "Sina Weibo, WeChat or Xiaohongshu", for example. Another option that can apply with culture-specific references is "translation by a more general word" (Baker, 2011 [1992]). Thus, "David Attenborough" in Box 6.1 can become "a documentary" or "an educational show". Similarly, a culture-specific food such as "croissant" can be translated as "pastry" (using a superordinate instead of a hyponym, if justifiable in the context).

6.2.2 *Relevance to audience*

The AUSIT *Recommended Protocols for the Translation of Community Communications* provide the following advice to organisations commissioning community translations: "Messages are more effective when they are relatable. Use real-life examples that your audience can identify with" (AUSIT, 2022: 4). The *Better Practice Guide for Multicultural Communications*, published by the Department of Families, Fairness and Housing of the State of Victoria, Australia, provides recommendations along the same lines:

> Provide relevance: People are drawn to messages they perceive as relevant to them personally or to their situation. Personalised communication makes it easier for people to understand the costs or benefits of a particular behaviour (such as complying with physical distancing requirements).
>
> (State of Victoria, 2023)

Similarly, the State of Queensland's *How to Choose Culturally Appropriate Education Resources: A Guide for Dietitians and Nutritionists* points out that among the characteristics of ineffective public messaging in multicultural societies are culturally inappropriate guidance, examples and graphics that are not relevant to different cultural groups and " 'word for word' translations that don't represent food practices or cultural/religious beliefs of the audience" (State of Queensland, 2018).

While these quotations relate to organisations designing public messaging campaigns and producing original contents for translation, they are also relevant to

104 *Translation and Community*

community translators. Cultural appropriateness and relevance to the target cultural groups need to be addressed at the resource development stage (AUSIT, 2022). However, this does not mean that community translators do not have a role to play.

First, not all organisations and source-document writers apply these recommendations and produce texts and materials from a multicultural perspective. Second, even when organisations are aware of the need for culturally relevant and appropriate resources and do their best to be inclusive, they are often unable to produce a culturally suitable text for every cultural group. This objective requires time-consuming research and consultation as well as human and financial resources, which are often limited. Third, the translator is "the sole true intercultural communicator" (Liddicoat, 2016: 356) with language and cultural knowledge and expertise to mediate the source text, whether it was written from a monocultural or multicultural perspective and regardless of how much cultural adaptation it underwent during the resource development process. Community translators can therefore make translated content more relevant to their target audience by undertaking cultural adaptations, especially at the level of figurative language and culture-specific examples. Consider the example in Box 6.3.

Box 6.3 Quality time with kids

Life is hectic. There is work, household chores, dropping kids at school, picking them up, **walking the dog,** getting the car serviced, going to the gym and so on. In this hectic lifestyle we have, it is important to have **quality time** with your kids. Setting aside quality time to share with your kids creates bonds between you and them; promotes their emotional, social and intellectual development and helps **fill their emotional cup,**
Here are some ideas for **quality time** with kids:

- Games: Want to have fun with your kids? How about **board games like Monopoly and Settlers of Catan**? Not your favourite games? How about Taco Cat Goat Cheese Pizza and Anomia?
- Movie nights: Try a movie night if your kids love movies or have a favourite series such as **Star Wars** or **John Hughes flicks**.
- Hobbies: **If you like music, you can pick up a guitar and ask your kids to grab percussion instruments.** You might be one of those who enjoy **skateboarding, swimming, bushwalking or horse riding**. It doesn't matter as long as you have a good time with your kids!

The text in Box 6.3 is full of activities that are relevant to some cultural groups but not necessarily to others. Spending "quality time" with family and friends is a universal way of bonding and socialising, but not all languages and cultures have a name for it, and the activities considered constitutive of quality time can vary

Translating culturally sensitive texts 105

significantly from one cultural group to another. Making the translation more relatable to the target cultural group may need to start at the conceptual level.

For some audiences, a literal translation of "quality time" may be meaningless or even alienating. They might find alternative translations such as "family time", "gathering time", "bonding time" or "storytelling time", for example, more relevant and culturally suitable. The point of the text is that parents need to dedicate some time to strengthening bonds with their children through different activities. The examples and suggestions provided are just that—examples and suggestions which can be adapted to the audience to make them more relatable. Thus, "walking the dog", "board games like Monopoly and Settlers of Catan", "Star Wars or John Hughes flicks", music and "percussion instruments", "skateboarding, swimming, bushwalking or horse riding" can all be partly or completely replaced with more relevant activities and examples. Naturally, when the required cultural adaptation is significant (i.e., when it goes beyond a couple of culture-specific references or includes changing examples and situations), consultation with the commissioner is necessary. This also needs to be communicated to other relevant colleagues involved in the translation project, such as the translation reviser (see Chapter 10) so that they are aware of the approach implemented.

6.2.3 *Politeness, power and distance*

Human communication—whether verbal or non-verbal, spoken or written—is governed by the politeness rules applicable in the relevant cultural context and situational context. Brown and Levinson (1987) explain that three factors determine politeness strategies: power, distance and rank of imposition.

Power refers to the distribution of interpersonal and social power, either real or perceived, between the speaker/writer and the addressee (i.e., whether one is more powerful than the other or the two are equal). Distance refers to the relative social distance existing or assumed to exist between the speaker/writer and the addressee (i.e., whether they are complete strangers, acquaintances or close friends/colleagues). Rank of imposition refers to the extent to which the utterance or the message communicated is likely to impose on the addressee or constitute a face-threatening act (e.g., an imposition or offence as in asking someone to perform an action for you, criticising someone or providing negative feedback). Although these three considerations are universally relevant, there are significant variations from one culture to another in terms of how they apply, how they are perceived and how much weight they are given. One major difference is that some cultures tend to prioritise social distance, deference and respect for the addressee's autonomy, while others value a sense of involvement and closeness (Brown and Levinson, 1987; Scollon et al., 2012).

Cultural differences often manifest themselves in writing. Different cultural groups may organise texts differently and may assume different levels of power or distance vis-à-vis their audience (Katan and Taibi, 2021: 306–320). As Hatim (1997) asserts, "different cultures handle text-type politeness differently (that is, text forms not judged 'polite' in English could be tolerated and accepted as 'polite' in Arabic)" (151).

106 *Translation and Community*

One aspect that is closely relevant to the work of community translators is the social distance assumed in the source text between writer and reader and the ensuing level of formality (register) and directness. Within the same text genre and comparable contextual parameters, German texts, for example, tend to be more formal and direct and less reader friendly than English texts (House, 2015; Jaworska, 2015). Additionally, English public messaging (e.g., health leaflets, website advice on different personal, family and community matters) tends to be direct and close in addressing the reader (e.g., using the pronoun 'you'), while similar texts in languages such as Spanish tend to be more impersonal (e.g., using the passive or pseudo-passive voice) (AUSIT-FECCA, n.d.a: 8). The AUSIT-FECCA *Style Guide for Community Translations into Chinese* notes that, in Australian public service publications, English tends to convey "a more friendly author-reader relationship than Chinese" (e.g., through personal pronouns), which "can seem overly friendly in Chinese, softening the impact a source text attempts to have. Sometimes they even sound awkward in Chinese. In such cases, more imperative expressions will better serve the translation function" (AUSIT-FECCA, n.d.c: 8).

Such cultural differences do not mean that public service texts are more polite or more aggressive in one culture than in another; they simply indicate different cultural practices and assumptions about the relationship between authorities and community members (power and distance). Scollon et al. (2012: 10–11, 16, 242) point out that one of the major issues in intercultural communication is that speakers and writers assume that the surface language refers the audience to the same shared semantic base. Something similar can be stated about some (community) translators: One of the major issues in their work is that they overlook their role as intercultural communicators and assume that the surface language of the source text can convey the same semantic base and the same message to the readers of their translations. The examples of surface language mentioned above (passive voice, formal or informal register, address terms, etc.) are manifestations of cultural assumptions in relation to politeness, power and distance.

In translating a text from one language to another, community translators need to apply the politeness and textual norms of the target language and culture. For instance, if the source text is too informal (less social distance than expected) for the target audience, the translator can make the necessary adjustments. If the source text consists of a list of dos and don'ts introduced with politeness markers such as "please" and this is not common in similar texts in the target language, such markers can be omitted. If an English text addresses the reader as "you" and the target language has more than one option available, the translator needs to decide which would be the most appropriate. For example, Spanish, French, German and Italian second-person pronouns distinguish between the formal 'you' (*vous* in French or *usted* in Spanish), indicating more social distance, and the familiar 'you', indicating less social distance (*tu* in French and *tú* in Spanish) (Katan and Taibi, 2021: 316).

Translating culturally sensitive texts 107

6.2.4 Political correctness

Ely et al. (2006) define political correctness cultures as those "where unspoken canons of propriety govern behaviour in cross-cultural interactions—that is, interactions among people of different races, genders, religions, and other potentially charged social identity groups". In terms of language use, political correctness consists of being careful with words to avoid disparaging or offending people, especially those who belong to oppressed or minority groups. The aim of the political correctness movement is "to make language less wounding or demeaning to those whose sex, race, physical condition or circumstances leave them vulnerable to the raw power of words" (Bryson, 2016: 502). According to Diversity Council Australia, an organisation seeking to promote inclusion in the workplace, "Language is a powerful tool for building inclusion and exclusion at work", but "Inclusive language is not about being 'politically correct'—it is about using language which is respectful, accurate, and relevant to everyone" (Diversity Council Australia, 2017).

There has been a considerable amount of controversy and debate over the notion of political correctness (see e.g., Ely et al., 2006; Marques, 2009; Hughes, 2010), but what is of interest here is that in a diverse sociocultural context, language use needs to be respectful and inclusive. Contents translated by community translators may refer to diverse cultural and social groups, which requires careful monitoring of language choices to avoid biased or hurtful language. As Katan and Taibi (2021: 123) put it, political correctness "affects the acceptability of a translation, and raises questions about the role of the translator/interpreter". Public services, especially in multicultural and democratic countries, usually strive to be inclusive, but the community translator still has a role to play, both when the writer of the source text failed to be politically correct and when they were compliant but the translation process itself involves different translation options and language sensitivities within the target sociocultural context.

One area where political correctness and inclusive language are required is gender. The AUSIT-FECCA style guides for community translations, for instance, remind community translators that their audiences consist of both women and men and that they therefore need to be inclusive and avoid generic masculine forms whenever possible (AUSIT-FECCA, n.d. a and b). The guides recommend that translators generally use gender-neutral lexical choices or both feminine and masculine as long as this does not impact understanding or readability. They also advise that community translators not use feminine forms exclusively when the source text relates to a topic that might be traditionally associated with women (e.g., housework or child nutrition). The same AUSIT-FECCA documents note, "It is safe to use feminine forms when the source text is addressed to women only (e.g., pregnancy tips), but sexist when it deals, for example, with childcare, home schooling or cooking" (n.d. a and b: 15).

At the same time, gender neutrality needs to be addressed within the resources and constraints of each target language. As the same AUSIT-FECCA style guides note, languages such as Arabic or Spanish are grammatically gendered (nouns, adjectives and pronouns, for example, have either a masculine or a feminine form),

108　*Translation and Community*

which means that when translating an English gender-neutral sentence referring to people (e.g., nurses, teachers, students), the translator needs to decide whether to use the masculine or feminine form (n.d. a and b: 15–16). In both Arabic and Spanish, masculine forms have been traditionally used as the default option, while feminine forms are used when the people referred to are specifically women.

To make community translations more inclusive, translators into Arabic, for example, can occasionally use both masculine and feminine forms (e.g., الممرضات والممرضون ["female nurses and male nurses"]), but if the text includes recurrent references to people and frequent affixed pronouns, gender inclusiveness becomes impractical due to language limitations. Unlike the English "he/she" or "his/her", the corresponding Arabic pronouns are suffixed to the noun, which makes it impractical to include two pronouns every time one is needed. In some cases, translators into gendered languages can also opt for more creative ways to achieve inclusiveness, such as by using lexical choices that help avoid gendered references (e.g., in Spanish *equipo médico* ["medical staff/team"] instead of *los médicos* ["the male doctors"]) (AUSIT-FECCA, n.d. a 15).

6.3 Dealing with culturally sensitive texts

6.3.1 *Sexuality and sexual abuse*

As Lung (2003: 256–257) points out, some concepts and topics are more readily expressed in some languages and cultures than in others, including love, sex and intimacy, which are more commonly and explicitly expressed—both verbally and nonverbally—in Western cultures than in more conservative societies. Lung notes that sexual references are more sensitive in Chinese than in European languages, for example. Similarly, Taibi and El-Madkouri Maataoui (2016) note that sex-related taboos are stronger in Arab cultures than in European ones. Lung suggests that "Translating sensitive concepts from an open to a conservative society . . . requires a tacit understanding and tactful use of languages" (257). The same author continues to say that the translation of taboo expressions and concepts into Chinese requires due attention to Chinese language and cultural acceptability norms.

In addition to language and cultural norms, translators also need to consider the type of text being translated and the specific context, as I repeat in this textbook. One aspect of this specific context is the position and relative importance of the taboo topics in the text. Baker (2011 [1992]): 234), for example, suggests that the translator "may decide to omit or replace whole stretches of text which violate the reader's expectations of how a taboo subject should be handled". This may be appropriate, for example, in literary translation, children's books or texts where taboo references only have an insignificant position (e.g., examples or one-off expressions) but not when the taboo topic is the focus of the entire text or a major section in it. Texts translated for local communities can include information and advice relating to a broad range of topics that may be sensitive for some cultural groups: sex-based discrimination, sexual consent, sexual abuse,

Translating culturally sensitive texts 109

sexually transmitted infections, reproduction, fertility treatment (assisted reproduction therapy) and so on. In these cases, avoidance, omission or substitution are not viable.

Translation through cultural adaptation is a feasible alternative. Lung (2003: 267) concludes that one of the major mistakes in the translation of sensitive texts is focussing on the surface structures of the source text without due attention to the way the relevant sensitive topic is communicated about in the target-language culture. She recommends that the translator strike a balance between being inside and outside the source text, that is, inside the cultural context of the source text and that of the translation and its audience. Given the differences between cultural practices and expectations in Chinese and English-speaking communities, she argues that "there is a need to coat the message with an appreciation of the way in which sensitive issues are presented within the confines of a set of cultural norms" (Lung, 2003: 257).

Coating the message, including by using euphemisms and circumlocutions, is another common strategy for communicating sensitive contents, including through translation. With reference to the South African context, for example, Mabule (2009) describes that references to human reproduction and body functions are taboo in Northern Sotho, one of the official languages of the country, and that "the use of euphemisms functions prominently for the translated text to be acceptable to the targeted readers" (45). However, Mabule notes that this strategy has its drawbacks, the main one of which is inaccuracy and loss of meaning: "During the process of translating these HIV/Aids materials, euphemism plays an important role, thus resulting in loss of the actual meaning in some instances" (49).

A common dilemma translators face is whether to lean more towards accuracy or towards cultural relativism and sensitivity. As Mabule (2009) explains, strategies such as euphemism or metaphorical expressions address cultural sensitivity but may fall short in terms of terminological precision; on the other hand, the use of taboo expressions may be accurate at the expense of user engagement and reception:

It is easy to name the organs of reproduction in English without the reader feeling offended, even if the reader is a Northern Sotho speaker, but immediately one names the very same parts in Northern Sotho, the reader feels offended or switches off.

(49)

Working mostly in the context of public service communication strategies, community translators need to achieve both accuracy and audience engagement or strike a balance between the two. A one-size-fits-all approach would not, of course, resolve the dilemma of community translators caught between accuracy requirements and cultural sensitivity. However, a few guidelines are suggested in Table 6.1.

110　*Translation and Community*

Table 6.1 Parameters to consider

Parameter	Explanation
Cultural differences	"Awareness of cross-cultural asymmetries in the perception of taboo and conflictual issues and attentiveness to diverging thresholds of acceptability in relation to sensitive topics may be the basis for more culturally sensitive professional practices" (Martín Ruano, 2018: 269).
Client instructions	Whether the client is happy to take a culturally sensitive approach or they prefer to push boundaries and introduce cultural change.
Ethical considerations	Translators need to be aware of their professional ethics and their positions in intercultural relations as "privileged agents who have the power to grant other parties the unique and enriching opportunity of accessing and getting acquainted with cultures different from their own" (Martín Ruano, 2018: 268).
Language resources and constraints	The strategies available to a community translator will vary depending on the lexical and other resources available in each language. This can be related to terminological development in certain areas (e.g., health or law) and/or cultural considerations. For example, English, French and German may have equivalent terms for 'sex-based discrimination', 'sexual consent' or 'sexual abuse', but community languages such as Urdu, Karen or Hausa, for instance, may not.
Text type	One main distinction needs to be made between public messaging (Chapter 4) and regulatory texts (Chapter 5). Translation of the former will generally prioritise acceptability, accessibility and audience engagement, while the latter will give more importance to terminological precision.
Status of sensitive references/topics in the source text	Adaptation or replacement is more appropriate if sex or similar taboo areas are only mentioned in passing (e.g., as examples or for humoristic purposes) than when they are the focus of the text.
Audience	While the broad cultural group may have conservative attitudes towards (language relating to) certain sensitive topics, some specific segments within the same community (e.g., younger people) may not share the same attitudes.
Language variety	The language variant used for the translation can facilitate or hinder communication about taboo topics. For example, a standard variant will normally be less offensive. This also relates to the dissemination medium (e.g., translation written to be read or to be spoken).

6.3.2　Domestic violence

Domestic violence is another area where language use—both in source texts and in translations—can be sensitive and controversial. Even the term 'domestic violence' itself can trigger different responses. Randell et al. (2012: 1193), for example, who use the term 'intimate partner violence' in their paper, report that women in the English-speaking groups taking part in their study cautioned against using 'domestic violence' in awareness materials, "feeling that it would be a turn-off for many women experiencing IPV [intimate partner violence]".

Translating culturally sensitive texts 111

Educational and awareness resources need to be developed with care and sensitivity, to accommodate not only broad cultural differences but also regional and local variations (Bell, 2015: 52). Similarly, community translators working on such resources must exercise caution to achieve accurate meaning transfer and at the same time avoid any culturally inappropriate references, discriminatory language or lexical choices with unintended connotations. As the text in Box 6.4 shows, language in relation to domestic violence or intimate partner violence is nuanced and constantly evolving.

In addition to undertaking training and research in this area to develop their understanding, community translators need to work closely with relevant parties (e.g., translation commissioner and/or content experts) to produce optimal and culturally suitable translations. For example, in gendered languages, the use of specific pronouns (both masculine and feminine or only one of them) can be problematic in this context. The AUSIT-FECCA style guides suggest, "When the source text includes sensitive content (e.g., domestic violence or sexual abuse), it is good practice to check with the translation commissioner whether the translation should use a gender-neutral or a gender-specific approach" (n.d. a and b: 15).

Box 6.4   The language we use

Words are powerful, so the language we use throughout this site was chosen with intention.

Domestic or intimate partner violence?

In the domestic violence service field, there are many different ways to describe relationship violence. Throughout this site you will see an interchanging of "domestic violence" and "intimate partner violence."

What's the difference and why do we use both phrases?

Domestic violence refers to violence among people in a domestic situation, and can thus include not only a spouse or partner (same sex or opposite sex), but also siblings, parents, aunts, uncles, cousins, etc.

Intimate partner violence is more specific in describing violence perpetrated by a partner in a romantic or dating relationship. This sort of abuse is Women Against Abuse's primary focus; however, the descriptor "intimate partner violence" is a more recent term. Many people still consider "domestic violence" as referring in fact to intimate/dating partners. It's a nuanced issue, and until the general public begins using a more inclusive term, we have decided to use both phrases interchangeably when we discuss relationship violence.

112   *Translation and Community*

> Furthermore, we recognize that abuse occurs within a spectrum of relationships, and it is our intention to ensure that anyone that is in an abusive relationship will be able to access interventions. Some of these relationships include: sex trafficking; relationships described as "hooking up," "dating;" "friends with benefits," or other terminology; abuse within an institutional setting; and other abusive relationships where there is a pattern of coercive (use of force or threats) behaviors or tactics utilized against the victim with a purpose of gaining and keeping power or control over them.
>
> **Victim/Survivor**
>
> How do we describe individuals who seek help during or after they have left a violent relationship? The word "victim" is used by members of law enforcement and within the context of courtroom proceedings, but for many of our organizations, "survivor" speaks to the sense of empowerment our coordinated response aims to encourage in the people we serve. In the end, it is imperative to follow the lead of the person seeking support, since the journey from victim to survivor is unique to each person. To that end, many are beginning to use the term Victim/Survivor (V/S) to represent this continuum.
>
> (www.womenagainstabuse.org/education-resources/the-language-we-use)

6.3.3   Religion

Religious sensitivity in the context of community translation does not relate to the translation of sacred or religious texts (see e.g., Nida, 1994; Abdul-Raof, 2004 or Israel, 2023 on this area of translation), as these are not usually the focus of communication between public services and community members. It relates to other types of texts (e.g., political statements, community leaders' media releases; public service texts about social services, education, social cohesion, religious tolerance, etc.) which may contain religious references or trigger religious sensitivities.

Translators—and communicators in the public sphere, in general, for that matter—need to be aware that religion is not always a safe topic; in some societies, it is safer to discuss and make references to religion than in others. We also need to be aware that labelling religious denominations and practices can involve sensitivities, which requires maximal caution when selecting from lexical choices in translation. Often, taboos relating to other areas (e.g., sex) are also related to religion.

Even apparently neutral references can have religious connotations in some sociocultural contexts (socializing with friends, romantic relationships, etc.). This does not mean that source text writers or community translators should exercise self-censorship and avoid all religion-related topics that might cause

Translating culturally sensitive texts 113

sensitivities, but communication about such topics, including through translation, needs to be conducted in a culturally sensitive manner. Again, as I pointed out in subsection 6.3.1, the translation approach and strategies will depend on several parameters, including whether religion is the central topic of the source text and whether the text is regulatory or not. If references to religion or religious groups are essential parts of the source text, the community translator must assess the potential connotations and impacts of their own lexical choices and make sure that their translation approach does not cause any (additional) offense to any religious group.

6.3.4 Offensive language

Offensive language can refer to any word, utterance or stretch of text or discourse that can cause offense (taboo language) or to utterances that cause offense on a given occasion (O'Driscoll, 2020: 4–5). In the first sense, offensive language can encompass most of the areas covered in this chapter so far, including textual impoliteness, politically incorrect language and language relating to taboo areas such as sex, domestic violence and religion. In this subsection, I use 'offensive language' to refer to profanity, obscene language or swearwords.

Generally, public service texts are unlikely to contain such language; however, profanity may occasionally appear in spontaneous statements by politicians or community leaders, for instance. The occurrence of such language in communication intended for the public will be governed by the norms of the culture in question, as the acceptability of swear words (e.g., for emphasis) is culturally relative, and the threshold of tolerance varies from one culture and context to another. Some American politicians, for example, are famous for expletives. The way to approach such offensive language will depend on the nature of the text and on the target culture and audience; see the examples in Box 6.5).

Box 6.5 Profanity in public discourse

1) **Informative text:** Seething Trump accuses Rep. Shiff of treason and denounces the current impeachment inquiry as "bullshit".
2) **Educational resource:** Most Americans agree that politicians such as President Trump are not good role models for children. The President has become notorious for his foul language. Expressions such as "a bad motherf—er" or "a pain in the ass" coming from a high-profile leader are having an impact on our kids.
3) **Election campaign:** Would you vote for a candidate who uses offensive language against your country of origin? Well, Trump refers to Haiti and African countries as "shithole countries".

114   *Translation and Community*

In informative and educational resources such as Examples 1 and 2 in Box 6.5, offensive language can be translated using softening or cushioning strategies. Thus, "bullshit" can be translated as "nonsense", for instance. The swear words in Example 2 can even be omitted depending on the target culture because it would not affect the message "Foul language coming from a high-profile leader is having an impact on our kids". In Example 3, assuming that the text is intended to provoke a strong reaction from voters, it might be appropriate to use strong language but again within the constraints of the target culture. The bottom line is that the community translator needs to use their text analysis skills and cultural knowledge to decide whether some cultural adaptation is necessary. If unsure, consultation with the relevant stakeholders is key to effective and culturally sensitive communication.

Summary

As a professional service facilitating communication between public services and different language and cultural groups, community translation requires some level of cultural mediation and adaptation. Community translators are expected to demonstrate cultural knowledge and intercultural skills to ensure a successful, effective and culturally sensitive transfer of messages. Like other areas of translation, community translation often involves dealing with cultural assumptions and culture-specific concepts and figurative language. Like other areas of translation as well, it also requires mediation and adaptation in terms of culture-based textual conventions and norms. In addition to these common cultural challenges, community translation can cover a broad range of social, environmental and political topics, some of which may be quite sensitive and therefore require special attention to cultural mediation and sensitivity.

As Simms (1997: 3) notes, "all texts are at least potentially sensitive", but in this chapter I have focused on issues and aspects that are most relevant to the context of community translation. These range from innocuous instances of culture-specific references and examples to highly sensitive topics such as political correctness, sexuality, sexual abuse and domestic violence. In the case of culture-specific concepts and references, the community translator needs to undertake some level of cultural substitution and adaptation, where necessary, to ensure that the translations are relatable and more engaging for their target audience. As for contents that are likely to be highly culturally sensitive, the general recommendation is that the community translator, who in many cases is the first person with relevant cultural knowledge to identify potentially culturally sensitive concepts, needs to assess the overall communicative situation and make adjustments to facilitate inclusive and politically correct communication. When justified, cultural adaptations in translation

Translating culturally sensitive texts 115

are not distortions, but the translator needs to consider several factors to make informed decisions:

- Awareness of cultural differences: Being aware that differences between the source culture and the target culture can extend from shared knowledge to politeness norms in texts to belief systems relating to sensitive topics.
- Translation brief: Whether the client is keen to communicate with their audience in a culturally sensitive manner or not.
- Ethical considerations: Being aware that as a translator, you are in a position to expose readers to different—or even shocking—cultural perspectives or mediate cultural differences.
- Language resources and constraints: Strategies to ensure cultural inclusiveness and sensitivity will be subject to the resources available in the target language.
- Text type: A distinction needs to be made between public messaging and regulatory texts.
- Status of sensitive references/topics in the source text: Whether sensitivity relates to specific words or examples or to the topic of the entire document.
- Audience: Whether the translation is aimed at all community users who speak the target language or a specific group (e.g., age group).
- Language variety: Whether the text is being translated into a standard variety (e.g., print translation) or a dialect (e.g., dubbed video).

Suggested activities

1) Collect five source texts about sensitive topics (e.g., child abuse, sexual abuse, domestic violence or cults) and their translations. Make sure the texts are relevant to community translation (not, for example, literary translation). Underline all the instances of culturally sensitive concepts and expressions. Examine the translation of these instances in terms of translation strategies and the degree of translator intervention to mediate between source and target cultures.
2) Discuss the text in Box 6.4 in small groups. Is the content consistent with what you knew about domestic violence and intimate partner violence? Is the content applicable to your other language(s)?
3) Translate the text in Box 6.4 into your other working language and write a 200-word commentary on the cultural adaptations you undertook in the translation process (e.g., did you omit "hooking up", "dating" and "friends with benefits"? Did you translate them literally? Did you find culturally appropriate equivalents?). If you did not make any cultural adjustments, please explain why.

116 *Translation and Community*

Further reading

- Katan, David and Taibi, Mustapha (2021). *Translating cultures: An introduction for translators, interpreters and mediators* (Third Edition). London and New York: Routledge.

Chapters 5, 9 and 11 of this resource are particularly relevant to cultural mediation in translation (and interpreting). In Chapter 5, my colleague and I focus on the links between language and culture, and among other things, we discuss the contexts of situation and culture, the lexicon, categorisation and political correctness. In Chapter 9, we examine cultural orientations, that is, tendencies towards particular ways of perceiving the world and doing things. Then in Chapter 11, we discuss cultural differences in communication styles, cultural preferences for spoken or written communication and cross-cultural variations in terms of the importance given to clarity or formality in written communication.

- Simms, Karl (Ed.) (1997). *Translating sensitive texts: Linguistic aspects*. Amsterdam: Rodopi.

Although this edited volume does not focus on cultural sensitivity in the context of community translation, the insights it offers in relation to sensitivity in translation are likely to enhance your understanding of the issues involved. The book covers sensitivity in translating novels, legal documents, religious texts, travel brochures, and so on. The authors offer a wide variety of approaches to addressing issues of (cultural, political, religious and sexual) sensitivity in translations and to address the competing needs of authors and audiences, source cultures and target cultures. The editor's introduction also provides an overview of the key issues surrounding the translation of sensitive texts.

References

Abdul-Raof, Hussein (2004). The Qur'an: Limits of translatability. In Faiq, Said (Ed.), *Cultural encounters in translation from Arabic*. Bristol: Multilingual Matters: 91–106.

AUSIT (2022). *Recommended protocols for the translation of community communications*. https://ausit.org/wp-content/uploads/2024/03/AUSIT-FECCA-Recommended-Protocols-for-the-Translation-of-Community-Communications_042023.pdf.

AUSIT-FECCA (n.d.a). *Style guide for community translations into Spanish*. https://ausit.org/wp-content/uploads/2024/03/AUSIT-Style-Guide-for-Spanish-Community-Translations_042023.pdf.

AUSIT-FECCA (n.d.b). *Style guide for community translations into Arabic*. https://ausit.org/wp-content/uploads/2024/03/AUSIT-Style-Guide-for-Arabic-Community-Translations_042023.pdf.

AUSIT-FECCA (n.d.c). *Style guide for community translations into Chinese*. https://ausit.org/wp-content/uploads/2023/05/AUSIT-Style-Guide-for-Chinese-Community-Translations_CLEAN_042023.pdf.

Baker, Mona (2011 [1992]). *In other words: A coursebook on translation*. Abingdon: Routledge.

Translating culturally sensitive texts 117

Bassnett, Susan (2002 [1980]). *Translation Studies* (3rd Edition). London and New York: Routledge.

Bedeker, Laetitia and Feinauer, Ilse (2006). The translator as cultural mediator. *Southern African Linguistics and Applied Language Studies*, 24(2): 133–141. DOI: 10.2989/16073610609486412.

Bell, Erica (2015). Cultural translation of a domestic violence intervention for small children: Key policy and practice directions. *International Journal on Disability and Human Development*, 14(1): 45–58.

Brown, Penelope and Levinson, Stephen (1987). *Politeness: Some universals in language usage*. Cambridge: Cambridge University Press.

Bryson, Bill (2016). *Made in America: An informal history of American English*. London: Black Swan.

Diversity Council Australia (2017). *Words at work: Building inclusion through the power of language*. www.dca.org.au/research/wordsatwork-building-inclusion-through-power-language.

Ely, Robin J.; Meyerson, Debra and Davidson, Martin N. (2006). Rethinking political correctness. *Harvard Business Review*. https://hbr.org/2006/09/rethinking-political-correctness.

Hatim, Basil (1997). *Communication across cultures*. Exeter: University of Exeter Press.

Hatim, Basil and Mason, Ian (2013 [1990]). *Discourse and the translator*. London and New York: Routledge.

House, Juliane (2015). *Translation quality assessment: Past and present*. Abingdon: Routledge.

Hughes, Geoffrey (2010). *Political correctness: A history of semantics and culture*. Maldon, MA: Wiley-Blackwell.

Israel, Hephzibah (2023). *The Routledge handbook of translation and religion*. London and New York: Routledge.

Jaworska, Sylvia (2015). Review of recent research (1998–2012) in German for Academic Purposes (GAP) in comparison with English for Academic Purposes (EAP): Cross-influences, synergies and implications for further research. *Language Teaching*, 48(2): 163–197.

Katan, David and Taibi, Mustapha (2021). *Translating cultures: An introduction for translators, interpreters and mediators* (3rd Edition). London and New York: Routledge.

Liddicoat, Anthony J. (2016). Intercultural mediation, intercultural communication and translation. *Perspectives: Studies in Translatology*, 24(3): 354–364. DOI: 10.1080/0907676X.2014.980279.

Lung, Rachel (2003). Translating sensitive texts. *Perspectives*, 11(4): 255–268. DOI: 10.1080/0907676X.2003.9961479.

Mabule, Dorah Riah (2009). The taboos attached to the translation of biological terms from English into Northern Sotho. *South African Journal of African Languages*, 29(1). DOI: 10.1080/02572117.2009.10587316.

Marques, Joan F. (2009). How politically correct is political correctness? A SWOT analysis of this phenomenon. *Business & Society*, 48(2): 257–266.

Martín Ruano, Rosario (2018). Issues in cultural translation: Sensitivity, politeness, taboo, censorship. In Harding, Sue-Ann and Carbonell Cortés, Ovidi (Eds.), *The Routledge handbook of translation and culture*. Abingdon and New York: Routledge: 258–278.

Molina Martínez, Lucía (2022). Techniques/strategies (of translation). *ENTI (Encyclopedia of translation & interpreting)*. AIETI. www.aieti.eu/enti/techniques_ENG/.

Nida, Eugene A. (1994). The sociolinguistics of translating canonical religious texts. *TTR*, 7(1): 191–217. DOI: 10.7202/037173ar.

O'Driscoll, Jim (2020). *Offensive language: Taboo, offence and social control*. London, New York and Dublin: Bloomsbury.

Pym, Anthony (2010 [1992]). *Translation and text transfer: An essay on the principles of intercultural communication*. Tarragona: Intercultural Studies Group.

118 *Translation and Community*

Randell, Kimberly A.; Bledsoe, Linda K.; Shroff, Purvi L. and Pierce, Mary Clyde (2012). Educational interventions for intimate partner violence: Guidance from survivors. *Pediatric Emergency Care*, 28: 1190–1196.

Reiss, Katharina and Vermeer, Hans (2014 [1984]). *Towards a general theory of translational action: Skopos theory explained*. Translated by Christiane Nord. Routledge.

Scollon, Ron; Scollon, Suzanne and Jones, Rodney (2012). *Intercultural communication: A discourse approach*. Malden, MA: Wiley–Blackwell.

Simms, Karl (1997). Introduction. In Simms, Karl (Ed.), *Translating sensitive texts: Linguistic aspects*. Amsterdam: Rodopi: 1–26.

Snell-Hornby, Mary (1995 [1988]). *Translation studies: An integrated approach*. Amsterdam and Philadelphia: John Benjamins.

State of Queensland (Metro South Health) (2018). *How to choose culturally appropriate education resources: A guide for dietitians and nutritionists*. https://metrosouth.health. qld.gov.au/sites/default/files/content/how_to_choose_culturally_appropriate_education_ resources.pdf.

State of Victoria, Australia, Department of Families, Fairness and Housing (2023). *Better practice guide for multicultural communications*. https://content.vic.gov.au/sites/default/ files/2023-08/Better-practice-guide-for-multicultural-communications.pdf.

Taibi, Mustapha and El-Madkouri Maataoui, Mohamed (2016). Interpreting taboo: The case of Arabic interpreters in Spanish public services. In Taibi, Mustapha (Ed.), *New insights into Arabic translation and interpreting*. Bristol: Multilingual Matters: 69–90.

Taibi, Mustapha and Ozolins, Uldis (2016). *Community translation*. London and New York: Bloomsbury.

Vermeer, Hans (1986). Übersetzen als kultureller transfer. In Snell-Hornby, Mary (Ed.), *Übersetzungswissenschaft—Eine Neuorientierung*. Tübingen: Francke: 30–53.

Vinay, Jean Paul and Darbelnet, Jean (1995 [1958]). *Comparative stylistics of French and English: A methodology for translation*. Translated and edited by Juan Sager and M.-J. Hamel. Amsterdam and Philadelphia: John Benjamins.

7 Translating for different dissemination media

Community translations are not always disseminated as written texts (in print or online). To take the example of the COVID-19 awareness campaigns in different countries, multilingual information was made available in audio and video formats as well. Audiovisual resources were also developed using different communication options (e.g., video with community language speakers vs. subtitling). In this chapter, I discuss the differences between dissemination media and the language and translation options applicable in each case. The chapter covers the following points:

- Need for different and complementary dissemination media for community translations;
- Resources and constraints in different modes of communication;
- Language and textual variations across modes (e.g., oral vs. written);
- Adaptation of translation strategies to the dissemination medium.

7.1 Diversity in communities and communication methods

As I highlighted in Chapter 1 (see also Taibi and Ozolins, 2016), community translation is needed in local contexts characterised by linguistic and cultural diversity. Different social or ethnic groups will speak different languages and have different cultural preferences, orientations and practices. At the same time, users from the same language group (e.g., Chinese, Vietnamese or Spanish speakers in the United States) come from different parts of the world and different socioeconomic backgrounds, have varying literacy levels and are classifiable into further subcategories (e.g., youth vs. older people, established vs. recent migrants, men vs. women). This sociolinguistic and sociocultural diversity in multilingual societies poses several challenges for both public services and community translators (Burke, 2018). For both, it is essential to conceive of community translation as part of an effective communication strategy.

DOI: 10.4324/9781003367741-8

120   *Translation and Community*

For public services, an effective communication strategy starts with knowing the different target audiences and identifying their communication needs and preferences. An effective communication strategy cannot be based on a one-size-fits-all approach (Hajek et al., 2022: 6). As far as community translation is concerned, effectiveness means not only content accuracy but also relevance and accessibility for the target audience.

Translation accessibility is relative and therefore needs to be based on community feedback and research-informed knowledge about each target group (Taibi, 2018). This is consistent with an extensive body of literature, especially in health care communication and social marketing, which shows that language and cultural variations affect access to public services and therefore need to be effectively accommodated (e.g. Andrulis and Brach, 2007; Schouten and Meeuwesen, 2006; Schyve, 2007). As I described, such language and cultural variations often exist within what is considered the same language or cultural group, which creates a need for message targeting, which, as Schmid et al. (2008) explain,

> involves defining a subgroup of a population based on common characteristics and providing information in a manner consistent with those characteristics. This approach assumes that if group members possess enough similar characteristics and motivations, they will be influenced by the same message.

Knowledge about the target population, including its different segments and subgroups, "allows message developers to allocate campaign resources economically and strategically by targeting their relevant audience" (Schmid et al., 2008).

One area where communities vary is preferences relating to dissemination media. The *NSW Government Language Services Guidelines*, for example, recognise that "Communications that are tailored and accessible for target audiences are likely to be more effective in their 'reach'. It is therefore important to consider the target audience's preferred format and channel of communication" (Multicultural NSW, 2022: 15). The same document continues, "Options other than written translations should be considered, particularly when seeking to communicate to a group of people. This approach may be helpful where there is a low level of literacy within communities that speak a language other than English" (Multicultural NSW, 2022: 15). The National Health and Medical Research Council's (2019) *Guidelines for Guidelines: Dissemination and Communication* also recognises the need for assessment of each target audience or segment and for messages to be designed and disseminated in accordance with the findings of that assessment: "Conducting a communication needs assessment of these segments will help you tailor your dissemination strategy towards their particular requirements". As I illustrate in the following section, differences in community profiles and preferences may require different translation dissemination methods.

7.2   Community preferences and communication effectiveness

For sociocultural reasons, different communities and social groups may prefer to receive public service information through different formats and channels. Sociocultural factors may include cultural traditions and orientations (e.g., preference for oral rather than written communication), literacy levels, age, gender or levels of engagement with technology and social media. There are also factors that are inherent to the dissemination media themselves (e.g., audiovisual materials facilitating visual explanation and illustration or print resources enabling in-depth engagement with content and easy retrieval and recall of information).

Shin and Song (2021), in their survey on effective COVID-19 communications with Asian Australian communities, found that respondents reported traditional news media such as television or newspapers as the most used sources of information in relation to the pandemic. They also found variations among their participants in terms of length of residence in Australia: "immigrants within the last 10 years tend to rely more on personal networks, the Internet and social media for information on COVID-19". The authors found that ethnic language resources (e.g., SBS, Australia's multicultural and multilingual national broadcaster) and news from countries of origin were among the least used sources of COVID-19 information. The authors attributed this low use of multilingual resources to the fact that most of their participants had been in Australia for many years and reported good or very good English proficiency. The authors also suggest that another reason could be the perceived quality and utility of those multilingual sources.

Also in relation to COVID-19, Hajek et al. (2022) explored the communication needs and preferences of seven broadly classified groups: African, Pasifika, Afghan, Myanmar, Indian subcontinent, Arabic-speaking and Chinese-speaking. They did so through interviews with relatively small groups of community leaders (ranging from 2 to 19 participants in each group), which may not necessarily be representative of the ethnic and language groups they spoke for, as the same authors acknowledge: "We acknowledge that individuals' contributions may not be representative of the community and that a community is likely to be heterogenous in terms of knowledge, attitudes and practices" (Hajek et al., 2022: 6). However, the point they make is that while there are some preferences that are common to most audiences, communities vary in terms of their perception of what works better for them when it comes to receiving health care information.

Because of the inherent advantages of audiovisual media, Hajek et al. (2022) found that this "format is preferred by most communities. Specifically, the Afghan, African, Arabic-speaking and Myanmar communities identified videos about COVID-19 as a particularly effective medium for receiving information" (9). Participants from Africa, Pacific Islands, the Indian subcontinent, the Arab world, Afghanistan and Myanmar preferred to receive information through social media. Understandably, oral communication was preferred by those whose cultural background was oriented towards orality, especially when literacy was low. The study findings also revealed that all ethnic and national groups preferred social media for receiving health care information, with Facebook being the most popular except in the Chinese community, who preferred to use WeChat (9).

However, while communication strategies need to be designed in line with the target audience's preferences (National Health and Medical Research Council, 2019; Migration Council Australia, 2022), a large body of research and guidelines for good practice recommends using a combination of dissemination channels (Schipper et al., 2016). The Australian Commission on Safety and Quality

122 *Translation and Community*

in Healthcare (2014), for example, advises that combining oral and written information is likely to enhance the effectiveness of health care communication and reinforce key health messages. Johnson and Sandford (2005) also demonstrated that combining verbal and written health information was more effective among parents of children who were discharged from hospital. The participants in the study (Americans and Canadians) scored significantly higher for knowledge and satisfaction when the two communication modes were combined.

More recently, both Hajek et al. (2022) and Dickson et al. (2023) recommend a multimodal approach to dissemination. Hajek et al. (2022: 13) stress the need for both audiovisual (e.g., videos) and non-digital formats (e.g., leaflets and brochures) with visual aids to enhance comprehension. Dickson et al.'s (2023) participants "recommended using a multipronged approach of print and digital strategies to disseminate health information". These strategies or channels include posters in places frequented by culturally and linguistically diverse community members, websites and social media platforms (e.g., Facebook, WhatsApp and Instagram).

As the Australian Commission on Safety and Quality in Health Care (2014: 42) notes, "people need to be provided with multiple opportunities to access, understand and act on health information. . . . This could be done using strategies such as providing information in different formats". While this and other citations in this section relate to health care communication, the same applies to communication with culturally and linguistically diverse communities in other areas (e.g., education, social services, legal advice, the environment). Multimodal dissemination strategies are likely to address community preferences (cultural), user preferences (individual), differences in literacy levels and physical constraints (e.g., eyesight in relation to print translations), and for those who can use more than one medium, it reinforces messaging and improves comprehension and retention of information.

While the points I have made apply to public services in the first instance, community translators also need to be aware of dominant user preferences in their target community and, if necessary, act as expert advisers (see Section 2.4). More importantly, they need to distinguish between one dissemination medium and another and use the language variety and translation strategies that are most consistent with the communication strategy and medium. This is what I turn to in the following sections.

Box 7.1   Questions to consider/discuss

1) Does it make any difference to the community translator whether their translation is going to be published (in print or online) or whether it is going to be used as a script for audiovisual production?
2) The community translator should advise the client/commissioner on language variants to be used depending on the format in which their translation is to be disseminated. Do you agree? Is this consistent with their role as discussed in Chapter 2?

Translating for different dissemination media 123

3) Translating texts intended for dissemination on social media may require language and style adaptations. Do you agree? Does this apply to your working languages and target communities?
4) Language acceptability relates to the cultural and community context as well as the applicable language and stylistic norms. It has nothing to do with the communication channel. How do you feel about this statement?
5) A translator receives a long interview to translate without a translation brief. They know that the interviewee is a community leader, but they do not know whether the translation is going to be published and if so in what dissemination format. What should they do?

7.3 Variations between media/modes of communication

With the advances in technology and communication systems, public services in many countries have diversified the dissemination methods of their public messaging, including translated or multilingual contents. A case in point was health care communication during the COVID-19 pandemic (2020–2023). Awareness campaigns relating to risks, symptoms, vaccination and other behavioural aspects were launched through online written texts, dubbed or subtitled video files, downloadable audio files, hyperlinked PDFs, digital images and posters (Gerber et al., 2021), as well as mass media, community leaders, community health workers, telephone dissemination and leaflets and posters displayed in public places (Fergus et al., 2021).

As far as communication with multilingual communities is concerned, our focus is on those dissemination channels that require community translation, not community interpreting, which is not within the scope of this textbook. Written texts (in digital or non-digital format) and dubbed or subtitled audiovisual materials, for example, may need translation, while face-to-face or technology-mediated communication with community leaders or health providers may require interpreting if the speaker is not proficient in the relevant community language. At the same time, technology has enabled easy transition from verbal or audiovisual dissemination to written communication and vice versa, such as an awareness Zoom webinar being automatically transcribed and subsequently translated for further dissemination. Whatever the case, community translators, as communicators, need to be aware that different dissemination channels may have different resources and constraints and may require different translation strategies.

Every text—or communicative event for that matter—involves a transmitter, a channel and a receiver (Shannon and Weaver, 1963 [1949]); in other words, a sender/speaker/writer, a medium (of communication) and a receiver/addressee/audience. Without going into the debate on whether communication consists of a simple transmission of messages (the sender–receiver model) or co-construction and exchange of meanings between participants in a communicative event, as the

124   *Translation and Community*

Semiotic School argues (Wright, 2008: 27), suffice it to note for our purposes here that the channel or medium of communication plays an important role in the communication process.

The medium is "the means or vehicle which conveys the text to the reader (in communication theory, "channel" stands for sound waves or print on paper)" (Nord, 2005: 62). It therefore not only enables communication between author and audience but can also determine or influence the language used. As Nord (2005: 62) asserts, the medium affects not only the reception of texts but also their production. This includes text organisation, syntactical structures, lexical choices, register and style, which are all important aspects for the community translator and their target community.

The role of the medium has been recognised in the translation studies literature, especially translation quality assessment models based on Hallidayan linguistics such as House's (1977, 1997, 2001). House offers a functionalist model of translation quality assessment which revolves around equivalence at two basic levels: ideational and interpersonal. The ideational level relates to content or ideas, while the interpersonal level relates to the relationship between author and reader. Central to House's model is the notion of register, with its three elements: field (the ideational component of the text; content or subject matter), tenor (the relationship between the author and the reader, e.g., whether it involves power and distance) and mode, which

> refers to both the channel—spoken or written (which can be "simple," i.e., "written to be read" or "complex," e.g. "written to be spoken as if not written"), and the degree to which potential or real participation is allowed for between writer and reader.
>
> (House, 2001: 248)

What is of importance to us as community translators is that, as I have discussed, different dissemination channels and modes of communication vary in terms of resources, constraints as well as textual and linguistic manifestations (language use).

It is well known, for example, that oral and written communication are quite different. Comparing the two, Biber (1988: 35–40) notes the following, among other differences:

1) Writing is limited to the lexical and syntactic resources (words and structures) as well as typographical conventions (e.g., boldface or underlining for emphasis), while speaking involves other resources, such as prosody and non-verbal communication (e.g., facial expressions, gestures, intonation and stress).
2) The attitudes towards spoken and written communication vary from one social or cultural group to another (e.g., Kress, 2010). This applies both to contexts where either writing or speaking is preferred and to how the societies involved evaluate the two channels.
3) Written texts and spoken discourse have different conventions in relation to cohesion, internal coherence and information structure.

Although many authors (e.g., Biber, 1988: 24; Crystal, 1995; Tanskanen, 2006) argue that there is no absolute distinction between spoken and written communication, it is generally accepted that oral communication is aural and transient while writing is visual and more permanent; speech is produced in real time without planning, while writing involves planning and editing; speech involves interaction and feedback, while writing generally does not (exceptions are text messaging and online enquiries) and oral communication generally takes place in a situational context that is shared by the participants, whereas that is not usually the case for written communication (Cameron and Panović, 2014: 21).

However, while these distinctions might apply to typical conversational and written communication, some of them do not necessarily apply to the type of public service communication handled by community translators. In terms of spontaneity vs. planning, for instance, public messaging is usually planned and carefully presented, whether it is delivered in writing (e.g., leaflets and websites), orally (e.g., radio) or audiovisually (e.g., television and videos on social media). As Tanskanen (2006: 75) states, "not all spoken language is unplanned nor all written language planned, and differences due to the degree of planning exist even within the modes".

Another difference between the written and spoken modes, which is probably more relevant to the work of translators, relates to how text is organised, namely syntactical complexity, cohesion and the way informational structure is marked. The written mode has been found to display more structural complexity, although it must be noted that this applies to typical formal writing in contrast to typical informal speech. Chafe (1982: 36), for example, found "formal written language to differ from informal spoken language by having a larger proportion of nominalizations, genitive subjects and objects, participles, attributive adjectives, conjoined phrases, series, sequences of prepositional phrases, complement clauses, and relative clauses".

Greenbaum and Nelson (1995: 17), in their comparison of spontaneous conversations, broadcast discussions, unscripted monologues, personal letters and academic and non-academic writing, also conclude that conversations, as the stereotypical form of oral discourse, show the least complexity (fewer coordinate and subordinate clauses). In terms of cohesion, oral discourse is known to tolerate or even rely on reiteration or repetition more than writing for several purposes. While repetition may be considered a sign of redundancy in written texts, it functions as a cohesive device in speech and serves other functions as well, including as an intensifier of the point or as a comprehension enabler. As Bazzanella (2011: 249) says, "Repetition, besides being a useful cognitive device (as a simplifying/clarifying device, a filler, and a support both for understanding and memorizing), an efficient text-building mechanism, and a widespread literacy and rhetorical device, is a powerful conversational and interactional resource".

However, many authors have suggested that mode alone (written vs. spoken) cannot explain the surface language variation between texts (Tanskanen, 2006: 75). Tannen (1982) argues that register and genre can explain such differences better than mode and that focus on interpersonal involvement or on content is key.

126 *Translation and Community*

Mazzie (1987) believes that the content of the text (abstract vs. narrative) plays a more decisive role than mode in determining language and textual similarities and differences. Meanwhile, Greenbaum and Nelson (1995) suggest that whether the discourse is planned or unplanned is a key factor in variation even between texts or discourses in the same mode.

It can be asserted, however, that all these views are partially correct and complementary rather than mutually exclusive. Tannen's (1982) point about register probably summarises the key determinants of language variations in text and discourse, as register is based on field (subject matter), mode (medium of communication) and tenor (the assumed relationship, distance and power between author and reader). For example, we often find texts which cover the same topic and use the same mode (writing) but vary significantly in terms of the projected relationship between participants in the communication (tenor), as the excerpts in Box 7.2 illustrate.

Box 7.2 Texts with different levels of involvement (tenor)

1) Air pollution is contamination of the indoor or outdoor environment by any chemical, physical or biological agent that modifies the natural characteristics of the atmosphere.

   Household combustion devices, motor vehicles, industrial facilities and forest fires are common sources of air pollution. Pollutants of major public health concern include particulate matter, carbon monoxide, ozone, nitrogen dioxide and sulfur dioxide. Outdoor and indoor air pollution cause respiratory and other diseases and are important sources of morbidity and mortality (www.who.int/health-topics/air-pollution#tab=tab_1).

2) On a clear breezy day, the air smells fresh and clean. Clean air is air that has no harmful levels of pollutants (dirt and chemicals) in it. Clean air is good for people to breathe. On a hot day with no wind, the air can feel heavy and have a bad smell. once in a while, the air can even make your chest feel tight, or make you cough. When too much dirt and chemicals get into the air, the air is dirty or polluted. Dirty air is not good for people to breathe. When the air has some dust, soot or chemicals floating in it, people who are inside probably won't notice it. People who are outside might notice it. People with asthma, a disease that can make it hard to breathe, and children who play outside a lot might feel a little strange. When you are active outdoors, for example, when you run and jump a lot, you breathe faster and take in more air. Any pollutants in the air go into your lungs. (www.airnow.gov/education/students/clean-and-dirty-air-part-one)

Translating for different dissemination media   127

> 3) Depressive disorder (also known as depression) is a common mental disorder. It involves a depressed mood or loss of pleasure or interest in activities for long periods of time.
>
> Depression is different from regular mood changes and feelings about everyday life. It can affect all aspects of life, including relationships with family, friends and community. It can result from or lead to problems at school and at work.
>
> Depression can happen to anyone. People who have lived through abuse, severe losses or other stressful events are more likely to develop depression. Women are more likely to have depression than men (www.who.int/news-room/fact-sheets/detail/depression).
>
> 4) Please believe me, after many years of experience, that depression can be totally wiped out! You are not weak, you are not worthless, you are not a permanent burden, you are not any of the other negatives that the illness tries to tell you . . . you have a very common illness which WILL pass. And you are not alone, just ask for help (https://depression.com.au).

All the passages in Box 7.2 are written texts taken from different websites offering information to the public about issues of interest. Both Excerpts 1 and 2 are about air pollution, and both Excerpts 3 and 4 deal with depression. However, readers will undoubtedly notice certain differences among them: For instance, Excerpts 1 and 3 are more formal than Excerpts 2 and 4.

Consider the difference between the lexical choices, for example, in "Pollutants of major public health concern include particulate matter, carbon monoxide, ozone, nitrogen dioxide and sulfur dioxide" (Excerpt 1) and "When too much dirt and chemicals get into the air, the air is dirty or polluted" (Excerpt 2), or between "Depressive disorder (also known as depression) is a common mental disorder" (Excerpt 3) and "Please believe me, after many years of experience, that depression can be totally wiped out!" (Excerpt 4). Another difference that is also related to formality, is the presence or absence of personal pronouns (e.g., "You are not weak, you are not worthless, you are not a permanent burden, you are not any of the other negatives that the illness tries to tell you" in Excerpt 4). The presence and frequency of such pronouns denotes a closer interpersonal relationship between writer (i.e., public service in our case) and reader (target community). It suggests a higher degree of involvement, which is typical in the discourse of professional services characterised by empathy, such as counselling, social work and social services.

A third difference is the amount of repetition, which is used more in Excerpts 2 and 4 than in Excerpts 1 and 3: Repetition is less frequent in the formal examples than in the less formal ones. Excerpt 4 shows the most repetition, to the extent that it reads as if someone was speaking rather than writing. Interestingly, Excerpt 4 is introduced as follows on the website: "Note from clinical A/Prof David Horgan",

128 *Translation and Community*

which supports this observation and the point made earlier in this section about re-iteration being associated with spoken discourse. The orality of Excerpt 4 is further indicated with capital letters replacing paralanguage to convey additional emphasis ("you have a very common illness which WILL pass").

Other modes of communication commonly used in public service communication and in community contexts in general are pictograms, which combine visual and textual elements; unsubtitled videos that contain visual and oral features or subtitled videos that contain visual, oral and textual resources at the same time. In videos, the visual element includes not only images or footage but also the non-verbal aspects of communication displayed by presenters and interviewees (e.g., facial expressions, hand gestures). In such multimodal communication, language, with all its lexical and grammatical resources, is only one component of what Kress and Van Leeuwen (2001) call a "communicational ensemble" and Gambier (2023: 1) refers to as a "complex system of signs". The different elements are not used separately but as a combination of connected semiotic resources (meaning-making resources) which complement one another.

As Díaz-Cintas and Remael (2014: 5) note, "Audiovisual programmes use two codes, image and sound, and whereas literature and poetry evoke, films represent and actualize a particular reality based on specific images that have been put together by a director". While reference here is to entertainment films in the first instance, the same applies to audiovisual materials produced for educational, awareness or public messaging purposes. Whether such resources consist mainly of an expert presentation; interviews with authorities, experts or community members or a script read by a broadcaster in addition to visual illustration, there are multiple modes of communication that are simultaneously used and drawn upon.

7.4 Different translation strategies for different dissemination channels

Due attention to the communicative context requires, among other things, attention to the mode of communication. Community translators particularly need to consider the practices, requirements and expectations associated with each medium because as Kress (2010) explains, each has its own traditions and conventions. This includes not only the inherent differences between any given modes (e.g., print translation with text only, print translation with illustrations, video) but also any applicable variations that are specific to the target community (e.g., written communication using a standard variety and videos using a vernacular of the same language).

Awareness of differences between dissemination media and the sociolinguistic context of the target community will often lead community translators to adapt their translation strategies to ensure they are consistent with the communication strategy and medium. For example, if the translation is going to be delivered orally (e.g., speaker using it as a script for a community awareness event), the translator will probably need to make structural adaptations in terms of sentence length and

Translating for different dissemination media   129

complexity. Although accessibility is key to community translation in general, as we have seen in this textbook (e.g., Chapters 1 and 4), oral delivery, especially in community contexts, requires more accessible and simple structures. While a reader can follow an idea through a long sentence or a long sequence of embedded clauses, this might be a challenge for listeners, as they do not have access to a written text and would therefore need a greater cognitive effort to remember all the sequence.

Other adaptations may be of a cultural nature; for example, the terms of address used in writing might not be culturally appropriate for a face-to-face encounter involving oral communication of information. Similarly, if the material to be translated consists of a pictogram (text supported with visual illustrations) with space limitations, the translator may find "translation by illustration" (Baker, 2011 [1992]; See Chapter 3) quite useful. If the concept or process is already illustrated in the poster or pictogram, the translator may leave certain terms in the source language or use fewer words than they would in other circumstances. This is especially convenient when there is no equivalent term in the target language or when the target language is analytic and requires a long segment to paraphrase a single term (e.g., "chair with wheels for obese people" for 'bariatric wheelchair').

In audiovisual translation, in addition to space constraints, there are timing requirements and considerations relating to the shift from orality to writing. Díaz-Cintas and Remael (2014: 5) explain that in subtitling, the screen space available is limited, and "the target text will have to accommodate to the width of the screen. Although the figures vary, this means that a subtitle will have some 32 to 41 characters per line in a maximum of two lines". As subtitling involves a change from the oral to the written mode, translators often need to leave out lexical items from the source discourse (Díaz-Cintas and Remael, 2014: 5) because of both space limitations and the differences between the two communication modes. In terms of timing, the same authors point out that subtitles need to be synchronised with what speakers are doing and saying on screen. Synchronicity is one of the key requirements in audiovisual translation. The *Code of Good Subtitling Practice* (Carroll and Ivarsson, 1998), for instance, stresses that "There must be a close correlation between film dialogue and subtitle content; source language and target language should be synchronized as far as possible". In relation to language and accessibility, the same document recommends the following:

- Using simple syntactic structures; this makes syntactic units more manageable on screen, saves spaces and reduces the user's cognitive effort);
- Condensing text and ensuring conciseness without impacting on text coherence (see Box 7.3 for examples of text editing for conciseness);
- Using syntactically self-contained subtitles (i.e., so that the user does not need to wait for the next subtitle to comprehend a message);
- Using appropriate language register; this applies to all translation types and contexts.

130 *Translation and Community*

Box 7.3   Editing for conciseness

1) - **From the government's perspective**, we know we need better national laws.
   - As government, we know we need better national laws.
2) - However, **it must be remembered** that community cooperation **will have positive effects** on community safety.
   - However, community cooperation will enhance community safety.
3) - This is one of the eligibility criteria **for obtaining a mortgage loan.**
   - This is one of the mortgage loan eligibility criteria.
4) - We believe that you should feel safe at your workplace **independent of whether you have a visa or not and what type of visa you have.**
   - We believe that you should feel safe at your workplace regardless of visa status.
5) - Older people face **the challenge of having** a higher risk of heat-related health problems.
   - Older people face a higher risk of heat-related health problems.
6) - Encourage the person to drink small sips of water or juice if **they have survived and they are still able** to swallow.
   - Encourage the person to drink small sips of water or juice if able to swallow.
7) - First **and foremost**, we need to be role models for our children **to follow, imitate and learn from**.
   - First, we need to be role models for our children.

Gambier (2023) highlights accessibility as a key consideration in audiovisual translation. He defines it in the following broad terms: "Accessibility allows anybody to achieve specific goals with effectiveness, efficiency, and satisfaction in a specific context of use, and allows communication to go beyond any social, cognitive, age, gender divide and mental, sensory, or physical impairment" (3). For Gambier, accessibility takes central stage in the assessment of audiovisual translation quality. Accessibility covers the following criteria, which can also be taken as translation quality criteria in this context:

- Acceptability: The extent to which the translation is consistent with the language norms and the stylistic choices, rhetorical patterns and terminology are acceptable;
- Legibility: Whether technical aspects such as font, position of the subtitles and subtitle rate facilitate the reading of subtitles;
- Readability: Text complexity, cognitive load in relation to text complexity, shot changes and speech rates;

Translating for different dissemination media 131

- Synchronicity: Synchronisation of speech and lip movements (in the case of dubbing); synchronisation of speech/subtitling and footage (what is said in speech or text and what is shown in pictures).
- Relevance: Information to be translated, clarified, left out or added in order to improve user experience and not increase their cognitive effort (Gambier, 2023: 12–13).

Gambier (2023) concludes that with these criteria being predominant in the audiovisual translation industry, "the usual ones (accuracy, appropriateness, and coherence) become secondary and even minor if the time and space constraints have priority" (13). This, however, should be taken with caution in the context of community translation. As I pointed out earlier, the *Code of Good Subtitling Practice* itself (Carroll and Ivarsson, 1998) recommends that conciseness not be at the expense of coherence.

In addition, while accuracy, appropriateness and coherence may not be essential in the translation of films, sitcoms or other entertainment products, in community translation they are indispensable. Community translation involves working with high-stakes contents (health care advice, legal information, social and environmental issues, etc.), which require accurate, meaningful and appropriate communication across languages and cultures. Díaz-Cintas and Remael (2014) point out that the adaptations often required due to the constraints of audiovisual translation have led some to look down on this type of translation, "considering it as a type of adaptation rather than translation", while others use the adaptation involved in audiovisual translation as "an excuse to carry out a linguistic transfer that is clearly inadequate" (5).

In community translation, we need to consider audiovisual translation as well as other translation dissemination media as different communication channels with different resources and constraints. While community translators are expected to adapt their translation strategies and choices to the dissemination medium, the key quality parameters and expectations (i.e., accuracy, accessibility, language appropriateness, coherence and cultural sensitivity) remain the same. Sometimes it is a challenge to strike a balance between the technical requirements of the medium and other quality parameters, but a key skill for community translators to develop is the ability to weigh up the risks involved against the options available.

Summary

With the steady advances in technology and dissemination media, community translation cannot be envisaged as only written translation. As governments and civic organisations diversify the communication channels they use to reach out to the public (social media, videos, leaflets, etc.), community translators are expected to work with different types of texts and modes of communication. Modes of communication (e.g., oral vs. written, oral vs. audiovisual)

132 *Translation and Community*

are inherently different and vary in terms of conventions, resources and con-straints. As part of their assessment of the communicative context, commu-nity translators need to be aware of these differences and use appropriate language and translation strategies. Adaptations to the medium include using one language variety rather than another, stylistic adjustments, simplifying syntactical structures, editing for conciseness, changing address terms and politeness markers and so on. Medium-specific adaptations, however, are not to be made at the expense of the essence of community translation: accurate, effective and empowering communication across languages and cultures.

Suggested activities

1) Choose a written text in one of your working languages which provides general advice on an issue of public interest (e.g., violence, crime, health and wellbe-ing, inter-ethnic relations in the local community). Translate it into your other working language bearing in mind that your translation is not going to be pub-lished but used by a community leader who is going to speak at an upcom-ing awareness workshop. When you have finished, check whether you (should) have made any adaptations in terms of lexical choices, structures and cohesive devices given that the content will be delivered orally.
2) Now go back to both the source text and your own translation and identify 10 sentences or phrases in each which could be edited for conciseness (conveying the same message in fewer words).
3) Locate an awareness video and a leaflet in the same language and on the same topic. Analyse their language (syntactical complexity, formality of lexical choices, cohesive devices, etc.). If you have identified any differences, do you think these are due to the mode of communication or idiosyncratic differences between authors or producers?
4) Search the internet for an awareness video (on COVID-19, bullying, tax evasion, etc.) that has been subtitled into one of your working languages. Write a 200-word commentary on the quality of the subtitles based on the criteria in Section 7.4.

Further reading

- Kress, Gunther (2010). *Multimodality: A social semiotic approach to contem-porary communication*. London and New York: Routledge.

While Kress does not address translation, his book is a good reference for understand-ing multimodality in general. He discusses the multiple modes people use in differ-ent spheres of life to communicate and make meaning (images, writing, speech and sound, gestures, 3D objects and so on). In his Chapter 5 in particular, he addresses the affordances of different communication modes, differences and similarities between them, as well as cultural variations in preferences for and usage of different modes.

References

Andrulis, Dennis P. and Brach, Cindy (2007). Integrating literacy, culture, and language to improve health care quality for diverse populations. *American Journal of Health Behavior*, 31(Suppl): S122–S133.

Australian Commission on Safety and Quality in Health Care (2014). *Health literacy: Taking action to improve safety and quality*. Australian Commission on Safety and Quality in Health Care. www.safetyandquality.gov.au/publications-and-resources/resource-library/health-literacy-taking-action-improve-safety-and-quality.

Baker, Mona (2011 [1992]). *In other words: A coursebook on translation*. Abingdon: Routledge.

Bazzanella, Carla (2011). Redundancy, repetition, and intensity in discourse. *Language Sciences*, 33: 243–254.

Biber, Douglas (1988). *Variation across speech and writing*. Cambridge: Cambridge University Press.

Cameron, Deborah and Panović, Ivan (2014). *Working with written discourse*. Los Angeles, London and New Delhi: Springer.

Carroll, Mary and Ivarsson, Jan (1998). *Code of good subtitling practice*. www.esist.org/wp-content/uploads/2016/06/Code-of-Good-Subtitling-Practice.PDF.pdf.

Chafe, Wallace (1982). Integration and involvement in speaking, writing and oral literature. In Tannen, Deborah (Ed.), *Spoken and written language: Exploring orality and literacy*. Norwood, NJ: Ablex: 35–53.

Crystal, David (1995). Speaking of writing and writing of speaking. *Longman Language Review*, 1: 5–8.

Díaz-Cintas, Jorge and Remael, Aline (2014). *Audiovisual translation: Subtitling*. London and New York: Routledge.

Dickson, Kara; Aboltins, Craig; Pelly, Janet and Jessup, Leigh (2023). Effective communication of COVID-19 vaccine information to recently-arrived culturally and linguistically diverse communities from the perspective of community engagement and partnership organisations: A qualitative study. *BMC Health Services Research*, 23(1): 877. DOI: 10.1186/s12913-023-09836-3.

Fergus, Cristin Alexis; Storer, Elizabeth; Arinaitwe, Moses; Kamurari, Solomon and Adriko, Moses (2021). COVID-19 information dissemination in Uganda: Perspectives from sub-national health workers. *MC Health Services Research*, 21: 1061. DOI: 10.1186/s12913-021-07068-x.

Gambier, Yves (2023). Audiovisual translation and multimodality: What future? *Media and Intercultural Communication: A Multidisciplinary Journal*, 1(1): 1–16. DOI: 10.22034/mic.2023.167451.

Gerber, Leah; Wilson, Rita; Hlavac, Jim and Avella Archila, Alex (2021). *Developing multilingual communication strategies for CALD communities during the COVID-19 vaccination rollout*. https://lens.monash.edu/@politics-society/2021/05/31/1383335/developing-multilingual-communication-strategies-for-cald-communities-during-the-covid-19-vaccination-rollout.

Greenbaum, Sidney and Nelson, Gerald (1995). Clause relationships in spoken and written English. *Functions of Language*, 2(1): 1–21.

Hajek, John; Karidakis, Maria; Amorati, Riccardo; Hao, Yu; Sengupta, Medha; Pym, Anthony and Woodward-Kron, Robyn (2022). *Understanding the experiences and communication needs of culturally and linguistically diverse communities during the COVID-19 pandemic*. https://rest.neptune-prod.its.unimelb.edu.au/server/api/core/bitstreams/d6b30546-ded4-56ce-8b2c-3625bf8d0215/content.

House, Juliane (1977). *A model for translation quality assessment*. Tübingen: Gunter Narr Verlag.

House, Juliane (1997). *Translation quality assessment: A model revisited*. Tübingen: Gunter Narr Verlag.

134 *Translation and Community*

House, Juliane (2001). Translation quality assessment: Linguistic description versus social evaluation. *Meta*, 46(2): 243–257.

Johnson, Anne and Sandford, Jayne (2005). Written and verbal information versus verbal information only for patients being discharged from acute hospital settings to home: Systematic review. *Health Education Research*, 20(4): 423–429. DOI: 10.1093/her/cyg141.

Kress, Gunther (2010). *Multimodality: A social semiotic approach to contemporary communication*. London and New York: Routledge.

Kress, Gunther and van Leeuwen, Theo (2001). *Multimodal discourse: The modes and media of contemporary communication*. London: Arnold.

Mazzie, Claudia A. (1987). An experimental investigation of the determinants of implicitness in spoken and written discourse. *Discourse Processes*, 10: 31–42.

Migration Council Australia (2022). *Integrating culturally, ethnically and linguistically diverse communities in rapid responses to public health crise*. https://migrationcouncil.org.au/wp-content/uploads/2022/02/Communication-Guide-CALD-communities-in-public-health-crises.pdf.

Multicultural NSW (2022). *NSW Government language services guidelines*. https://multicultural.nsw.gov.au/wp-content/uploads/2022/11/Language-Services_Guidelines_OCT22.pdf.

NationalHealth and Medical Research Council (2019). *Guidelines for guidelines: Dissemination and communication*. www.nhmrc.gov.au/guidelinesforguidelines/implement/dissemination-and-communication.

Nord, Christiane (2005). *Text analysis in translation: Theory, methodology, and didactic application of a model for translation-oriented text analysis*. Amsterdam and New York: Rodopi.

Schipper, Karen; Bakker, Minne; de Wit, Maarten P. T.; Ket, Johannes and Abma, Tineke A. (2016). Strategies for disseminating recommendations or guidelines to patients: A systematic review. *Implementation Science*, 11: 82.

Schmid, Kristina L.; Rivers, Susan E.; Latimer, Amy E. and Salovey, Peter (2008). Targeting or tailoring? Maximizing resources to create effective health communications. *Marketing Health Services*, 28(1): 32–37. www.ncbi.nlm.nih.gov/pmc/articles/PMC2728473/.

Schouten, Barbara C. and Meeuwesen, Ludwien (2006). Cultural differences in medical communication: A review of the literature. *Patient Education and Counseling*, 64(1): 21–34.

Schyve, Paul M. (2007). Language differences as a barrier to quality and safety in health care: The joint commission perspective. *Journal of General Internal Medicine*, 22(Suppl 2): 360–361.

Shannon, Claude and Weaver, Warren (1963 [1949]). *The mathematical theory of communication*. Urbana: University of Illinois Press.

Shin, Wonsun and Song, Jay (2021). What our survey found about effective COVID-19 communications in Asian Australian communities. *Melbourne Asia Review*, 5. DOI: 10.37839/mar2652-550x5.16.

Taibi, Mustapha (2018). Quality assurance in community translation. In Taibi, M. (Ed.), *Translating for the community*. Bristol: Multilingual Matters: 7–25.

Taibi, Mustapha and Ozolins, Uldis (2016). *Community translation*. London and New York: Bloomsbury.

Tannen, Deborah (1982). Oral and literate strategies in spoken and written discourse. *Language*, 58: 1–20.

Tanskanen, Sanna Kaisa (2006). *Collaborating towards coherence*. Amsterdam and Philadelphia: John Benjamins.

Wright, Scott (2008). Language, communication and the public sphere: Definitions. In Wodak, Ruth and Koller, Veronika (Eds.), *Handbook of communication in the public sphere*. Berlin: Mouton de Gruyter: 21–43.

8 Translating personal official documents

> This chapter focuses on translating personal official documents (civil registry certificates, driver's licence, academic qualifications, etc.) as a special area of translation practice. Although these documents fall under the category of administrative or legal texts, their translations are often part of the language services offered to migrants, refugees and other minority group members to facilitate their access to services and their social integration. This chapter covers the following:
>
> - Features, challenges and requirements of translating official documents;
> - A functional approach to translating official documents;
> - Quality criteria in this area;
> - Practical guidelines (accuracy, language appropriateness, document integrity and presentation).

8.1 Translation of official documents as community translation

Practically, an official document for translation can be any type of document "if it falls within a judicial process or a request of acknowledgement of rights before any kind of administrative body" (Mayoral Asensio, 2014: 4), such as personal letters or text messages for a court proceeding. However, this type of translation typically involves personal official documents such as civil registry certificates (e.g., birth, marriage, death, or filiation certificates), driver's licences, penal records (police checks) or academic qualifications (enrolment certificate, testamur, academic transcript, etc.).

As such, these documents are not the staple material in community translation as defined in Chapter 1 and are completely different from the typical public messaging or regulatory texts translated by community translators (Chapters 4 and 5). They can be classified as legal or administrative translations, but they have been included in this textbook because their translations are often part of the language services offered to migrants, refugees and other minority group members to facilitate

DOI: 10.4324/9781003367741-9

136   *Translation and Community*

their access to services and their social integration. Translating personal official documents can, of course, be required by diplomats, businesspeople, students and so on who need to prove a status or lodge an application or claim internationally, but it is also often an essential part of community members' access to public services in the countries where they live or where they are moving.

Massive population movements have characterised the last century, especially after World War II, as a result of armed and political conflicts and economic needs in both the countries of origin and host countries. The latter had to have infrastructures in place to regulate migration flows, including through official translations, even before they started considering language services such as community translation. First, administrators needed to verify identities and backgrounds, assess risks and facilitate the administrative access and integration of migrants and refugees, which took place through official translators, sworn translators or any other person who was deemed qualified or eligible.

Only decades later did host countries start to offer community translation services in the form of multilingual public messaging. In Australia, for example, language services had their beginnings in 1947, when the country had to respond to the post-World War II migration needs (Department of Home Affairs, 2023). As new migrants settled in the country, the government and organisations such as the Red Cross started to provide translation services, which were focused mainly on administrative or official documents. Banks were also among the first organisations to offer free translation services in the early post-war years, for obvious economic interests (Chesher, 1997: 282). Community translations in the sense of translations of public-interest information followed later, especially in the 1970s and 1980s (Chesher, 1997: 282).

8.2   Special type of translation

Certification is the most distinctive feature that sets the translation of official documents apart from other types of translation: Translators must be certified or officially recognised, and they must certify their translations, often with a stamp, signature and other details. Comparing this area of translation practice with community translation, Taibi and Ozolins (2016) note,

> Whereas other areas of community translation largely provide information, and often persuasion, warning or instruction, official documents are a gateway to having rights or status recognized. As this can be a high-stakes issue, these translations come under scrutiny in a way no other community translation document will.

(79)

Official documents are "a gateway to having rights or status recognized", and so are their translations. This is why governments and administrations around the world usually have stringent systems to regulate access to this specialised translation area and to select and recognise translators who are qualified to offer services within it.

Thus, you will find translators—with or without qualifications—translating literature, audiovisual content, public messaging and so on, but unless they are duly certified or recognised by the relevant authority, their translation of a birth certificate or a driver's licence will not be recognised as valid.

In many countries (e.g., France, Morocco, Spain), translators who are approved to translate official documents are called sworn translators, and they gain this status through a test organised by the Ministry of Justice, the Ministry of Foreign Affairs or a similar government department or agency. In Mexico, the name is slightly different (*perito traductor oficial*, 'expert official translator'), but the qualification process is similar: Applicants apply to the relevant Superior Court of Justice and sit a written and oral exam (Translated, 2023). In Australia, the same NAATI-certified translators who translate public messaging (and other texts) are qualified to translate official documents as well. In the United States, the system is less rigorous, as "anyone can certify a translation. A translator does not need to be certified in order to provide a certified translation. The individual translator can certify their translations, as can an employee of a translation company" (American Translators Association, 2023).

In addition to the translator's certification and stamp, translations of official documents may also be required to include an affidavit (see example in Box 8.1), as is the case when the translations are presented in a court case. As is explained in the *Best Practices for the Translation of Official and Legal Documents*, published by the Australian Institute of Interpreters and Translators,

> An affidavit sets out the translator's qualifications, lists and certifies each source document and lists the associated translations and certifies them as true and correct. Affidavits are usually prepared by the lawyers requesting the translation and need to be sworn or affirmed before a Justice of the Peace or other person authorised to take an oath or affirmation, who will stamp and sign the affidavit. They may also stamp and sign source documents (copies) and translations.
>
> (AUSIT, 2022: 9)

Box 8.1   Example of affidavit

I, [name], of [address] in the State of [your state, e.g., NSW], translator, AFFIRM/MAKE OATH AND SAY:

1) I am familiar with both the [XXXX] language and the [XXXX] language and I am competent to make a translation of the document produced to me and marked "A" into the English language.
2) Produced and shown to me at the time of making this my affidavit and marked with the letter "A" is an original/a certified copy/fax copy/of a marriage certificate in the [XXXX] language.

138 *Translation and Community*

> 3) Produced and shown to me at the time of making this my affidavit and marked with the letter "B" is a correct translation of the document marked "A" into the [XXXX] language.
>
> AFFIRMED/SWORN by the (Deponent)
>
> [Name]
> At: [Name of city or town]
> on the day of: [Date]
> Signature of deponent
> Before me:
> This Affidavit was prepared by [XXXX]

Depending on common practice or professional directives in each country or state, such translations may also include a disclaimer such as the following: "The translator, in providing this certification, gives no warrant as to the authenticity of the source document. Any unauthorised change to the translation renders this certification invalid" (AUSIT, 2022: 9).

As the translations of personal official documents usually travel from one country to another, legalisation or authentication is also required. This is done through municipal authorities, a notary public, the consulate of the destination country, the Ministry of Foreign Affairs, the Ministry of Justice or combinations of these authorities depending on the country (Mayoral Asensio, 2014: 7). This process is applicable when the two countries do not have a mutual recognition agreement for official translations, and it serves as an additional security layer to ensure that the content of the document was accurately translated by an identifiable and qualified translator.

Another distinctive feature of translating personal official documents is that because of the special ethical and legal responsibilities involved in it, it is quite documentary. Nord (2018 [1997]) uses the label 'documentary' to describe translations that are focused on the source text, describe source-text elements, follow source-language norms in relation to language and layout and clearly read like a translation, not like an original piece of writing. Such translations are in clear contrast with 'instrumental' translations, which are expected to convey source-text messages in a natural and conventionally acceptable manner in the target language and culture (e.g., community translations discussed in the other chapters of this textbook).

In documentary translations, the translation "is a text about a text" (Nord, 2018 [1997]: 47), and this is perhaps nowhere as evident as in the case of translations of personal official documents: The translator not only translates the information in the source document but also describes and refers to relevant features in the document (e.g., stamps, signatures, using [sic] for errors and misspellings, inserting [illegible] when part of the text is illegible, and so on).

8.3 Challenges

Like other legal and administrative texts, personal official documents are often characterised by rigid, complex or archaic grammatical structures, frequent use of passive constructions and highly formal register, in some cases even for something as simple as stating the date or affixing the issuer's signature (Żralka, 2007). In English, we often find expressions such as "witness my hand this . . .", "I have hereunto set my hand this . . .", "never validly married", "hereby certify that this is a true copy of particulars recorded . . ." and "to all privileges attached to the same by Royal Charter in token whereof . . .". Such language requires research at both the comprehension and translation stages: the translator of official documents, especially at the beginning of their career, needs to find out what such expressions mean in their context and subsequently identify equally formal and appropriate expressions in the target language.

In a study on the translation of personal official documents in Australia, Taibi and Ozolins (2022) found that among the challenges translators faced were the diversity of issuing countries and administration systems, variation in the type and amount of information provided in the source documents, poor legibility (e.g., handwritten certificates or old documents) and differences in naming conventions. In terms of diversity in documents from different states or regions, 66.07% of the translators identified this as an issue in the case of birth records, and 46.36% and 44.95% of them said the same about driver licences and police clearances (penal records), respectively. Such linguistic, cultural and administrative diversity was noted earlier by Fuentes Luque (2002), who was referring to the situation of the United States: "The influx of immigrants from developing countries poses new challenges not only for politicians and social agents, but also for translators, who are confronted with official documents of varied and often unfamiliar ethnic, legal, and cultural backgrounds". In terms of variation in the amount of information included in the source document, 64.86% of the translators in Taibi and Ozolins' (2022) study identified this variation as an issue in the case of birth records, 51.38% in the case of driver licences and 47.66% for police clearances.

Whether the original document was issued by a local administration, a legal institution, an education provider or another type of organisation, variations in the cultural context, the legal and administrative systems and the associated terminology pose many challenges to translators. Especially in their early career stages, translators need to undertake extensive research to familiarise themselves with the different systems, institutions and concepts. Educational qualifications, for instance, are identified as one of the most problematic types of documents. Most countries have education systems with primary, secondary and tertiary levels, but within each level there are variations from one country to another (in terms of nomenclature, duration of studies, further classifications and streams, awards and certificates, etc.).

As one translator in a study of mine noted, the translation of the terms found in educational qualifications "should be direct, not free interpretation, but at the same

140 *Translation and Community*

time meaningful and not confusing or misleading. No attempt should be made to put what the translator may believe is the equivalent of overseas qualifications" as this is the role of the institutions processing translations in the destination country (Taibi and Ozolins, 2022: 263). The challenge therefore lies in 1) understanding original terms in their cultural and institutional context, 2) translating those terms in a meaningful way for the end user (administrators in another country who will be using the translation as part of their assessment of an application or case and 3) doing so without unwittingly assuming equivalence between qualifications in the country of origin and the destination country. Box 8.2 offers some questions to consider.

Box 8.2 Questions to consider

1) The translation of personal official documents is in stark contrast with what I have said about community translation in previous chapters. What makes this type of translation special?
2) Do you find the rationale for including the translation of personal official documents in community translation convincing?
3) Do you agree that the translation of personal official documents involves special ethical and legal responsibilities?

8.4 A functional approach to the translation of official documents

In a paper about the sworn translation of legal documents, Prieto Ramos (2002) argues for applying Skopos theory to such documents. Although the author refers mainly to court documents such as summonses, his argument can be understood to encompass the translation of official documents in general. He notes that traditionally, the fidelity (accuracy) requirements in this area of translation practice have been closely tied to formal and semantic equivalence, which "often leads to literalisms which may obscure style, undermine textual coherence, and thus hinder comprehension. If literality is embraced uncritically, we may indeed fail to be 'loyal' to the intrinsic communicative nature of any translational interaction" (28).

Instead, the author believes that the Skopos rule can be applied to sworn translations as well by considering the function of the translation in its communicative situation (the intended effect), the translator's role as a "linguist–notary public" and the cultural systems in which both the source document and the translation are produced (Prieto Ramos, 2002: 28). Based on these considerations, Prieto Ramos (2002) argues, the translator can determine the best methods and strategies to achieve the aims of the translation, with due attention to the intercultural dimension inherent to the translation task. He affirms that the target text should

- Comply with the formal requirements of sworn translation, viz.: inclusion of all ST content elements, official formula, description of paralinguistic information, translator's comments between square brackets;

Translating personal official documents 141

- Fulfil the same function(s) and have essentially the same effects as those of the ST;
- Facilitate the identification and understanding of the relevant SC [source culture] judicial institutions and legal parameters referred to in the ST;
- Achieve "stylistic clarity or faithfulness" by possibly following the basic TC [target culture] legal discourse and text typology conventions which may be deemed appropriate to enhance comprehension, without departing from the ST content (Prieto Ramos, 2002: 30).

What I said in Section 8.2 about the translation of personal official documents being 'documentary' might suggest that this type of translation cannot be approached functionally. The fact that translators in this area are expected to focus on the source text; describe relevant source-text features and reflect source-text patterns, organisation and presentation suggests a literal rather than functional approach to translation.

In translating official documents, "established, conceptual, neutral and morphological formulations centred on the ST-SC [source text-source culture] pole normally take priority over functional renderings, due to the core conditions of authenticity and accuracy" (Prieto Ramos, 2002: 33). However, this should not be synonymous with literalism: "Nonetheless, these should not imply imitating original segments uncritically or ruling out, for instance, alternative hybrid combinations, information explicitations or stylistic and structural adaptations whenever these are justified by the communicative components of the sub-*skopos*" (Prieto Ramos, 2002: 33). In addition, peculiar practices common in translating official documents, such as descriptions of official features (e.g., stamps and signatures) or anomalies (e.g., crossed-out segments), can be understood and justified within a functional framework.

The purpose of this type of translation is not to communicate messages to the public but to let authorities in the destination country know the contents of official documents issued in the country of origin. The purpose is also to convey the official nature of the source document (through the description/translation of seals, stamps and authentications) and to flag any aspects that undermine the integrity or validity of the official document (e.g., by using appropriate conventions to note illegible, modified or crossed-out text). As Mayoral Asensio (2014: 3) contends, in this area of translation practice, "the translator becomes a *public authenticator* of the contents of the translation" (italics in the source). Translators in this context are concerned not only with content accuracy but also with the ethical and professional implications of handling what might be fraudulent documents (Taibi and Ozolins, 2022: 265).

A functional approach can also help in clarifying the translator's loyalties in this area of translation practice. As Mayoral Asensio (1999) noted, the translation of official documents involves conflicting "fidelities" which pose ethical dilemmas for the translator. The translator is expected to be faithful or loyal not only to the original document but also to the holder of the document and the end user, i.e. the organisation receiving the translation for processing (Taibi and Ozolins, 2016, 2022: 258).

142   *Translation and Community*

The commissioner of the translation may be an organisation or a direct client (the document holder or their relative). The direct client may, for instance, instruct the translator to update or complete the full name that appears in the source document, either because the client has changed (part of) their name, because the name in the document is incomplete or because the spelling is not consistent with their current identity documents (e.g., national identify card or passport). They might also insist that certain terms appearing in the source document (e.g., 'diploma', 'certificate', 'enrolment status') be translated in the most favourable way (e.g., 'Bachelor of Arts', 'completion letter').

Although it is not always easy to deal with the deontological dilemmas triggered by this type of translation and the intricate loyalties it involves, a functional understanding of the communicative context will help. The direct client may provide helpful background information and a translation brief, but the translator of official documents must be guided by the different professional and institutional requirements as well. Most importantly, they are guided by the fact that the translation task at hand relates to an official document issued by an official body and that the translation will be used by an institutional end user to prove an official identity, status, qualification or kinship relationship.

Finally, and in relation to professional and institutional requirements, a functional approach can explain the difference between a full translation and a template (extract) translation and can help determine which would be more appropriate. As its name suggests, a full translation consists of a complete translation of the entire source document including the names of the issuing institution and officers; the factual content of the document, the stamps, signatures, notes and so on. A template/extract translation (see sample in Box 8.3), on the other hand, is a summary translation focusing on "those parts of the text that are common to all official documents of a given type" (Lambert-Tierrafría, 2007: 222). Thus, a marriage certificate template, for instance, would consist of a table with rows relating to the particulars of the bride and bridegroom; rows relating to information such as date, place and registration of the marriage and other rows relating to the marriage celebrant or authority.

An official template translation is the most functional in the sense that it practically, efficiently and cost-effectively serves the purpose of proving the bearer's identity, status or other circumstances. However, whether it is appropriate or not will need to be determined based on the type of document (e.g., not appropriate for a contract), professional practice in the national context (in some countries, full translations are the norm) and, in some cases, the requirements of the institutional end user. For example, extract translations are commonly accepted by Australian government agencies and non-government organisations, but the Australian Health Practitioner Regulation Agency does not accept them for degrees, diplomas, certificates and transcripts (AHPRA, 2023).

Box 8.3 Sample template

Translator's name, surname, address, professional number, etc.

Translated   From: To:

Original Sighted	**Certified Copy Sighted ***	**Original Not Sighted**

Extract Translation of Driver's Licence

PARTICULARS OF BEARER	
Given Name(s)	**Surname**
Not Stated	Not Stated
Date of Birth	**Age**
Not Stated	Not Stated
Place of Birth	**Nationality**
Not Stated	Not Stated

PARTICULARS OF REGISTRATION	
Licence Number	**Country of Issue**
Not Stated	Not Stated
Categories of Vehicles for which Licence is Issued	
Not Stated	
Date of Issue	**Valid Until**
Not Stated	Not Stated
Place of Issue	**Issuing Authority**
Not Stated	Not Stated
Other Relevant Data in Source Document Nil	

Translator's Disclaimer
This is a true and accurate translation of the text provided on the attached document.
I give no warranty as to the authenticity or otherwise of the document submitted for
translation. Any unsealed alteration to this translation renders it invalid.

144 *Translation and Community*

8.5 Quality criteria

Taibi and Ozolins (2023a) proposed quality criteria for translating personal official documents. These were based on literature relating to translation quality (e.g., House, 1977, 2014; Nord, 2018 [1997]) or the translation of official documents (Mayoral Asensio, 2014), as well as on the NAATI translation testing criteria and standards and findings from a survey conducted in Australia with participants including translators, language service managers, and end users of translations of official documents (Taibi and Ozolins, 2022, 2023b). The quality criteria are the following (Taibi and Ozolins, 2023a):

1) Accuracy:

- Accurately translates propositional content and intent of source text;
- Accurately reproduces details such as names of persons, places and administrations;
- Includes all essential information for type of document.

2) Integrity:

- States whether the document sighted is an original, a certified copy or a non-certified copy;
- Describes official features of the source document (stamps, signatures, etc.);
- Describes unusual features (obliterated text, cross-outs, corrections);
- Uses square brackets for the translator's in-text descriptions or notes or uses translator's notes elsewhere in the translation;
- Includes translator disclaimer, such as the one recommended by AUSIT (2022: 9): "The translator, in providing this certification, gives no warrant as to the authenticity of the source document. Any unauthorised change to the translation renders this certification invalid".

3) Language and style:

- Uses formal register appropriate for the translation of official documents;
- Uses language structures and lexicon correctly.

4) Presentation: Presents contents in a clear, organised and user-friendly manner.

8.6 Guidelines

I led a team in developing the guidelines in Box 8.4 as part of the research project "Translation of official documents: Ensuring quality and enhancing security", funded by NAATI and Multicultural NSW. We developed the guidelines in the Australian context, hence references to NAATI, AUSIT, the Department of Foreign Affairs and Trade (DFAT) and LOTE (languages other than English). However, most of the recommendations in the guidelines are applicable and useful in other national contexts.

Box 8.4   Guidelines for translating personal official documents

This document provides guidelines for professionals and organisations producing or using translations of personal official documents. These include government organisations, language services and professional translators.

Section I provides general information about the translation of personal official documents.
Section II includes general guidelines for end users (organisations using translated personal documents).
Section III covers good practice for translation agencies and language services.
Section IV provides detailed guidelines for professional translators working with personal documents.

I.   General information about translated personal documents

1.   What are translations of personal official documents?

Translated documents which are likely to be used in institutional settings to certify identity, status, qualifications or other attributes. These typically include civil registry certificates (e.g., marriage, divorce, birth, filiation), police certificates (e.g., police check), driver licences and academic qualifications. In practice, they may include any type of document "if it falls within a judicial process or a request of acknowledgement of rights before any kind of administrative body" (Mayoral Asensio, *Translating Official Documents).*

2.   Who is qualified to translate personal official documents?

In Australia, translators must be certified by the National Accreditation Authority for Translators and Interpreters (NAATI) to be able to translate official documents. Certified translators use their NAATI stamp, which includes their certification number, languages they are qualified to translate from and into and (in post-2018 stamps) the expiry date of their certification. However, there are languages for which NAATI certification is unavailable. Where there are no certified or recognised practising translators, advice should be sought from the relevant public service or language service provider on available options.

   The expiry date on the translator's NAATI stamp is the date their recertification is due; it is not the expiry date of the translation.

146   *Translation and Community*

3.   *What to expect?*

Translators may provide a full translation or an extract translation of the source document (please see 2.1 and 2.2 under Section II below). In either case, official translations include the contact details of the translator and their NAATI stamp. A copy of the source document is also stamped with the translator's NAATI stamp and attached to the translation. This stamping is only intended to indicate the source document used for the translation; it is not an authentication of the source document itself.

When translations of personal documents are commissioned through language services or translation agencies, the translation may show the details of the agency rather than those of the translator.

II.   For end users (organisations using translated personal documents)

1.   *What information do you need translated?*

1.1. Personal documents relate to the identity, status or qualifications of an individual, which need to be recognised or validated by Australian institutions.

1.2. Translations need to give an accurate rendition of the information which is essential for the purposes in your organisation.

1.3. The type of translation you will need depends on the amount of information you need and how much you need to scrutinise personal documents.

2.   *What kinds of translation will you receive?*

There are two ways the information in personal documents can be translated for you:

2.1. A full translation, which reproduces not only all the information in the document but may also include particular formatting and style which represents the source document.

2.2. An extract translation gives the essential information you need in compact form, usually when there is a limited number of items of information that you need translated. Templates exist for translation of the most common forms of personal documents (e.g. status, identity, licenses, qualifications, work experience).

3.   *Information you need to provide*

Clients and translators need clear information (e.g., on institution websites) as to the kind of translation (full or extract) accepted and any other requirements for translation.

A good example of the information to include is the section "Foreign Documents" available on the DFAT Australian Passport Office website.

4. *Authenticity*

4.1. While translators may occasionally identify authenticity issues with documents, they are usually not equipped or trained to detect irregularities or forgeries. Institutions need to have their own mechanisms of investigation if the authenticity of documents is in doubt.

4.2. The increasing and now nearly ubiquitous use of electronic transfer of documents means translators will not always see an actual original document. Translators will translate what is sent to them, but they are expected to indicate the type of copy they are translating from (original, certified copy, faxed or electronic uncertified copy, etc.).

4.3. Translators are not responsible for the authenticity of the source documents and may make a disclaimer on their translation to this effect.

5. *Quality*

5.1. Translations should be undertaken by a NAATI Certified Translator, a NAATI Recognised Practising Translator or another authorised translator where a certified or recognised translator does not exist.

5.2. Translations must be done by a translator with relevant certification or credentials in the relevant direction (i.e., LOTE into English or English into LOTE).

5.3. Translators with NAATI credentials will stamp their translations with a NAATI stamp.

6. *Translations from English into other languages*

The procedures that need to be followed for translations of personal documents from English into foreign languages may differ as follows:

6.1. Extract translations are less widely known or accepted outside Australia; it is more likely that full translations will be required.

6.2. Foreign governments may need additional procedures (e.g., Apostille) for documents presented at their official institutions. DFAT has guidelines in this regard, and relevant embassies or consulates as well as translation companies can usually assist with information.

6.3. For some translations into LOTE, the translator's signature may need to be authenticated. In these cases, translators should have their signature registered with DFAT.

148 *Translation and Community*

III. For translation agencies and language services

1. *Client brief and holder details*

1.1. When source documents are submitted to a translation agency or language service rather than to the individual translator, it is essential to establish the purpose of the translation and whether a full or extract translation is required. It is also important to take note of relevant holder details (especially name spelling) and provide them to the translator. A copy of the holder's identity document showing the name(s) and surname(s) in Latin alphabet is recommended.

2. *Processing documents*

2.1 When forwarding source documents to the translator, please ensure that the documents or copies are complete and legible. In some cases, administrative staff at agencies and language services may not be proficient in the relevant language to determine legibility, but every effort should be made to ensure that the document submitted for translation is either an original or a copy in a good condition.

For different reasons, some clients may only have highly illegible documents, in which case they should be encouraged to obtain legible ones or otherwise be advised that the translator will only be able to translate what is legible.

3. *Guidelines, style guides and templates*

3.1 It is good practice for agencies and language services, especially large ones and those receiving large quantities of personal documents, to have clear guidelines and style guides for their translators or contractors. If a language service does not have its own guidelines, translators should be advised and periodically reminded to follow AUSIT's *Best Practices for the Translation of Official and Legal Documents*. Similarly, language services may develop templates of standard personal documents or use those available on the AUSIT website. Standardised templates will ensure consistency, especially for extract translations.

4. *Translation checking*

4.1 In the translation of personal documents, even minor errors and typos such as misspelling of names may have a significant impact on clients. Translation checking by another colleague is an essential step in the translation process. It ensures that errors and typos overlooked by the translator are identified and corrected before the translation is forwarded to the client.

When another certified translator is in charge of translation checking, suggested amendments need to be forwarded to the first translator for approval or a response.

Translating personal official documents   149

To minimise the potential impact on the translator's workload, it is advisable to have translations checked before printing and stamping.

IV.   For translators of personal documents

This section covers guidelines to be followed in **all official translations,** followed by specific guidelines for cases of *full translation*, and cases of *extract (template) translation* in jurisdictions where these are used.

1.   *Guidelines for all personal document translations: all translations*

1.1.   Clearly identify the translation as a translation by indicating which language it has been translated from.

1.2.   Specify the nature of the source document—original, [electronic] copy, certified/uncertified copy, etc.

1.3.   Include translators' notes where particular issues need the attention of the receiver/reader. Translator notes should be clearly marked as such.

1.4.   Reproduce persons' names exactly as in the source document if written in Latin letters. Otherwise, they should be transliterated following the norms applicable to the source language or in the issuing country. If the holder provides an ID document in Latin alphabet, this can be used as a reference.

1.5.   Translate names of official institutions. In some cases, they may be left in the source language (when in Latin alphabet) or transliterated (when in a different script). When using the latter option, a translation of the name should be added between square brackets.

1.6.   If receiving the source document from the client directly, it is important to take note of relevant holder details (especially the spelling of person names in the document). A copy of the holder's identity document showing the name(s) and surname(s) in Latin alphabet is recommended.

1.7.   If the document submitted by the client is partly or mostly illegible, they should be made aware that because of ethical considerations, you will only be able to translate legible text, indicating illegible portions as such.

1.8.   Abbreviations need to be spelt out when known.

1.9.   Follow house style of agencies/translation companies if receiving commissions for such translations through them.

1.10.   For academic qualifications, do not attest to equivalence of qualifications, education levels, ranks or other characteristics to those of the receiving country. These need to be assessed and determined by competent institutions in the country where the personal document translations are lodged.

1.11.   Convey special features such as erasures, overwriting, illegible text and so on.

150 *Translation and Community*

1.12. If the source document contains an incomplete sentence, information in the wrong place (e.g., date of issue in the box for place of issue) or spelling inconsistencies, this should be indicated by inserting [sic] immediately after the error in question.

1.13. Include a disclaimer as to the authenticity of the source document and the fact that any changes or erasures to the translation render it invalid.

1.14. Authorise the translation by adding the translation date and your NAATI stamp, signature or other attribute of yourself as the translator as required in your jurisdiction.

1.15. In jurisdictions where extract translations are widely used for standard personal documents, explain extract or full translation options to direct clients who may be unaware of this distinction.

2. *For full translations*

2.1. Full translations may be required by the client or by the institution they plan to submit the translation to. As a general rule, the following types of documents must be translated fully: academic qualifications, contracts, agreements, financial statements and any personal documents that are to be submitted as part of a court proceeding.

2.2. Provide a complete and accurate translation of all information on the source document, including institutional marks, stamps, seals, headings and signatures, by describing it between square brackets if not reproducing it (e.g. [illegible signature]; [rectangular stamp]).

2.3. Reproduce format where required and feasible.

2.4. If the document has multiple pages, ensure pagination and provide means of identifying this as one translation (e.g. page 1 of 4).

3. *For extract translations*

3.1. Find out which Australian institutions accept extract translations and which do not; in the case of a translation into LOTE, ask the client to request this information from the relevant authority (e.g., embassy or consulate).

3.2. Use approved templates if institutionally available or create your own templates based on known institutional paradigms. Please refer to templates available on the AUSIT website.

3.3. Clearly identify (in the form of a heading) that this is an extract translation.

3.4. Provide an accurate translation of essential information in the source document in the required template.

Translating personal official documents   151

> **Summary**
>
> Translating personal official documents is a special area of translation practice that involves legal and administrative documents such as those relating to personal status, criminal records, driver licences and educational qualifications. It is not like community translation as presented in the rest of the textbook, but I have included it because of the role it plays in facilitating the integration of migrants, refugees and other minority groups and their involvement in society, including education, employment and other areas. Given that these translations are used for administrative or legal purposes (to prove a status to authorities, usually in a country other than the issuing country), they need to be done with two main criteria in mind: accuracy of content (conveying the factual information and personal details exactly as they appear in the source document) and document integrity (describing/translating both official features such as stamps and signatures as well as anomalies such as illegible or crossed-out text). As practice in this area of translation varies from one country to another, the translator must comply with the norms and conventions applicable in the country or locality. When translating such documents through a translation agency or language service, there may also be specific standards and conventions to comply with.

Further reading

- AUSIT. (2022). *Best practices for the translation of official and legal documents*. https://ausit.org/wp-content/uploads/2022/07/220422_AUSIT-Best-Practices-2022-v1.1-clean-version.pdf

AUSIT's guidelines provide practical instructions and recommendations regarding translating personal official documents (and legal documents in general). The guidelines cover a wide range of aspects relating to these documents, including accuracy, completeness, documenting special features in the source text, translator notes, names and so on.

- Mayoral Asensio, Roberto (2014). *Translating official documents*. London and New York: Routledge.

Although it was first published in 2003, this is a must-read book for those interested in working in translating official documents. The book provides an overview of the social context, characteristics and challenges of this area of translation practice. It

152 *Translation and Community*

also offers useful insights into the roles of official translators and different document types and translation approaches, as well as solutions for common issues.

- Taibi, Mustapha and Ozolins, Uldis (2022). Translation of personal official documents: What Australian practitioners say. *The Journal of Specialised Translation* 38: 254–276.

This paper is one of the outcomes of the research project "Translation of official documents: Ensuring quality and enhancing security", mentioned above. It reports the views of Australian translators on the challenges and practices in this area.

- Taibi, Mustapha and Ozolins, Uldis (2023a). Quality and integrity in the translation of official documents, *Perspectives 31(5)*: 882–899. https://doi.org/10.1080/0907676X.2022.2053176

This is another research publication based on the project this chapter derives from. For this part of the project, we report on assessing the quality of translations of official documents from Arabic, Chinese and Spanish into English. The quality criteria we propose in the paper are worth considering for other languages.

- Taibi, Mustapha and Ozolins, Uldis (2023b). Translation of personal official documents: Examining Australian norms and practice, *Meta Journal des traducteurs Translators' Journal* 68 (2), 341–360. https://doi.org/10.7202/1109341ar

This paper complements "Quality and integrity in the translation of official documents". In this report, we discuss the findings of three surveys on quality, integrity and authenticity in the translation of official personal documents with three key stakeholders (translators, language service providers and institutional end users).

Suggested activities

1) If you have never translated a personal official document, take two or three of your own documents (birth certificate, passport, academic qualifications, etc.) and translate them into your other working language. As you are translating, note down the challenges you face, the research you undertake and the decisions you make (including revisions, if any).
2) Find out from your national professional association for translators (or a relevant government body) whether they have guidelines in relation to translating official documents and whether they have templates for extract translations. Compare your findings with the guidelines proposed in this chapter.

References

AHPRA-Australian Health Practitioner Regulation Agency (2023). *Translating documents.* www.ahpra.gov.au/Registration/Registration-Process/Translating-Documents.aspx.

American Translators Association (2023). *What is a certified translation?* www.atanet.org/client-assistance/what-is-a-certified-translation/.

AUSIT (2022). *Best practices for the translation of official and legal documents.* https://ausit.org/wp-content/uploads/2022/07/220422_AUSIT-Best-Practices-2022-v1.1-clean-version.pdf.

Chesher, Terry (1997). Rhetoric and reality: Two decades of community interpreting and translating in Australia. In Carr, Silvana E.; Roberts, Roda; Dufour, Aideen and Steyn, Dini (Eds.), *The critical link: Interpreters in the community.* Amsterdam and Philadelphia: John Benjamins: 277–289.

Department of Home Affairs (2023). *History of TIS National.* www.tisnational.gov.au/About-TIS-National/History-of-TIS-National.aspx. (Accessed 3 April 2023).

Fuentes Luque, Adrian (2002). Translating official documents for African immigrants. *ATA Chronicle*, 31: 2.

House, Juliane (1977). *A model for translation quality assessment.* Tübingen: Gunter Narr Verlag.

House, Juliane (2014). Translation quality assessment: Past and present. In House, Juliane (Ed.), *Translation: A multidisciplinary approach.* Palgrave Macmillan: 241–264.

Lambert-Tierrafría, Sylvie (2007). Templating as a strategy for translating official documents from Spanish to English. *Meta Journal des traducteurs Translators' Journal*, 52(2): 215–238.

Mayoral Asensio, Roberto (1999). Las fidelidades del traductor jurado: Batalla imprecisa. In Feria García, Manuel C. (Ed.), *Traducir para la justicia.* Granada: Comares: 17–57.

Mayoral Asensio, Roberto (2014). *Translating official documents.* London and New York: Routledge.

Nord, Christiane (2018 [1997]). *Translating as a purposeful activity: Functionalist approaches explained.* Abingdon: Routledge.

Prieto Ramos, Fernando (2002). Beyond the confines of literality: A functionalist approach to the sworn translation of legal documents. *Puentes*, 2: 27–35.

Taibi, Mustapha and Ozolins, Uldis (2016). *Community translation.* London and New York: Bloomsbury.

Taibi, Mustapha and Ozolins, Uldis (2022). Translation of personal official documents: What Australian practitioners say. *The Journal of Specialised Translation*, 38: 254–276.

Taibi, Mustapha and Ozolins, Uldis (2023a). Quality and integrity in the translation of official documents. *Perspectives*, 31(5): 882–899. DOI: 10.1080/0907676X.2022.2053176.

Taibi, Mustapha and Ozolins, Uldis (2023b). Translation of personal official documents: Examining Australian norms and practice. *Meta Journal des traducteurs Translators' Journal*, 68(2): 341–360. DOI: 10.7202/1109341ar.

Translated (2023). *Official translations (sworn and certified).* https://translated.com/sworn-certified-official-translation. (Accessed 30 May 2023).

Żralka, Edyta (2007). Teaching specialised translation through official documents. *Journal of Specialised Translation*, 7: 74–91.

9 Locating and using resources

This chapter provides practical advice on how to locate and use resources. It is intended to enable you to use a variety of research tools and methods to search for information, especially country-, institution- or domain-specific terminology. As I discuss the different resources available to community translators, I also show how to locate and assess the reliability of different language and thematic resources. The chapter covers the following:

- Dictionaries, thesauri and glossaries;
- Encyclopaedias;
- Parallel texts;
- Published translations;
- Machine translation and artificial intelligence;
- The impact of technology on community translation quality and skills.

9.1 Dictionaries, thesauri and glossaries

A dictionary is a collection of words in one language (monolingual), two languages (bilingual) or more (multilingual) listed alphabetically. It provides meanings, definitions, pronunciations (phonetic transcription or, in the case of online dictionaries, audio icon), etymologies (origin or history of the word) and parts of speech (e.g., whether the word is a verb or a noun), as well as examples of usage (sentences showing how the word can be used). Dictionaries can also be classified into general (e.g., the Cambridge Dictionary, the Merriam-Webster Dictionary, the Oxford English Dictionary) or specialised (e.g., the World Health Organization's Unified Medical Dictionary; https://iris.who.int/handle/10665/119845). Naturally, a domain-specific dictionary will provide more relevant information and terminology than a general one.

A thesaurus presents words as word families, grouping synonyms—alternative words with the same or similar meanings—together without explaining their meanings. It helps you find synonyms and sometimes contrasting words, antonyms. Unlike dictionaries, thesauri do not contain all the words of a language but focus on providing synonyms.

DOI: 10.4324/9781003367741-10

Locating and using resources 155

A glossary is a specialized list of terms related to a specific field, discipline or subject (e.g., COVID-19, social welfare, disability services, or primary schooling). It defines technical or domain-specific terms and is often found in textbooks, manuals, academic works or particular institutions (e.g., Department of Immigration, Taxation Office). Glossaries are useful for understanding jargon or terminology within a specific institutional context, specialisation area or even country. Unlike dictionaries and thesauri, glossaries are narrower in scope and focus on specific topics. Many translation students and translators compile their own glossaries; this ensures that they make the most of the time invested in researching terms at some stage of their learning or professional career.

In summary, dictionaries provide a comprehensive list of possible word meanings, thesauri offer synonyms (and sometimes antonyms as well) and glossaries define specialized terms. Combining these resources can enhance your vocabulary effectively and can provide solutions to translation problems. However, these are the most basic translator resources, and they should not be used as the only support. Other resources such as encyclopaedias, parallel texts and published translations (See next sections) also need to be used as references when the content of the source text is new to you or not completely clear or when you are in doubt about the appropriateness of certain lexical choices.

The way you use such resources can also determine the extent to which your vocabulary search and translation solutions are successful. Many students tend to rely on bilingual dictionaries because they offer readily available 'equivalents'. However, as Samuelsson-Brown (2010: 90) reminds us, a monolingual dictionary can be more helpful than we might think as it provides explanations which can help us understand concepts. A common error among translation students is to look up a word in a bilingual dictionary and use an 'equivalent' word in the target language without considering the specific context the word appears in. Sometimes only one potential equivalent in a long list of senses will be appropriate. In some cases, none of the equivalents proposed in a bilingual dictionary will be suitable. Consider, for example, the word 'community' in Box 9.1, which is recurrent throughout this textbook.

Box 9.1   Different senses of 'community'

The Merriam-Webster online dictionary defines 'community' as follows:

1) a unified body of individuals: such as

   a) the people with common interests living in a particular area
      broadly: the area itself
      the problems of a large *community*
   b) a group of people with a common characteristic or interest living together within a larger society (a *community* of retired persons, a monastic *community*)

156 *Translation and Community*

c) a body of persons of common and especially professional interests scattered through a larger society (the academic *community*, the scientific *community*)
d) a body of persons or nations having a common history or common social, economic, and political interests (the international *community*)
e) a group linked by a common policy
f) an interacting population of various kinds of individuals (such as species) in a common location
g) STATE, COMMONWEALTH

2) a) a social state or condition

The school encourages a sense of *community* in its students.
b) joint ownership or participation (*community* of goods)
c) common character: LIKENESS (*community* of interests)
d) social activity: FELLOWSHIP

3) society at large (the interests of the *community*)

(www.merriam-webster.com/dictionary/community)

When you search for 'community' in your bilingual dictionary, you might find equivalents (in your other language) that translate as 'society', 'group', 'social group' or 'public'. Some bilingual dictionaries may also include a lexical equivalent meaning 'neighbourhood' or 'municipality'. If you have to translate a text such as, "Twelve communities in Boki Local Government Area of Cross River have been flooded following two days of heavy rain, while more than 3,000 farmlands were equally destroyed" (https://sunnewsonline.com/cross-river-floods-affects-12-communities-destroys-3000-farmlands), you should have comprehension and critical analytical skills to understand that the word 'communities' does not refer to a society, group, social group or public but rather to the sense of 'neighbourhood', 'municipality' or 'local territorial area'. Similarly, the fact that a thesaurus lists several lexical items which are presumably synonyms does not mean that they are interchangeable and can all be used for your translation context. Please see the example in Box 9.2.

Box 9.2 Using a thesaurus entry

Read the following thesaurus entry for 'major' and consider whether any of the matches can be used to replace 'major' in the sentences listed below:

Strongest matches: big, considerable, dominant, extensive, large, large-scale, leading, main, primary, sizable

Locating and using resources 157

> **Strong matches:** above, better, chief, elder, exceeding, extreme, senior, superior, upper
>
> **Weak matches:** greater, hefty, higher, larger, most, oversized, supreme, ultra, uppermost (www.thesaurus.com/browse/major)
>
> To determine which options might be appropriate substitutes for 'major' in the following sentences, you might need to use a monolingual dictionary or locate instances in which each potential synonym is used (collocation). In many cases, you will need to rule out all the strong and weak matches and focus on the strongest matches. Even here, only one or two might be appropriate. If none is suitable, you might need to look elsewhere. Be guided by the context of use and the level of formality (register).
>
> 1) The organisation needs a *major* overhaul.
> 2) They have made a *major* contribution to equity within the community.
> 3) The *major* source of income for councils is rates and annual charges.
> 4) The Government's decision represents a *major* blow to the economy and the environment.
> 5) The Sokoto River is the *major* river in north-west Nigeria.
> 6) The federal police have launched a *major* anti-drug crackdown in *major* cities.
> 7) This is the *major* community news publication in the country.

9.2   Encyclopaedias

An encyclopaedia is a valuable resource for translators and translation students as it provides a wealth of information across various subjects. When translating a text, understanding the concepts, specialised terms and context is crucial. An encyclopaedia offers detailed information on historical events, geographical features, ethnic groups, cultural practices, scientific and technical concepts and so on. Translators and trainees can use it to gain insights into the background of a topic, ensuring accurate and contextually appropriate translations.

Encyclopaedias contain definitions of terms, which can be especially helpful when dealing with specialised vocabulary. Unlike dictionaries, encyclopaedias do not provide definitions and examples only but also give extensive information about the concept, phenomenon, process, person or place in question. In addition, when there are cultural nuances or sensitivities involved, as is often the case in community translation, encyclopaedias can be particularly useful in providing information about customs, traditions and beliefs specific to different cultures. Translators and trainees can use this knowledge both to understand and convey the culture-specific meaning effectively and sensitively (see Chapter 6).

158   *Translation and Community*

Box 9.3   Using an encyclopaedia as a translator's resource

Below is a text about cirrhosis. The term and the topic might be completely
new to you. While the text itself provides some explanation, you might need
to undertake research to find out more or to check your understanding of
certain concepts. Please underline or note down the concepts you need to
understand and look them up in an encyclopaedia (e.g., Encyclopaedia Brit-
tanica; see www.britannica.com). If an encyclopaedia is available in your
other working language(s), you can browse it too.

Cirrhosis

Cirrhosis is a chronic condition characterised by extensive scarring and fibrosis within the liver tissue. Here are a few facts about it:

1) Pathogenesis:

- **Liver Damage**: Cirrhosis results from prolonged liver damage caused
  by various factors such as chronic alcohol abuse, viral hepatitis (especially hepatitis B or C), non-alcoholic fatty liver disease and other
  underlying conditions.
- **Scar Formation**: Over time, the liver responds to injury by replacing
  healthy tissue with fibrous scar tissue. These scars disrupt the normal
  architecture of the liver.

2) Structural Changes:

- **Nodules and Fibrosis**: Irregular nodules replace the smooth liver tissue, leading to a lumpy appearance. These nodules consist of fibrotic
  tissue.
- **Hardening**: The liver becomes progressively harder due to the accu-
  mulation of scar tissue.

3) Functional Implications:

- **Impaired Blood Flow**: Scar tissue obstructs blood flow through the
  liver, affecting its vital functions.
- **Portal Hypertension**: The slowed blood flow causes high blood pressure in the portal vein, leading to complications like ascites (fluid buildup
  in the abdomen), varices (enlarged veins in the oesophagus or stomach)
  and hepatic encephalopathy (brain dysfunction due to toxin buildup).
- **Increased Risk of Liver Cancer**: Cirrhosis significantly elevates the
  risk of developing liver cancer.
- **Liver Failure**: In advanced stages, cirrhosis can lead to liver failure,
  where the liver's ability to function is severely compromised.

Locating and using resources 159

4) Clinical Presentation:

- **Asymptomatic Early Stages**: Many individuals remain asymptomatic during initial stages of cirrhosis.
- **Late Symptoms**: As the liver damage progresses, symptoms may include weakness, fatigue, muscle cramps, weight loss, nausea, vomiting, upper abdominal pain, easy bruising, jaundice and leg swelling.

5) Diagnosis and Management:

- **Liver Function Tests**: Blood tests assess liver enzymes, bilirubin and kidney function.
- **Imaging**: Ultrasound and elastography detect structural changes.
- **Biopsy**: A liver tissue sample confirms the severity and cause of cirrhosis.
- **Treatment**: Focuses on managing symptoms, addressing the underlying cause and preventing further damage. A liver transplant may be necessary in severe cases.

9.3 Parallel texts

The notion of parallel texts is used in different senses by different authors and disciplines. The first sense is parallel texts as original texts written in different languages by native or competent speakers of the language that correspond to each other in terms of content, text type, communicative situation and/or purpose (Hartmann, 1980; Snell-Hornby, 1995; Bowker, 2001). The other sense, used for instance in natural language processing and computational linguistics, refers to versions of the same text in two or more languages placed together or side by side, as is the case in translation memories (Simard, 2019). The two senses of the term correspond respectively to Baker's (1995) 'multilingual' and 'parallel' corpora. In this chapter, I mainly refer to parallel texts in the first sense, that is, as authentic texts in two or more languages of interest (basically, your working languages) which cover the same topic and do so in a comparable communicative situation (e.g., formal vs. informal; specialised vs. non-specialised; journalistic vs. official communication).

Parallel texts can be useful resources for translators in several ways. As Gallego-Hernández (2015) concludes, most translators refer to such texts to learn about terminology and phraseology and use different functions of corpus linguistics tools, including wordlists, concordances and collocations (words co-occurring with others).

1) **Terminology:** By comparing how specific concepts and phenomena are communicated about in similar contexts but different languages and cultures, you can identify the most common terms and expressions to use when translating.

160 *Translation and Community*

2) **Phraseology:** Finding natural phrasing, as in determining how words are organised and what phrases are common in a given language. Seeing how a sentence is structured and phrased in another language can help you find a natural-sounding way to express the same idea in the target language.

In short, before translating a text in the community context, it is worth spending some time exploring the Internet (or print resources, if applicable) for comparable texts in the target language. This will enhance your understanding of the topic at hand and expose you to the type of language that native speakers (e.g., government agencies, the media, political and community leaders) use to discuss content that is similar to what you have in the source text. However, this always needs to be done with due attention to the level of formality (whether communication is academic, official or informal) and the origin of the resources being consulted (e.g., in case there are lexical and terminological variations between the countries where the resources were produced and your local target community).

Parallel texts in the second sense (i.e., translation memory; compiled corpora of texts and their translations) are also useful for the following reasons among others:

1) **Consistency check:** Parallel texts can be used to ensure consistency in translation style and terminology throughout a project, especially when working on lengthy documents.
2) **Building a translation memory:** By storing previously translated segments from parallel texts, translators can leverage past work for future projects, thus improving efficiency.

However, this type of parallel text is mainly applicable to professional translators who have demonstrable translation skills and experience. As a learner, you will find the process of developing a translation memory useful (i.e., learning how to use translation memory software such as Trados or memoQ and retrieve past translations), but the stored translations will not necessarily be a reliable source in terms of translation solutions and terminological accuracy and consistency.

9.4 Published translations

Published translations are also a good resource. There are online directories that provide community and institutional translations classified by language and subject matter. There are also government and non-government websites which include community-relevant content available in different languages. You should be able to locate those relevant to your language and target community by browsing, for example, the websites of ministries of health, justice, immigration, social security or education, as well as the websites of local governments (e.g., state government or city council). The following are only examples of where translations can be located:

• Find a Translation, website managed by All Graduates Interpreting and Translation Services, Australia (https://findatranslation.com.au/#google_vignette);

Locating and using resources 161

- The Victoria State Government's Health Translations directory, Australia (www.healthtranslations.vic.gov.au);
- Dental Health Services Victoria, Australia (www.dhsv.org.au/oral-health-advice/Professionals/oral-health-resources/translated-materials);
- The South African Department of Justice and Constitutional Development (www.justice.gov.za/brochure/brochure_list.html);
- The Hong Kong government Multi-language Platform (www.gov.hk/en/theme/multilanguage/mlp/index.htm);
- Ministry of the Interior, National Immigration Agency, Taiwan (www.immigration.gov.tw/5382/5385/7445/7451/7454/208092);
- Affiliation of Multicultural Societies and Service Agencies, Canada (www.amssa.org/resources);
- McGill University Health Centre, Canada, Health Resources in Many Languages (www.muhclibraries.ca/patients/health-topics/multilingual/);
- National Social Inclusion Office, Ireland, Multilingual resources and translated information (www.hse.ie/eng/about/who/primarycare/socialinclusion/about-social-inclusion/translation-hub/multilingual-resources-and-translated-material/);
- Swiss Red Cross, Switzerland, All Migesplus Publications (www.migesplus.ch/en/publications);
- Asylex, Legal Advice for Asylum Seekers, Switzerland (www.asylex.ch);
- National Online Health Services in Norway—health care for asylum seekers and refugees in Norway (www.helsenorge.no/utlendinger-i-norge/flyktninger-og-asylsokere);
- Department of Health, United Kingdom, Publications in Other Languages (https://webarchive.nationalarchives.gov.uk/ukgwa/20130105165548/www.dh.gov.uk/en/Publicationsandstatistics/Publications/DH_4123594);
- North Yorkshire Police, United Kingdom, Victims Code in other languages (www.northyorkshire.police.uk/police-forces/north-yorkshire-police/areas/about-us/about-us/equality-and-diversity/victims-code-in-other-languages/);
- Substance Abuse and Mental Health Services Administration, United States (https://store.samhsa.gov/?f%5B0%5D=language%3A1459);
- National Institute on Minority Health and Health Disparities, United States (www.nimhd.nih.gov/programs/edu-training/language-access/health-information/index.html);
- Food and Drug Administration, United States, Minority Health and Health Equity Resources (www.fda.gov/consumers/minority-health-and-health-equity/minority-health-and-health-equity-resources);
- Medline Plus, United States (https://medlineplus.gov/languages/languages.html);
- Health Information Translations, United States (www.healthinfotranslations.org);
- Limited English Proficiency, Department of Justice, United States (www.lep.gov).

However, such translations need to be approached with a critical mind. They should be used as guides or as learning materials, not model translations. The fact that they were published does not necessarily guarantee that they were prepared

162   *Translation and Community*

by professional translators, that they were revised or that they are of optimal quality.

For example, González and Amanatidou's (2023: 11–12) survey with 18 Australian language service providers showed that the industry has varying standards of quality assurance. Only 16.65% of the respondents reported that their translations were checked by both NAATI-certified translators and community reviewers, 33.33% confirmed that translations were always revised by a certified translator and approximately 45% advised that this was the case only sometimes. Several other studies (e.g., Antonini et al., 2017; Gigliotti, 2017) show that community translations in many parts of the world are provided by non-qualified volunteers, which raises concerns about their quality and reliability as resources for students and translators.

9.5   Machine translation and artificial intelligence

Technology has influenced the translation profession in several ways (see e.g., O'Hagan, 2019). Whether you are a translation student or a practitioner, you will be already using technological resources in one way or another. Svoboda and Sosoni (2023) conducted a survey with 412 translators working in institutional settings in 26 countries (mostly European). Most of the participants worked for international institutions, 37.7% worked for national administrations and organisations and a small minority worked for non-governmental organisations or the banking sector. The survey findings revealed that 97.6% of these translators used translation technology in their professional activities. Out of these, 81% reported daily use of translation memory or localisation tools such as Trados Studio, Memsource or MemoQ. Forty per cent (40%) of the respondents reported that they used machine translation daily, 20% did so weekly, and only 18% did not use it at all.

In addition to machine translation, artificial intelligence (AI) has emerged as a revolutionary translator resource in the last few years. Both are steadily and quickly advancing, so by the time this textbook is published or by the time you read it, major developments may have taken place. Machine translation refers to the use of software (e.g., Google Translate or DeepL) to translate text or speech from one language to another without human intervention. Forcada Zubizarreta (2022) defines it as "the process by which a computer program produces, from a source-language computer-readable text, a target-language computer-readable text which is intended to be an approximate translation of the former, and does so without any human intervention".

Generative AI (e.g., ChatGPT or Copilot), on the other hand, refers to the ability of a digital computer or computer-controlled robot to perform tasks commonly associated with humans. AI can simulate human intelligence and can be used for different purposes in different disciplines and professions (e.g., design, medical diagnosis, creative writing). It draws from different disciplines including computer science, cognitive science, mathematics, linguistics, psychology, neuroscience and philosophy. Its focus is on designing algorithms, data structures and computer systems to simulate human intelligence in performing tasks and processes, including

Locating and using resources   163

perception, reasoning, synthesising, problem-solving, learning and language understanding (Enríquez Raído, forthcoming; see also Pym and Hao, 2025).

AI can also be used as a type of machine translation, but that is not the only task it can perform. AI software is a powerful tool that leverages deep learning algorithms and computational methods to convert text or speech from one language to another. AI translators are trained on vast multilingual datasets, allowing them to analyse patterns, grammar rules and contextual cues. Unlike human translators, AI systems do not need to read and understand the entire text before translating, resulting in remarkably fast generation of translation outputs. These systems use neural networks to recognise language patterns, ensuring what is claimed to be accurate and natural-sounding translations. They learn from context and continue improving over time. After translation, AI systems apply post-processing techniques to refine the output, addressing any remaining inaccuracies.

Efficiency is a key advantage of both 'traditional' machine translation and AI translation. It is significantly faster than human translation, making it ideal for industries like e-commerce, where speed matters. Large volumes of text can be translated speedily, meeting customer demands. Additionally, machine translation and AI translation are generally less expensive than human translation, making them cost-effective for businesses and organizations. AI advocates also claim that the consistency of AI translations is another benefit. AI ensures consistent translations every time, maintaining uniformity in terminology and phrases. This reliability is essential for branding and communication. AI translation tools are also able to handle multiple languages simultaneously, making them efficient for localising global contents.

However, both machine translation and AI translation have raised concerns. As Mellinger and Pokorn (2018: 337) note, the technologisation of the translation industry has wide-ranging impacts: "Continuous innovation in the field has led scholars to examine the technological impact on translation workflows, products, and processes, and their conclusions have ranged from accolades to concern". For example, the contributors to Chan's (2015) edited volume _The Routledge Encyclopedia of Translation Technology_ point out some of the drawbacks of technology, but their views are generally positive about the impact of technology on the translation industry.

It is undeniable that there has been significant progress in machine translation in the last few years, to the extent that some consider it comparable with human translation (Oliver, 2020). However, one major concern is about translation quality, as the quality of automated translations is still not on par with human (professional) translations. Machine and AI translation can struggle with capturing language ambiguity and complexity, linguistic nuances, idiomatic expressions and cultural context (Bowker and Buitrago-Ciro, 2019). For instance, humour, slang, and figurative language pose major challenges.

Another limitation is that automated translation has limited ability and poor quality in languages with limited data (e.g., emerging community languages). The quality of output varies depending on how much training data (body of texts) is available: While machine translation and AI translation may perform well for

164 *Translation and Community*

widely spoken (and written) languages, it may struggle with lesser-used languages or dialects. This is especially the case for minority languages in which community translations are often needed.

In relation to the impact of AI on education, there have been opposing responses from higher education providers and educators. Some consider that the technology can play a positive role in alleviating routine tasks and assisting both teachers and students in focusing on critical issues and skills, while others are more concerned about unethical use of AI in education and its potential impact on academic integrity (Vicerrectorado de Innovación Educativa, 2023; Shah, 2023). While it is common to have opposing attitudes towards innovation and change, the use of AI in education is here to stay, which requires a shift of attention towards how the technology can be integrated effectively, responsibly and ethically to augment the learning experience (Vicerrectorado de Innovación Educativa, 2023: 4).

In relation to the impact of technology in translator education, there are again opposing views and findings. Zhang (2023) undertook a study with 20 Chinese undergraduate students to explore their attitudes towards machine translation. The participants "reported that they were generally more confident when translating and were more confident about the quality of their translations when using MT as a reference" (Zhang, 2023: 9). The students thought that machine translation did not have a negative impact on the quality of their translations; on the contrary, some of the participants believed that the impact was in fact positive. However, Zhang notes that despite this generally positive attitude towards machine translation, the students were reluctant to learn machine translation at their stage of study:

> They were concerned about over-reliance on MT, which would affect their creativity. They thought that MT was good to a certain extent; however, they did not want to be limited by machines and wanted to produce better quality translations than those produced by machines.
>
> (Zhang, 2023: 9)

In another study, Zhang and Qian (2023) found that students' translations which were completed from scratch were of a better quality than those they did with the assistance of machine translation and they later post-edited (revised): "The overall score, the accuracy sub-score and the fluency sub-score for the PEMT-assisted translations were significantly lower than those for the from-scratch translations" (107). The student participants felt more confident when starting their translation task based on a machine translation and were more positive about the expected translation outcome. However, post-edited machine translation did not improve their translation efficiency and yielded translation products that were of lower quality. Most students reported frustration and additional burden as they had to correct "weird" expressions in the raw machine translation. The students attributed the increase in cognitive effort to lack of knowledge about and training in machine translation and postediting (Zhang and Qian, 2023: 107). As the students who took part in the study were at an early stage of their translator education, the authors

Locating and using resources   165

conclude that machine translation "may not benefit undergraduate students in the early stages of translator training" without adequate training in machine translation and post-editing.

9.6   Automation, translation quality and translation skills

Zhang (2023: 9) argues, "As it will become increasingly difficult to prevent students from accessing freely available MT online, it makes more sense to inform students about the positive and negative impacts of MT, which should be based on sound research findings". The same applies to AI-generated translation.

One aspect about which there is general agreement is that machine translation, including AI-facilitated translation, requires postediting (revision by a human translator) to meet quality standards (Thunes, 2017: 112; Nitzke and Hansen-Schirra, 2021; AUSIT, 2022; Monguilod and Vitalaru, 2023). Thunes (2017: 112) adds that revision is also necessary with human translations, which I argue is correct in Chapter 10, especially for translations by non-qualified translators. As one of the language service providers in González and Amanatidou's study (2023: 15) reported, "many customers often use an unqualified staff member to translate or get a machine translation. . . . Then, we are asked to proof check and the mistakes are incredible and large parts need to be re-translated". However, automated translation requires special attention because of these limitations and because it might be over-trusted as it gives a false sense of reliability to both students and translation users. To illustrate the quality and reliability issues, Box 9.4 includes two translations of a Korean text, one provided by Google Translate and the other by Microsoft Copilot.

Box 9.4   Google translation and AI translation

Google translation

1.2 million people use 'K-Pass', all your questions will be answered here.

The Ministry of Land, Infrastructure and Transport announced yesterday that since the launch of K-Pass, it has compiled the most curious questions from users and will guide them through the K-Pass application (app).

The Ministry of Land, Infrastructure and Transport explained that since its launch on the 1st, K-Pass has exceeded 1.2 million members, including 850,000 people who switched to economical transportation cards and 350,000 new subscribers.

Since the launch of the business, 28,930 inquiries have been received through the K-Pass app, with the main inquiries being about the business content (33.5%) and usage methods and procedures (21.4%).

Regarding the business content, most of the information was about what kind of business K-Pass is and what the conditions are for receiving a refund.

166　*Translation and Community*

Regarding the usage method and procedures, questions were about where to receive a card issuance and how to sign up for membership. was counted as the largest number.

Accordingly, the Ministry of Land, Infrastructure and Transport included related information in the 'Frequently Asked Questions' menu of the K-Pass app and website so that users can easily resolve their questions. In addition, we plan to periodically update the 'Frequently Asked Questions' to make it easier for users to use the K-Pass. In addition, with the Korea Transportation Safety Authority, the K-Pass entrusted operation agency, K-Pass will be available at Seoul Station from May 22nd to 24th. We operate a pass promotion booth and provide information offline.

Copilot translation

K-패스, the Korean Transportation Card Service, has garnered over 1.2 million members since its launch on May 1st. Among the most frequently asked questions by users, the following topics stand out:

1) What is K-패스?: Many inquiries revolved around understanding the purpose and scope of K-패스.
2) How to Use K-패스: Users sought guidance on card issuance locations and membership registration procedures.
3) Refund Conditions for K-패스: Questions related to eligibility criteria for refunds were also prevalent.

To address these queries, the Ministry of Land, Infrastructure, and Transport has updated the "Frequently Asked Questions" section on the K-패스 app and website, ensuring that users can easily find answers to their doubts. Additionally, an offline K-패스 promotion booth will operate at Seoul Station from May 22nd to 24th, providing in-person assistance and further promoting the service. The booth, designed with input from a youth advisory committee, features the slogan "Pass Your Transportation Worries with K-패스" and creatively incorporates gate-like structures reminiscent of transit facilities. As K-패스 continues to gain popularity, the ministry remains committed to promptly addressing user inquiries and enhancing convenience for all passengers.

It is not necessary to refer to the source text or understand Korean to realise that the two versions are quite different:

1) The Google translation consists of 251 words, while the AI translation has 208 only;

Locating and using resources 167

2) There are several details in the Google translation that are missing in the AI translation (e.g., numbers and percentages of people and enquiries);
3) Google translates all instances of "K-Pass", while the AI translation leaves "Pass" in the source language;
4) The ideational content is not the same (compare, for example, the messages we have in the first paragraph of each version).

This reflects how it is possible to end up with considerably different versions of the same source text depending on the automated translation software that is used. Indeed, DeepL, another machine translation software, provided a different rendition for the first paragraph of the same source text: "1.2 million K-Pass users have questions, here's everything you need to know. The Ministry of Land, Infrastructure, and Transport (MOLIT) announced yesterday that it has compiled the most frequently asked questions on the K-Pass application (app) since its launch". So, we are not sure whether the source text says "1.2 million people use 'K-Pass'", as the Google translation suggests or "1.2 million K-Pass users have questions", as DeepL tells us.

At any rate, DeepL's (and Copilot's) "the most frequently asked questions" is likely to be more accurate and idiomatic than Google's "the most curious questions from users". What this amounts to is that for a user to be confident about the quality of a machine or AI translation, they need to have the necessary language skills in both the source and target languages (in this case, Korean and English). Similarly, for a reviser or posteditor to check and improve the quality of the automated translation, they need to have the necessary linguistic and translation skills, including, among other types of knowledge and ability, intercultural competence.

This argument leads to the conclusion that for advanced translation students, postediting automated translation could be a useful exercise for developing critical and revision skills, and for qualified practitioners, it could be an efficient manner of processing large volumes of texts. However, for translation students at early stages of their training, automated translation could pose more risks than benefits. AI, for example, could be used to interact with the system and develop language skills further (by using AI as a subject expert, encyclopaedia or even as a language instructor), but relying on it to generate translations for assignments will only reduce students' cognitive effort and negatively influence their development of translation skills.

Relying on automated translation outputs before developing basic skills in comprehension, analysis of meaning in context, text types, translation strategies, reformulation, revision and so on is likely to create a situation of dependence without critical skills. This situation would be like a mechanic relying on a robot to repair machinery without having the necessary knowledge, technical skills or problem-solving abilities. Translation trainees also need to be aware that they will be unable to use machine translation or AI for their final examinations and accreditation tests, if applicable, unless the examination is specifically designed to test postediting skills.

168　*Translation and Community*

> **Summary**
>
> Both translators and translation students have a variety of resources and tools at their disposal. These range from traditional (e.g., dictionaries and glossaries) to technological and revolutionary (machine translation and AI). Each resource or tool has its affordances and limitations, so it is essential for translators and translation students to be aware of them and to have the critical capacity to assess their reliability and use them wisely. Many of these resources can be used to develop your language skills (e.g., vocabulary, grammar, comprehension in context, etc.) and cultural competence, which in turn should enable you to address translation problems. Technological tools, especially artificial intelligence, offer a vast amount of data (encyclopaedic, linguistic, cultural, institutional, specialised, etc.) and can provide raw translations. This calls for caution, as it can be tempting for trainees to rely on technology to complete their translation assignments before developing their language and translation skills. "Don't give me fish; rather, teach me how to fish" is a saying that encapsulates the position translation students should adopt.

Suggested activities

1) Look for 10 published community translations in your area (either in print or on websites like the ones mentioned in Section 9.4). Compare them with their source texts and decide whether they can be used as references for your own translation assignments.
2) Choose a text that is relevant to your community context. Before translating it into your other working language, underline all the challenging terms, expressions and ideas (concepts, terminology or ideas you find difficult to understand or to translate). Decide which resources would be most useful for each item and conduct the necessary research. Reflect on and, if possible, discuss with your peers whether your choice of resource was appropriate and whether the search was effective.
3) Choose another text and follow the same procedure, but this time with AI only (e.g., ChatGPT, Copilot or any other AI tool). Do not prompt the AI system to translate the text for you, but ask it specific questions about the concepts, terms or ideas you found challenging. Reflect on and, if possible, discuss with your peers whether the responses you received were useful for the translation task.

Further reading

- Rothwell, Andrew; Moorkens, Joss; Fernández Parra, Maria; Drugan, Joanna and Austermuehl, Frank (2023). *Translation tools and technologies*. London and New York: Routledge.

Locating and using resources 169

The book introduces translation tools and technologies, including, among other things, the principles of computer-assisted translation, translation memory, corpora and machine translation. The book also covers translation project management, subtitle editing tools and translation quality assurance. Although you might not find all the chapters relevant to community translation or to your own work pattern, the book is likely to enhance your technical and instrumental competence.

References

Antonini, Rachele; Cirillo, Letizia; Rossato, Linda and Torresi, Ira (2017). *Non-professional interpreting and translation: State of the art and future of an emerging field of research.* Amsterdam and Philadelphia: John Benjamins.

AUSIT (2022). *Recommended protocols for the translation of community communications.* https://ausit.org/wp-content/uploads/2024/03/AUSIT-FECCA-Recommended-Protocols-for-the-Translation-of-Community-Communications_042023.pdf.

Baker, Mona (1995). Corpora in translation studies: An overview and some suggestions for future research. *Target,* 7(2): 223–243.

Bowker, Lynne (2001). Towards a methodology for a corpus-based approach to translation evaluation. *Meta,* 46(2): 345–364. DOI: 10.7202/002135ar.

Bowker, Lynne and Buitrago-Ciro, Jairo (2019). *Machine translation and global research.* Bingley: Emerald Publishing.

Chan, Sin-wai (Ed.) (2015). *The Routledge encyclopedia of translation technology.* London and New York: Routledge.

Enríquez Raído, Vanessa (forthcoming). *Leveraging large language models for translator education: An accessible resource framework.*

Forcada Zubizarreta, Mikel L. (2022). Machine translation. *ENTI (Encyclopedia of translation & interpreting).* AIETI. www.aieti.eu/enti/machine_ENG/https://doi.org/10.5281/zenodo.6369130.

Gallego-Hernández, Daniel (2015). The use of corpora as translation resources: A study based on a survey of Spanish professional translators. *Perspectives,* 23(3): 375–391. DOI: 10.1080/0907676X.2014.964269.

Gigliotti, Giulia (2017). The quality of mercy: A corpus-based analysis of the quality of volunteer translations for non-profit organizations (NPOs). *New Voices in Translation Studies,* 17: 52–81.

González, Erika and Despina Amanatidou (2023). Challenges in community translation service provision: The Australian perspective. In González, Erika; Stachowiak-Szymczak, Katarzyna and Amanatidou, Despina (Eds.), *Community translation: Research and practice.* London: Routledge: 5–22.

Hartmann, Reinhard (1980). *Contrastive textology: Comparative discourse analysis in applied linguistics.* Heidelberg: Groos.

Mellinger, Chirstopher and Pokorn, Nike (2018). Community interpreting, translation, and technology. *Translation and Interpreting Studies,* 13(3): 337–341. DOI: 10.1075/tis.00019.int.

Monguilod, Laura and Vitalaru, Bianca (2023). Machine translation, translation errors, and adequacy: Spanish-English vs. Spanish-Romanian. In *Proceedings of the First Workshop on NLP Tools and Resources for Translation and Interpreting Applications.* Varna, Bulgaria: INCOMA Ltd., Shoumen, Bulgaria: 4–12.

Nitzke, Jean and Hansen-Schirra, Silvia (2021). *A short guide to postediting.* Berlin: Language Science Press.

O'hagan, Minako (Ed.) (2019). *The Routledge handbook of translation and technology.* London and New York: Routledge.

170 Translation and Community

Oliver, Antoni (2020). Human translation and machine translation: Specificities, uses, advantages and disadvantages. *Linguapax Review*, 111–129.

Pym, Anthony and Hao, Yu (2025). *How to augment language skills. Generative AI and machine translation in language learning and translator training*. London and New York: Routledge.

Samuelsson-Brown, Geoffrey (2010). *A practical guide for translators*. Bristol, Buffalo and Toronto: Multilingual Matters.

Shah, Priten (2023). *AI and the future of education: Teaching in the age of artificial intelligence*. Hoboken and New Jersey: John Wiley & Sons.

Simard, Michel (2019). Building and using parallel text for translation. In O'hagan, Minako (Ed.), *The Routledge handbook of translation and technology*. London and New York: Routledge.

Snell-Hornby, Mary (1995). *Translation Studies: An integrated approach*. Amsterdam and Philadelphia: John Benjamins.

Svoboda, Tomáš and Sosoni, Vilelmini (2023). Institutional translator training in language and translation technologies. In Svoboda, Tomáš; Biel, Łucja and Sosoni, Vilelmini (Eds.), *Institutional translator training*. London and New York: Routledge: 73–91.

Thunes, Martha (2017). An analysis of text complexity in two text types. In Czulo, Oliver and Hansen-Schirra, Silvia (Eds.), *Crossroads between contrastive linguistics, translation studies and machine translation*. Berlin: Language Science Press: 92–120.

Vicerrectorado de Innovación Educativa—UNED (2023). *Guía para integrar las tecnologías basadas en inteligencia artificial generativa en los procesos de enseñanza y aprendizaje*. http://fediap.com.ar/wp-content/uploads/2023/12/Gu_a_para_integrar_las_tecnolog_as_basadas_en_IAG_1702048753-1.pdf.

Zhang, Jia (2023). Exploring undergraduate translation students' perceptions towards machine translation: A qualitative questionnaire survey. In *Proceedings of Machine Translation Summit XIX, Vol. 2: Users Track*. Macau SAR, China. Asia-Pacific Association for Machine Translation: 1–10.

Zhang, Jia and Qian, Hong (2023). The impact of machine translation on the translation quality of undergraduate translation students. In *Proceedings of Machine Translation Summit XIX, Vol. 2: Users Track*. Macau SAR, China. Asia-Pacific Association for Machine Translation: 99–108.

10 Revising your and another translator's work

In this chapter, I introduce translation revision as a step to ensure that translations meet quality criteria and are fit for purpose. This is followed by practical advice relating to revision in the context of community translation. Examples of translations and suggested revisions are provided in Arabic, Chinese, English and Spanish. The chapter covers the following:

- Translation revision as quality assurance;
- Required skills and qualifications;
- Revision parameters;
- Translation revision for community translations.

Box 10.1 Unrevised translation

The implications of social media on children before puberty

Social media has become a crucial part of our lives. However, its effects on children's cognition development before puberty are concerning and worth critical interest. Children before puberty go through a growing-up stage where they learn how to build social relationships and understand hints. However, online interactions lack accurate social differentiations, and thus it does not help children develop the basic skills in dealing with others.

It was proven that long-term memory has great importance in the learning process. However, the nature of social media which contains short and divided information, contradicts the mandatory cognition mechanisms that aim to improve children's memory, as The brain needs a continuous time of concentration to convey the information from short-term memory to long-term memory while passing the working memory, and this is important for tasks that require a larger cognition effort. Moreover, the continuous transition between social media and other tasks makes it difficult to store and remember information effectively, and this has long-term implications for academic success.

DOI: 10.4324/9781003367741-11

172 *Translation and Community*

The text in Box 10.1 is a translation of a text on the impact of social media on pre-teens. We do not need to check the source text to realise that there are issues with this translation at many levels. At the level of grammar, we say "cognitive development", not "cognition development" (adjective + noun, not noun + noun). Syntactically also, there is a lack of agreement between the subject (online interactions) in the first sentence and the pronoun "it" in the second sentence, which creates a cohesion issue: "However, online interactions lack accurate social differentiations, and thus it does not help children develop the basic skills in dealing with others".

At the level of accurate and clear transfer of meaning, the following long sentence fails to convey a clear message, mainly due to incorrect lexical choices (e.g., "divided information" and "mandatory") and a confusing clause structure which obscures the logical links between parts of the text: "However, the nature of social media which contains short and divided information, contradicts the mandatory cognition mechanisms that aim to improve children's memory, as the brain needs a continuous time of concentration to convey the information from short-term memory to long-term memory while passing the working memory, and this is important for tasks that require a larger cognition effort."

Unfortunately, inaccurate and/or awkward translations continue to be published on government and non-government websites and other types of resources. The publication of such sub-standard translations is evidence that the work was not sufficiently checked. For a translation to meet the minimum quality standards, it needs to be checked by the translator and at least one other reviewer.

10.1 Translation revision as quality assurance

As the example in Box 10.1 shows, translation revision is crucial to translation quality; it entails the bilingual revision of a translation by a translator or reviser who is proficient in the source language, to ensure that it conforms to the needs and the expectations of the recipient (Lee, 2006: 414). One or more reviewers check a draft translation against its source text and the translation brief to ensure that the translation is accurate in comparison with the source text, internally consistent, compliant with the language and textual norms of the target language and appropriate for the purpose for which it is intended.

Revision identifies language, translation and presentation errors so they can be addressed, either directly or by providing feedback to the translator. Translators can review and revise their own work before submitting it (self-revision), revise someone else's translation (other-revision) or check and improve the quality of a machine translation (postediting). Translation researchers and practitioners also describe revision work as checking, reviewing, editing and proofreading. Shih (2006), for instance, uses the terms 'self-checking' and 'revision' to refer to revision undertaken by the translator, Ko (2011) uses both 'checking' and 'revision' to refer to revision of someone else's translation and Mossop (2020) and Liang (2021) use 'revision' to refer to checking undertaken by a reviser, and 'other-revision'/ 'self-revision' when it is necessary to distinguish between the two. Mossop (2020)

Revising your and another translator's work 173

and Liang (2021) and others rightly consider that self-revision is an integral part of the translation process. In this chapter, I use Mossop's (2020: 248–250) terms and definitions, with the caveat that for me and my research colleague (Taibi and Ozolins, 2016; Taibi, 2018), quality assurance relates to all relevant stakeholders, not only the translating organization:

Revising/revision: The process of reading a translation in order to spot problematic passages, and then making or recommending any corrections or improvements that are needed to meet some standard of quality.

Self-revision: An integral part of the translation production process in which one checks and amends one's own translation.

Other-revision: Revising a translation prepared by another translator.

Postediting: Revising the output of machine translation.

Quality assurance: The whole set of procedures applied before, during and after the translation production process, by all members of a translating organization to ensure that quality objectives important to the client are being met (Mossop, 2020: 248–250).

As Mossop (2020: 1) notes, translation revision is required for a number of evident reasons, including the fact that nobody is perfect, not even experienced professional translators; that any writing process consists of drafting and redrafting and that translators may inadvertently produce sentences that are ambiguous or difficult to understand or disregard client specifications or the type of readership in preparing their translations. In community translation in particular, revision by the translator and by others (translation revisers, copyeditors and proofreaders) is an essential step in quality assurance.

Self- and other-revision can avoid problems ranging from minor grammatical and spelling inconsistencies that do not affect meaning to major distortions, omissions or language and style issues which are likely to influence the reception of the public messaging campaign as well as the image of the public service, private organisation and/or translation agency involved (Taibi, 2018: 21–22). As the revision guidelines of the Multicultural Health Communication Service (2019) acknowledge, translation revision

reduces the likelihood of error and should result in better quality in multilingual materials, scripts, ads and websites. The extra associated expense is usually justified. If serious mistakes come to light only at the printing or recording stage or even later, it is much more expensive to re-do a completed multilingual project, and can also cause delays to campaigns, research projects, etc.

To sum up, translation revision is an essential step in quality assurance, both self-revision and other-revision. It is beneficial for all the stakeholders involved. For translators and language service providers, translation revision is an indispensable step towards quality assurance, and failure to complete this step involves

174 *Translation and Community*

risks for the professional and/or organizational image and can even have budgetary or legal implications. For government and non-government organisations commissioning community translations, adequate translation revision ensures the effectiveness and appropriateness of public messaging, contributes to preserving the image of the organisation and can avoid additional costs (e.g., if funds need to be allocated to repair damages or to redo the entire production process). For end users (i.e., individuals and communities needing community translations), revision ensures communication effectiveness and appropriateness and a better user experience.

10.2 Required skills and qualifications

Translation revision "needs expertise, patience and attention to detail, and may take as much time as the translation did" (Multicultural Health Communication Service, 2019: 4). As Mellinger (2018) and Liang (2021) note, experienced and reliable translators are usually entrusted with translation revision based on a common assumption in the industry "that good translators are good revisers" (Liang, 2021: 95), although this assumption is not always supported by research findings (e.g., Hansen, 2008; Van Rensburg, 2017).

Liang's (2021) own study, which was conducted with Chinese translation trainees, showed that competent translation trainees tended to be good at revision and trainees who were weak at translation were also weak at revision, but there was no significant correlation in the intermediate group. Mossop (2020: 118–119) acknowledges that translation skills are a prerequisite for revisers and, in addition to those skills, lists the following competencies and attributes:

- Ability to detect errors or problems in translations;
- Translation experience;
- Knowledge of the procedures applicable to translation revision;
- Ability to make quick decisions;
- Ability to undertake revision to different degrees (depending on the purpose);
- Ability to justify suggested amendments and avoid unnecessary changes;
- Ability to revise through corrections rather than retranslation of the source text;
- Openness towards other translators' approaches and translation solutions;
- Diplomacy and tactfulness to avoid or deal with workplace conflicts;
- Cautiousness and awareness of one's limitations.

These competencies and qualities can be grouped under four categories:

1) Translation skills, experience and knowledge: In order to provide feedback on translations and suggest corrections or improvements, the reviser must have the necessary experience (to anticipate problem areas and compare the translation against its source text), translation skills (to propose corrections or solutions) and translation expertise (to provide and justify feedback using appropriate terminology).

Revising your and another translator's work 175

2) Analytical and observational skills: Not everybody is able to detect problems with translations. Künzli (2007), for instance, revealed that professional translators revising draft translations often failed to correct errors. While some errors are easy to identify (e.g., major distortions or clearly awkward constructions), others require closer attention, rigorous comparison of source and target texts and analysis of structural and logical relationships between sentences to identify any meaning or cohesion issues.

3) Procedural knowledge and skills: Different organisations have different procedures and formats for translation revision (templates with errors, corrections and explanations; tracked changes and comments; online system built specifically to process translations and revisions, etc.). The reviser needs to apply each client's standard or preferred procedure and format in each revision case, particularly freelancers who will serve multiple clients or organisations.

4) Interpersonal skills: Other-revision consists of providing feedback on someone else's translation and therefore involves interpersonal challenges and sensitivities. Feedback needs to be provided in a professional and neutral tone to avoid offending colleagues (inside the same organisation) or other translators in general, and it needs to focus on areas that are genuine problems with the translation, not personal stylistic preferences, which requires the reviser to be able to appreciate other translators' approaches and translation solutions. Künzli (2007: 124) found that "when professional translators are asked to revise draft translations, the proportion of unjustified changes . . . can be quite high".

Mossop (2020) also warns of the risk of treating others' work as one's own and making perfectionist but unnecessary changes: "However, when revising others, you have to keep in mind that they probably take pride in their work and will not be happy if you have made large numbers of unnecessary changes. The result will be poor working relationships" (198). Interpersonal skills are also needed when translation revision feedback is accessible to supervisors in the same organisation or where revisers prepare performance reports about translators. Diplomacy and professional conduct in such a context are needed to avoid workplace conflict (between translators and revisers).

In relation to reviser qualities and qualifications in community translation in particular, the AUSIT-FECCA *Revision Guidelines and Parameters for Community Translations*, which were developed in Australia during the COVID-19 pandemic and the ensuing public discussion on quality of health care translations, state the following (emphasis in the source):

> As a general rule, **a translation reviser must have qualifications that are equal to those required for the translation itself.** For example, if a translation was prepared by a NAATI-certified translator, the reviser needs to be certified at the same level at least. If the translation assignment falls within a specialised field such as medical or pharmaceutical translation, the reviser needs to have experience in translation and/or revision in the field (in addition to the relevant NAATI certification). Additional qualifications such as a

176 *Translation and Community*

tertiary degree in linguistics or translation studies are preferable, as advanced knowledge in these areas would enable the reviser to categorise errors appropriately and substantiate their feedback. **Monolingual readers may provide feedback on draft translations, but this will be limited to proofreading the translation and providing feedback on language and style, and how they might be perceived by an average end user.**

(n.d.: 1)

The guidelines do not mention interpersonal skills under the section about qualifications, but they do allude to these indispensable skills under the section on professional solidarity: 1) The reviser's feedback needs to be sent to the translator so that they can make the necessary changes or respond if they do not agree with the suggested amendments; 2) translation revisions must be sent through the same channel used to send the translation (e.g., no direct contact between the reviser and translator if the revision task was received through an agency) and 3) corrections need to be suggested in a professional and neutral tone, identifying only those instances that are considered errors, not personal preferences.

10.3 Parameters of translation revision

As I iterated in Section 10.1, translation revision is an integral part of quality assurance. It follows that the parameters of translation revision will vary depending on our understanding of translation quality. I am not going to discuss the different schools of translation quality assessment in this chapter, but it is worth quoting Koby et al.'s (2014: 416) broad definition, which provides a starting point for consensus: "A quality translation demonstrates accuracy and fluency required for the audience and purpose and complies with all other specifications negotiated between the requester and provider, taking into account end-user needs." Although the definition can raise many questions (Taibi, 2018), it addresses key quality criteria I have mentioned in this textbook (e.g., Chapters 3 and 4) such as accuracy, fluency (language appropriateness) and the translation brief (purpose of the translation, audience and other specifications). Koby et al. (2014) also offer a narrow definition of translation quality:

A high-quality translation is one in which the message embodied in the source text is transferred completely into the target text, including denotation, connotation, nuance, and style, and the target text is written in the target language using correct grammar and word order, to produce a culturally appropriate text that, in most cases, reads as if originally written by a native speaker of the target language for readers in the target culture.

(416–417)

In this definition, there is still due attention to accuracy, language appropriateness and audience (cultural appropriateness), but there is more detail, including references to completeness, nuanced meaning, appropriate style, correct language

Revising your and another translator's work   177

usage and naturalness (the translation reading as if it were an original piece of writing). However, Koby et al.'s narrow definition refers to the characteristics of "a high-quality translation", which raises the question of whether translation revision should aim to produce a high-quality translation or a translation that is just acceptable. As Mossop (2020: 160–166) explains in detail, this will depend on the importance of the document, the risks involved and the expectations of the client (intelligible translation, informative translation, publishable translation or polished translation).

Community translations are usually made available to the public, so the expectation is that the revised translation should be of a publishable quality, meaning that it is fully accurate, linguistically correct, tailored to the target audience, stylistically smooth and cohesive, internally consistent and compliant with the house style or specifications (Mossop, 2020: 165). In Chapter 4 of this textbook, I described that quality in community translations is determined based on the extent to which they are accurate, suitable, accessible, effective and impactful as well as linguistically, stylistically and culturally appropriate for the intended audience. Here, I outline some of the revision parameters proposed in the literature for translation in general (Lee, 2006; NAATI, 2018a, 2018b, 2018c; 2019a, 2019b, 2019c; Mossop, 2020) and AUSIT-FECCA's (n.d.) set for community translations in particular.

With reference to translation revision in general, Lee (2006) reviewed a few sets of revision parameters, including an older edition of Mossop (2020) and proposed the following four parameters:

1) Transfer: Whether the message of the source text was transmitted accurately;
2) Linguistic standard: Whether the norms and conventions of the target language are respected in the translation;
3) Readability: Whether the translation is coherent, logical and readable;
4) Functional adaptation: Whether the translation takes into account the purpose and the recipient (Lee, 2006: 418).

NAATI introduced translation revision as a component on its translation certification test in 2018. The revision task has eight parameters or error categories (NAATI, 2018a, 2018b, 2018c, 2019a, 2019b, 2019c): distortion, unjustified omission, unjustified insertion, inappropriate register, unidiomatic expression, errors of grammar/syntax, errors of spelling, and errors of punctuation:

1. Distortion: An element of meaning in the source text is altered in the target text. A distortion can occur in an individual word, phrase, clause or entire sentence.
2. Unjustified omission: An element of meaning in the source text is not transferred into the target text. An unjustified omission can occur with an individual word, phrase, clause or entire sentence.
3. Unjustified insertion: An element of meaning that does not exist in the source text is added to the target text. An unjustified insertion can occur with an individual word, phrase, clause or entire sentence.

178 *Translation and Community*

4. Inappropriate register: An expression or variety of language considered by a native speaker to be inappropriate to the specific context in which it is used.
5. Unidiomatic expression: An expression sounding unnatural or awkward to a native speaker irrespective of the context in which the expression is used, but the intended meaning can be understood.
6. Error of grammar, syntax: Errors in structuring words, clauses and phrases of a language. E.g. incorrect word type/form; incorrect verb tense/form; agreement error between subject-verb, noun-pronoun, adjective-noun, etc.
7. Error of spelling: Error in forming words with letters or characters. E.g. misspelling of a word/character, incorrect capitalisation.
8. Error of punctuation: Error in use of marks that separate sentences and their elements, and clarify meaning. E.g. incorrect comma, full-stop, apostrophe, inverted commas, etc.

Although NAATI's list of error categories refers to context, the revision parameters are mainly related to content accuracy and completeness and to language norms (from the perspective of a native speaker). There is no explicit mention of something similar to Lee's (2006) readability and functional adaptation, for example.

Mossop's (2020) revision parameters are probably the most comprehensive: 14 parameters under five categories: 1) transfer, 2) content, 3) language and style, 4) presentation and 5) specifications. I describe the parameters under these categories in Table 10.1.

Table 10.1 Mossop's five parameters for successful translation revision

Category	*Parameter*	*Specific questions to ask while revising*
Transfer	Accuracy	Does the translation accurately convey the messages of the source text?
	Completeness	Are there unjustified omissions or additions in relation to the source text?
Content	Logic	Do the translation and the sequence of ideas in it make sense (no contradictions, no temporal or logical inconsistencies)?
	Facts	Are there are any factual, conceptual or mathematical errors, either originating in the source text or introduced in the translation?
Language	Smoothness	Does the translation read smoothly or are there any awkward sentences or poor connections between sentences? **Mossop notes that the presence of acronyms and untranslated source-language words can affect smoothness.**
	Tailoring	Does the translation use the right register and tone for the type of text and the intended readers?

(Continued)

Revising your and another translator's work　179

Table 10.1 (Continued)

Category	Parameter	Specific questions to ask while revising
	Sub-language	Is the translation consistent with the source text in terms of genre and field-specific terminology? **Mossop notes that for translations intended for information only, specialised terminology might not be necessary.**
	Idiom	Is the translation idiomatic, i.e., are the combinations of words in it used by native speakers and is the translation consistent with the rhetorical norms of the target language?
	Mechanics	Are the grammar, spelling, punctuation and house style, if applicable, correctly applied?
Presenta-tion	Layout	Is the layout correct and consistent, including spacing, margins, indentations and so on?
	Typography	Are the typographic aspects (font size, bolded headings, underlining, etc.) appropriate and consistent?
	Organisation	Are the table of contents, headings, page numbers, etc. well organised?
Specifica-tions	Client specifications	Does the translation comply with the client's specifications?
	Employer policy	If applicable, does the translation comply with the organisation's translation policies?

Box 10.2　Monolingual revision task

Please revise the following translation from Arabic to English. In a normal translation revision, you would have access to the source text so that you can check the translation against it. As this textbook is aimed at students with different language combinations, use the English translation only. Translation revision in this case will be like monolingual editing; that is, you will be unable to revise it in terms of accuracy and completeness. Please identify all the problems that require attention (e.g., unclear meaning, incorrect grammatical structure, unidiomatic expression, lack of cohesion, incorrect punctuation).

Housing—a crisis that worries foreign workers in Saudi Arabia

According to experts "The lack of standards of safety, public hygiene, entertainment and services", four features that summarise the conditions of foreign labours housing in Saudi Arabia.

According to the expert of labourers housing, engineer Faisal Al-Sayegh; the labourers housing does not meet international standards and can have negative effects that puts Riyadh in embarrassment before the UN Human Rights Council.

180 *Translation and Community*

During a seminar on the "reality of the labourers housing in the kingdom ... in between hope and solutions". Al-Sayegh said, lack of enforcing regulations on workers accommodation, and the lack of awareness of society about their rights, further complicates the current situation.

The government estimates that the number of foreign workers in Saudi Arabia reaches 8.2 million, including 6.8 who work in the private sector establishments, and they are the most vulnerable to living in random areas or in dilapidated buildings, lacking many basic facilities and the reasons for a decent life. The Government figures show that 51% of these work in the construction sector.

According to the seminar's discussions, the end of the deteriorating labour housing situation has not yet been addressed, as the populated city of Jeddah (west) alone contains 54 random populations, of which workers constitute 80% of its population.

Al-Sayegh stressed the importance of supporting the "workers' residential villages" sector and activating clear and specific regulations and conditions for workers' housing. He said that the current conditions of workers in Saudi Arabia are contrary to the first clause of Article 25 of the Universal Declaration of Human Rights, which states that "everyone has the right to a standard of living sufficient to maintain the health and well-being of himself and his family, including nutrition, clothing, housing, medical care and the necessary social services." Al-Sayegh sharply criticized companies operating in the kingdom, saying they treat workers badly.

A previous Saudi study had proposed the establishment of a committee consisting of the ministries of interior, municipality, health, and justice to develop regulations and standards on workers' housing, but this has not been translated into reality until today. Those concerned with the conditions of workers are calling on the Saudi Ministry of Labour to adopt a system that imposes the improvement of labour housing and sets deterrent penalties on companies that are negligent in this area.

10.4 Community translation revision

Translation revision is translation revision, isn't it? Or should there be something special about the revision of community translations? Just like translation, revision is undertaken in a given context and for a given purpose. While general principles and quality criteria (e.g., accuracy, language and style, presentation, or client specifications) apply across the board, each field of translation and each communicative context will require a nuanced approach to translation and translation revision and a context-specific implementation of the common quality criteria.

In the case of community translations, one would expect aspects such as language accessibility (not only language norms and conventions), cultural appropriateness

Revising your and another translator's work   181

and the actual target user (not native speakers in general) to be at the centre of the revision process. AUSIT-FECCA's Revision Guidelines, developed in Australia to improve the quality of community translations, are a good point of reference. Although the guidelines are based on a generic framework applicable to different translation areas (Mossop, 2020), they are tailored to the community translation context. For example, one of the main revision considerations is cultural appropriateness:

> Does the translation contain any culturally inappropriate material, statements or references? Does the translation convey a stereotypical image of a given social or cultural group? Is the translation politically correct in light of the diversity in your community (gender, national, ethnic groups, etc.)?
>
> (AUSIT-FECCA, n.d.: 7)

Similarly, under the parameter of register and style, "Are the language structures and register likely to be accessible to the average user?" (AUSIT-FECCA, n.d.: 5). I present these revision parameters in Table 10.2 and illustrate some of them in more detail in Table 10.3.

Revision should not be approached as an exercise of error spotting only; with this approach, there is a risk of focusing on the mechanics of language (i.e., grammatical structure, word order, punctuation and spelling) and overlooking the function of the translation (whether it is fit for purpose).

Revision needs to be undertaken at both the macro and micro levels. At the macro level, the reviser checks the overall communicative function of the translation (i.e., whether it is meaningful, whether the messages are clearly expressed, whether there are any logical or conceptual inconsistencies—in short, whether the translation serves its communicative function). At the micro level, the reviser checks details such as localised inaccuracies, language errors or instances of inappropriate style or register.

Inexperienced and unqualified translators tend to start translating sentence by sentence before having a good understanding of the entire text and its communicative situation, Similarly. unqualified revisers may start checking a translation sentence by sentence. looking for language errors and any deviations from the source text at the surface level. A more appropriate and effective approach is to start with reading the whole translation to check whether it would make sense to the intended user from the first reading and whether its messages are logical and coherent. This initial reading can then be followed by a close comparison between the translation and its source text (and a closer look at the translation itself) to identify any of the error types I have described in this chapter.

A reviser should not miss the forest for the trees: Correcting localised errors is important, but it should not be at the expense of the overall assessment of the translation as a communicative instrument within a given context: "In the context of public messaging in particular, a final macro-level translation revision is necessary to ensure that the translation caters for the needs of the target users (i.e. it is culturally and linguistically suitable, accessible and communicatively effective)" (AUSIT-FECCA, n.d.: 2). In Table 10.4, I give some tips for your consideration and discussion.

182   *Translation and Community*

Table 10.2 AUSIT-FECCA parameters for revising translations

Broad category	*Parameters*	*Questions to consider while revising*
Meaning Transfer	Accuracy	Does the translation accurately convey the message of the source text? Are there any conceptual or factual errors?
	Completeness	Are there any unjustified omissions and/or additions? Have any parts of the source text been unjustifiably left in the source language?
	Logic/ coherence	Does the sequence of ideas make sense? Do ideas flow logically? **(Problems identified in a translation may be problems in the source text, which should be addressed at the translation and revision stages, if not identified earlier.)**
Language and Style	Cohesion	Are there good connections between sentences and clauses? Are sentences properly linked? Do they flow smoothly?
	Register and style	Do the language, style and tone fit the purpose of the translation (medium of dissemination and target audience)? **Are the language structures and register likely to be accessible to the average user?**
	Idiomaticity	Is the translation idiomatic? Does it follow the stylistic and rhetorical norms of the target language? Does the translation in general read/sound natural?
	Grammar	Are there any syntactical errors (e.g. subject–verb agreement, tense, prepositions, incomplete structure)?
	Lexical choice	Are the words and terms used correct and appropriate for the type of text and the intended users?
	Spelling	Are there any spelling errors or inconsistencies?
	Punctuation	Are there any punctuation errors, **especially those that may impact meaning or connection between sentences?**
Presentation	Layout	Is the layout appropriate and consistent (including spacing, margins, indentations, positioning of footnotes, relationship of text to graphics)?
	Typography	Are the typographic aspects (including bolding, underlining, font type and size) appropriate and consistent?
	Organisation	Are headings, page numbers, table of contents, etc. properly organised?
Cultural Appropriateness		Does the translation contain any culturally inappropriate material, statements or references? Does the translation convey a stereotypical image of a given social or cultural group? Is the translation politically correct in light of the diversity in your community (gender, national, ethnic groups, etc.)?
Specifications	Client specifications	If a translation brief has been provided, has this been complied with?
	Organisation policy and guidelines	If the organisation has policies and guidelines relating to translation, have these been complied with?

Revising your and another translator's work 183

Table 10.3 Examples of applying the AUSIT-FECCA translation revision parameters

Parameter	Example
Accuracy	ST: *La primera visita prenatal debe realizarse dentro del primer trimestre. Se debe realizar una visita de seguimiento aproximadamente cada 4–6 semanas, hasta llegar al final del embarazo.* TT: The first prenatal consultation should occur within the first trimester. There should be a follow-up consultation approximately every 4–6 weeks, <u>until the end of embarrassment</u>. REV: The first prenatal consultation should occur within the first trimester. There should be a follow-up consultation approximately every 4–6 weeks, **until the end of pregnancy**.
Logic/ coherence	ST: We know that by maintaining a healthy body weight, being physically active every day and enjoying a healthy diet, you can lower your risk of developing cancer. We know that <u>these factors</u> account for at least 30 per cent of all cancers. REV: We know that by maintaining a healthy body weight, being physically active every day and enjoying a healthy diet, you can lower your risk of developing cancer. We know that **failure to do so** accounts for at least 30 per cent of all cancers. Note: Sometimes logic/coherence problems can be in the source text. This does not mean that they should not be revised. If the translator failed to identify the problem, the reviser should do so.
Lexical choice	ST: ‫تُعتبر إمكانية تعرّض الأطفال إلى الاستغلال العاطفي عند استخدام الإنترنت معضلة عويصة.‬ TT: The possibility of children being <u>exhibited</u> to emotional exploitation when using the Internet is a serious dilemma. REV: The possibility of children being **exposed** to emotional exploitation when using the Internet is a serious dilemma.
Register and style	ST: Please note that vaccination is voluntary and free. TT: Es <u>menester</u> informarle que la vacunación es <u>potestativa</u> y está <u>exenta</u> de costo. REV: ***Para su información***, *la vacunación es* **voluntaria y gratuita**. Note: The unrevised Spanish translation is not inaccurate or grammatically incorrect, but it is excessively formal for an informative leaflet.
Cultural appro- priateness	ST: Mr Hunt said he welcomed the move TT: 亨特先生表示，他欢迎这一举措的实施 REV: 亨特部长表示，他欢迎这一举措的实施 Note: In the Chinese culture, it is more appropriate to refer to a minister using their title (Minister) and name, rather than Mr. + name. ST: Pork is a good source of phosphorus, selenium, and thiamine. TT: ‫لحم الخنزير مصدر جيد للفوسفور والسيلينيوم والثيامين‬ REV: ‫لحم الدجاج مصدر جيد للفوسفور والسيلينيوم والثيامين‬ Note: reference to pork is likely to be culturally inappropriate for Muslim readers of the Arabic translation. The revised translation replaces "pork" with "chicken".

Notes: ST, source text; TT, target text; REV, revision.

184   *Translation and Community*

Table 10.4 AUSIT-FECCA tips for translation revisers

Group discussion

AUSIT-FECCA *Revision Guidelines and Parameters for Community Translations* include the following tips for revisers. Please discuss them with a partner or in small groups. As you discuss the tips, please relate them to specific aspects of translation revision (qualifications, procedure, interpersonal skills and so on).

Dos	Don'ts
Ask yourself first whether you are qualified to revise this translation (e.g. if the text is specialised).	Don't take on to revise translations in an area you are not familiar with (unless you are ready to do a lot of research).
Read translations in a quiet environment, using the display format of your preference (when you have a choice). Traditionally, revisers were advised to read on paper, not on screen, but this will vary from one person to another.	Don't check translations on a phone screen or while doing something else. Translation revision requires as much attention and rigour as translation itself.
Start with a macro reading of the translation. This will give you a general idea about its coherence, cohesion and language appropriateness.	Don't start looking for errors straightaway.
Think of the translation revision task as a quality check exercise, not a skills and creativity contest.	Unless it is completely necessary, don't retranslate segments/texts. Work with the existing translation and fix only the items that need fixing.
Limit your corrections to what is necessary in light of the text type and translation brief. Examples: translation that is difficult to understand; inconsistent meanings; clearly ungrammatical sentence, inappropriate register, etc.	Don't make/suggest changes based on personal preferences only. Don't start looking for errors straightaway.
Check your own amendments and comments, especially if you are prone to mistakes when typing or editing text.	Don't introduce new errors in the revision process: meaning transfer errors due to comprehension issues; language errors while fixing inaccuracies or other meaning errors, etc.
Ensure consistency in your revision: e.g. if you correct a recurring item, make sure you correct it in the entire translation or, alternatively, indicate in a comment that this needs to be done.	Don't lose sight of the whole text while revising smaller items.
In public messaging in particular, revise translations with translation users in mind (e.g. meaning clarity, readability, accessible language, natural expression).	Don't suggest "improvements" based on a literal approach to translation.
If there are limitations (e.g. terminological challenges), acknowledge them to the client or agency.	Don't simply say the translation is OK because you don't know, are not sure, or don't have time to do further research.

> **Summary**
>
> Translation revision (both by the translator and by others) is an essential step in quality assurance. For translators and language service providers, it is a matter of quality assurance, professional or organizational image and, in some cases, risk management in terms of avoiding additional costs or legal liabilities. For public services, rigorous and competent translation revision contributes to ensuring that quality standards are met, and communication campaigns are effective. It can also minimise potential impact on the institutional image and avoid additional costs (e.g., in case problems are identified after publication). For communities using translated materials, revision ensures communication effectiveness and a better user experience.
>
> Although there are different parameters for translation revision in scholarly literature and in the industry, the existing parameters tend to agree on the need for translations to be revised in terms of accuracy, completeness, language and style, with an (implicit or explicit) expectation that translations will be appropriate for the context and purpose. For community translations, the AUSIT-FECCA *Revision Guidelines and Parameters for Community Translations* are highly useful. Although they are based on a generic framework applicable to different translation areas (Mossop, 2020), they are tailored to the community translation context. For example, they stress the importance of language accessibility, cultural appropriateness and the *actual* target user (not native speakers in general).

Suggested activities

1) Choose a text from the Internet that might be of interest to your community (e.g., leaflet on diet, information and advice for migrant workers, announcement to residents in a local community) and translate it into another language using machine translation. Read the translation (without reference to the source text) to see if it makes sense and if there are any logical or conceptual issues. Revise the translation using the parameters in Section 10.4.
2) Look for a website that provides information in more than one language and identify the most common translation and language issues. List examples under the main problem areas or error categories (e.g., accuracy, logic/coherence, grammar, idiomaticity, etc.)
3) List cultural issues that might be problematic in community translations (into one of your working languages) and that require special attention by both the translator and reviser.

186 *Translation and Community*

Further reading

- Mossop, Brian (with Jungmin Hong and Carlos Teixeira) (2020). *Revising and editing for translators.* London and New York: Routledge.

Written by a Canadian scholar with extensive experience in the Canadian Government's Translation Bureau as well as in teaching, this book is a comprehensive reference work on translation revision. It provides a detailed explanation of revision parameters, practical advice to revisers and real-life examples that will assist the reviser in determining the degree to which a revision needs to be undertaken. The fourth edition of the book also includes a chapter on trans-editing by Jungmin Hong and another on revising computer-mediated translations by Carlos Teixeira.

- AUSIT-FECCA (n.d.). *Revision guidelines and parameters for community translations.* https://ausit.org/ausit_fecca_translation_guidelines

The guidelines are specifically relevant to community translation. In addition to general recommendations, the guidelines outline key revision parameters and include illustrations in Arabic, Chinese and Spanish.

References

AUSIT-FECCA (n.d.). *Revision guidelines and parameters for community translations.* https://ausit.org/ausit_fecca_translation_guidelines.

Hansen, Gyde (2008). The speck in your brother's eye—the beam in your own: Quality management in translation and revision. In Hansen, Gyde; Chesterman, Andrew and Gerzymisch-Arbogast, Heidrun (Eds.), *Efforts and models in interpreting and translation research: A tribute to Daniel Gile.* Amsterdam: John Benjamins: 255–280.

Ko, Leong (2011). Translation checking: A view from the translation market. *Perspectives: Studies in Translatology*, 19(2): 123–134.

Koby, Geoffrey S.; Fields, Paul; Hague, Daryl; Lommel, Arle and Melby, Alan (2014). Defining translation quality. *Tradumàtica tecnologies de la traducció*, 12: 413–420.

Künzli, A. (2007). Translation revision: A study of the performance of ten professional translators revising a legal text. In Gambier, Yves; Shlesinger, Miriam and Stolze, Radegundis (Eds.), *Doubts and directions in translation studies: Selected contributions from the EST Congress, Lisbon 2004.* Amsterdam and Philadelphia: John Benjamins: 115–126.

Lee, Hyang (2006). Revision: Definitions and parameters. *Meta*, 51(2): 410–419.

Liang, Haiyan (2021). Initial translation interference to reviser trainees in English-LOTE translation revision tasks. *Translation & Interpreting: The International Journal of Translation and Interpreting Research.* DOI: 10.12807/ti.113202.2021.a06.

Mellinger, Christopher D. (2018). Re-thinking translation quality: Revision in the digital age. *Target: International Journal of Translation Studies*, 30(2): 310–331.

Mossop, Brian (with Hong, Jungmin and Teixeira, Carlos) (2020). *Revising and editing for translators.* London and New York: Routledge.

Multicultural Health Communication Service (2019). Can we just check it? *Guidelines for checking of health/medical translations.* www.mhcs.health.nsw.gov.au/about-us/services/translation/pdf/GuidelinesForChecking.pdf.

NAATI (2018a). *Revision of a non-specialised translation: List of error categories for candidates (English into Simplified Chinese).* www.naati.com.au/wp-content/uploads/2020/01/List-of-Error-Categories_Chinese-Simplified.pdf.

Revising your and another translator's work 187

NAATI (2018b). *Revision of a non-specialised translation: List of error categories for candidates (English into Spanish).* www.naati.com.au/wp-content/uploads/2020/01/List-of-Error-Categories_Spanish.pdf.

NAATI (2018c). *Revision of a non-specialised translation: List of error categories for candidates (English into Vietnamese).* www.naati.com.au/wp-content/uploads/2020/01/List-of-Error-Categories_Vietnamese.pdf.

NAATI (2019a). *Revision of a non-specialised translation: List of error categories for candidates (English into Arabic).* www.naati.com.au/wp-content/uploads/2020/01/List-of-Error-Categories_Arabic.pdf.

NAATI (2019b). *Revision of a non-specialised translation: List of error categories for candidates (English into Japanese).* www.naati.com.au/wp-content/uploads/2020/01/List-of-Error-Categories_Japanese.pdf.

NAATI (2019c). *Revision of a non-specialised translation: List of error categories for candidates (English into Korean).* www.naati.com.au/wp-content/uploads/2020/01/List-of-Error-Categories_Korean.pdf.

Shih, Claire Yi-yi (2006). Revision from translators' point of view: An interview study. *Target: International Journal of Translation Studies*, 18(2): 295–312.

Taibi, Mustapha (2018). Quality assurance in community translation. In Taibi, Mustapha (Ed.), *Translating for the community*. Bristol: Multilingual Matters: 7–25.

Taibi, Mustapha and Ozolins, Uldis (2016). *Community translation*. London and New York: Bloomsbury.

Van Rensburg, Alta (2017). Developing assessment instruments: The effect of a reviser's profile on the quality of the revision product. *Linguistica Antverpiensia, New Series: Themes in Translation Studies*, 16: 71–88.

11 Teamwork and community engagement

> The final chapter of this textbook focuses on the professional and community relationships of community translators (and translation students). Rather than a limited notion of the translator as a language expert working with texts and resources, I emphasise the role of community translators as members of (professional) groups and sociocultural communities. The chapter covers the following key aspects:
>
> - Translator competences, with a focus on interpersonal competence;
> - The importance of teamwork;
> - Teamwork for community translators;
> - Community engagement to connect with language-specific communities and societal organisations.

11.1 Interpersonal skills as part of translator competence

Kelly (2005, 2018) summarises the competences that translators are expected to demonstrate in the following: communicative and textual, cultural and intercultural, thematic (related to subject area), professional and instrumental, psycho-physiological or attitudinal, interpersonal and strategic (see also PACTE Group, e.g., Hurtado Albir, 2017). In her book chapter about education for community translators, Kelly (2018) argues that the same competences apply in the community translation context and explains them as follows:

- Communicative and textual competence in at least two languages and cultures: Active and passive skills in the two languages involved together with awareness of textuality and discourse and textual and discourse conventions in the cultures involved.
- Cultural and intercultural competence: Not only encyclopaedic knowledge of history, geography, institutions and so on of the cultures involved (including the translators' or students' own) but also and, more particularly, values, myths,

DOI: 10.4324/9781003367741-12

Teamwork and community engagement   189

perceptions, beliefs, behaviours and textual representations of these. Awareness of issues of intercultural communication and translation as a special form thereof.

- Subject area (thematic) competence: Basic knowledge of subject areas the future translator will/may work in to a degree sufficient to allow comprehension of source texts and access to specialised documentation to solve translation problems.
- Professional and instrumental competence: Use of documentary resources of all kinds, terminological research, information management, IT tools (word-processing, desktop publishing, data bases, Internet, email, etc.). Basic notions for managing professional activity: contracts, budgets, billing, tax; ethics, professional associations.
- Psycho-physiological or attitudinal elements: Self-concept, self-confidence, attention/concentration, memory, initiative.
- Interpersonal competence: Ability to work with other professionals involved in the translation process (translators, revisers, documentary researchers, terminologists, project managers, layout specialists) and other actors (clients, initiators, authors, users, subject area experts); teamwork, negotiation skills, leadership skills.
- Strategic competence: Organisational and planning skills, problem identification and problem-solving, monitoring, self-assessment and revision (Kelly, 2018: 30–32).

Much of this textbook is focused on communicative, textual, cultural and intercultural competences (e.g., Chapters 2, 3, 4, 5, 6, 7 and 8), although I have also addressed instrumental competence in Chapter 9. In this chapter, I focus on interpersonal competence and, to some extent, on psycho-physiological or attitudinal elements, especially the community translator's self-concept and self-confidence as a social agent.

Interpersonal competence is a critical skill for (community) translators, as it enables them to navigate complex linguistic and cultural interactions effectively within their workplace or professional relationships. As I pointed out in Chapter 2, community translators are also cultural mediators in a sense: They not only transfer messages from one language to another but also bridge gaps between people, cultures and contexts. To achieve this, they also navigate multiple concrete and abstract relationships and loyalties (e.g., direct communication and relationship with a translation reviser vs. identity-based relationship with the target community or cultural group).

Interpersonal competence encompasses a range of abilities that facilitate successful communication and collaboration with others. For community translators— and translators in general for that matter—these abilities extend beyond linguistic proficiency and involve empathy, adaptability, and cultural awareness. The following are aspects of interpersonal competence that community translators need in the course of their professional practice:

1) Active listening: Active listening is usually associated with interactional settings where participants speak (and listen) to one another, as is the case for

190   *Translation and Community*

community interpreting (e.g., in courts and hospitals). However, community translators also need to actively listen to their clients, colleagues and end users (the latter probably through written or indirect feedback). By understanding their needs, preferences and expectations, community translators can tailor their translation strategies to meet specific requirements. Active listening also helps in grasping contextual and culture-specific nuances, which are essential for accurate and appropriate translations.

2) Empathy: In addition to official documents and public messaging, community translators translate texts that convey emotions, opinions and personal experiences; empathy allows them to connect with the original author's intent and convey it appropriately and effectively in the target language. Whether translating an asylum seeker's narrative or a public appeal during a crisis, empathy ensures that the message resonates with the audience. Empathy, however, does not mean being biased or violating the principles of professional ethics and conduct (see Chapter 2).

3) Cultural sensitivity: Cultural competence is at the core of translation. As I explained in Chapter 6, community translators are expected to recognise cultural differences in norms, expectations and taboos. A culturally sensitive community translator avoids pitfalls like literal translations that may offend or misrepresent certain social, religious or political groups.

4) Negotiation skills: Interpersonal competence involves negotiation; translators, including community translators, negotiate terms, deadlines and expectations with clients. They may need to enquire about the client's entire communication campaign or the intended meaning in a particular segment. They may also need to discuss translation and dissemination options that would work best for the intended audience (see Chapter 7). Their negotiation skills will also be closely linked to, if not dependent on, components of their psycho-physiological competence such as self-concept and self-confidence. How much they are willing to negotiate and how they do it will depend to a large extent on their perception of themselves as persons and as professionals and their perception of their role and abilities.

5) Conflict resolution: In collaborative projects, conflicts may arise due to misunderstandings or differences in personality and approach. Interpersonal competence enables translators to resolve conflicts in a diplomatic manner. Whether it is a disagreement with a translation commissioner or reviser or feedback provided by community members/reviewers, a constructive approach fosters positive outcomes.

In translation and interpreting programs, it is now common for students to engage in at least one project-like assignment to develop their interpersonal skills further, especially those that are relevant to a translation project. Bilovesky (2023), for example, describes a model where students work in teams with one project manager and each team member is assigned a job position; in addition to the project manager, roles include terminologists, translators, editors and a copyeditor. The project manager oversees the entire translation project, including deadlines and time

Teamwork and community engagement   191

management, labour division (i.e. allocating parts of the translation to individuals and assigning tasks to each team member) and coordinates the activities and liaises between team members throughout the duration of the project. The terminologists undertake textual and contextual analysis of the source text(s), compile the necessary glossaries in Excel or another software, and search for relevant resources such as parallel texts.

Translators import the glossaries into their translation memory tool (e.g., Trados or MemoQ) and start to work on the translation assignment. When the translation is ready, it is sent to the project manager, who in turn forwards it to the editor (what I am calling a reviser in this textbook). The edited or revised translation is then forwarded to the copyeditor, who undertakes a final check in terms of language, style and formatting (Bilovesky, 2023).

If the copyeditor identifies major errors they are unable to correct, the translation is sent back to the project manager, who subsequently forwards it to the relevant team member. At the end of the project, each team member writes a team evaluation report and submits it to the project manager, who produces an overall evaluation of the teamwork, summarises the main issues that emerged during the collaboration, debriefs with the team members to provide advice and recommendations and assesses the overall satisfaction of team members with their colleagues. The tutor of the subject is only involved once the whole teamwork experience has been finalised (Bilovesky, 2023).

Assignments that simulate collaboration and relationships between team members are likely to give rise to different challenges and issues, putting members' interpersonal skills to the test and at the same time developing those skills for future use in professional contexts. As Bilovesky (2023) notes, one of the major advantages of such experiences is that they develop students' soft skills, including "communication, teamwork, conflict resolution, evaluation of team members, acceptance of assessment, criticism, justification of evaluation, analytical thinking, critical thinking, decision making and organization, healthy self-esteem, empathy, discipline, self-control, curiosity, and the ability to assert oneself" (319).

While, analytical thinking, critical thinking, decision-making and organization, healthy self-esteem, discipline, self-control, curiosity and the ability to assert oneself fall under the communicative, psycho-physiological and strategic competences I described earlier, competences often overlap (Kelly, 2002) and are enacted simultaneously. Interpersonal competence in particular is not an isolated skill but permeates every aspect of a translator's work and can influence their relationships not only with other language service professionals but also with clients and other stakeholders. While Bilovesky's (2023) model does not refer to clients and partners beyond those directly involved in the translation project, interpersonal skills will also be essential in a translator's interactions with institutions, community leaders and community members. Interpersonal skills for relationships with team members can be enhanced through project-based assignments, role play and reflection (see Box 11.1), while they can be developed further in a broader network of relationships through community engagement and internships (see Section 11.3).

192   *Translation and Community*

Box 11.1   Interpersonal scenarios

Consider the following scenarios and reflect on each situation and the relationships, behaviours and responses involved, especially your own responses. Discuss these behaviours and responses in pairs or groups.

Scenario 1: A community translation teacher asks Jing, Alex, Hiromi and Womba to work on a translation project together. The teacher does not specify roles but only explains the nature and expected outcome of the project (a 3000-word translation and a 1000-word report about the translation process) and leaves it up to the team members to discuss, decide roles and make the necessary arrangements. At their first meeting, Jing, who has been working as a part-time translator with several language service providers, takes the lead and starts assigning tasks to Alex, Hiromi and Womba. She believes that based on her work experience, she is sufficiently qualified to lead the team, decide each member's role and oversee the entire project. If you were Alex, Hiromi or Womba, what would you do and say?

Scenario 2: You have been working on a translation project with two other classmates, Sahar and Alejandra. While Sahar has been cooperative and has submitted her part of the translation, Alejandra has been lagging and has failed to respond to emails. What would you do? Would you inform the tutor/subject coordinator? Would you decide to do Alejandra's part together with Sahar to be able to meet the deadline? Would you find alternative ways to contact Alejandra? How would you communicate with her and what would you say? You are aware that Alejandra comes from a cultural background where directness (straightforward talk) is not the norm. Would you make any adaptations to your communication style?

Scenario 3: You are managing a community translation project consisting of a multilingual translation of a guide for newly arrived migrants and refugees. Everything is going well, and everybody is working smoothly, except for the team of three translators working into one specific language. You have received personal communication from the most senior translator in the group denigrating the quality of the work completed by the other two, and you have also received complaints from the other two team members that the senior translator is "bossy" and has an old-fashioned approach to translation. How would you proceed? How would you communicate with the team members?

Scenario 4: You translated twenty personal official documents for a language service provider and submitted the translations on time. You submitted them as Word documents so that a translation reviser could check them before you stamped them with your sworn/certified translator stamp. The language service provider sent you PDF versions of the documents saying that the translation reviser had corrected several factual and language errors without highlighting where the amendments had been made. You find you must check all the PDF versions against your Word files and the original documents as well. In the end, you realise that you do not agree with the reviser on several corrections. How would you proceed? (You might want to refer to Chapter 10).

Scenario 5: Your tutor has chosen your translation for discussion and feedback in the class. The tutor is always careful to de-identify student translations so that they can be discussed anonymously, but you know that it is your translation. One of your classmates starts to comment on the translation saying that it does not make sense and that it appears to be a case of copy-and-paste from Google Translate. Would you respond to them? If so, how would you do it?

11.2 Teamwork for community translators

The ability to work on a team is one of the most valued soft skills and attitudes in the modern workplace (Lucas and Grebing, 2023). Among other things, teamwork means collaboration and synergy: When individuals collaborate as a team, they contribute diverse and complementary skills, perspectives, experience and problem-solving strategies; by combining their strengths, they can achieve more than they would individually. Synergy arises when the collective effort produces results beyond what each person could achieve alone.

Teamwork also means enhanced problem-solving capacity: As the team puts their knowledge and problem-solving skills together, their capacity to address issues and challenges increases and improves. In addition, teamwork improves efficiency and productivity: As tasks are distributed (division of labour) and each member of the team contributes to the project, productivity is enhanced, and timely completion becomes more feasible. However, this does not mean that all teams working together will achieve complementarity, efficiency and increased productivity; team members must have effective communication and interpersonal skills and be able to recognise and deal with different personality types. As Carnevale and Smith (2013: 495) point out, "Interpersonal and negotiation skills are the cornerstones of successful teamwork. Unresolved conflicts can sap productivity and short-circuit strategic plans".

As far as translation is concerned, it has historically been perceived as a solitary individual job. However, while this was probably the case in the past, recent advances in technology, communication and industrial relationships have drastically changed translators' work patterns and environments. As Gummerus and Paro (2001: 142) put it,

The belief, often repeated, that translation is solitary work for lone wolves who sit in their chambers, buried under dusty dictionaries and piles of paper,

194 *Translation and Community*

is no longer valid in the age of modern technology. Increasingly, translation is based on teamwork.

(142)

Translation today is rarely a solitary endeavour, not even for literary translators who spend months translating a single work. In today's interconnected world, collaboration among translators (and other professionals) is not only beneficial but also essential and in some workplaces even mandatory.

Translation teams—translators, revisers, graphic designers, subtitlers—bring diverse skills to the table. Even within roles, for instance, some translators may excel in legal translation, while others specialise in health care or education; by working together, they pool their expertise, ensuring that each project receives the attention it deserves. Translation team diversity can also encompass complementary language skills, necessary for producing multilingual translated versions of the same work.

In terms of quality assurance, teamwork enhances quality standards. Multiple pairs of eyes can catch errors, inconsistencies and cultural nuances that an individual might overlook. Collaborative revision and proofreading lead to translations of better quality. As I showed in Chapters 8 and 10, quality assurance is especially crucial for high-stakes projects like personal official documents and legal or medical texts. Finally, teamwork in translation usually improves efficiency: Dividing tasks among team members accelerates the process; while one translator works on the initial draft, another can focus on research or terminology management. Efficient workflows reduce turnaround time, meeting tight deadlines without compromising quality.

For community translators, teamwork might consist of collaboration on large multistakeholder community translation projects that involve not only translators and revisers but typesetters, community reviewers, community leaders and staff representing the relevant public service. Apart from tensions and sensitivities that can arise in any workplace, two areas where teamwork in community translation can require special attention to interpersonal skills are translation revision and community feedback. As I have noted in the past, user feedback is currently an essential part of quality assurance in different industries, and community translation is not an exception (Taibi, 2018: 22).

Both revision by a professional reviser and community feedback are necessary because of the real-life risks involved in community translation. While professional revisers check translations based on their expertise (see Chapter 10), community leaders, focus groups or representative members will provide feedback based on their own experiences and expectations. Professional translators can be sensitive to feedback, especially when it comes from non-experts such as community members without translation qualifications. However, they need to understand that community members are not consulted to criticise the work of translators but to provide feedback on whether the translation will be fit for purpose.

While community translators are recognised as qualified language, communication and translation professionals, target community members or representatives

Teamwork and community engagement 195

and the organisation initiating translation projects can bring extremely helpful perspectives, insights and solutions; regular consultations with these community members ensure that translations resonate with their lived experiences. As I outlined in Taibi (2018), consultation with the community before, during and after the translation process is an essential step towards ensuring community translation quality. As long as reviser and community feedback is provided in a respectful manner and translators have the necessary interpersonal and psycho-physiological or attitudinal competences, neither formal nor informal feedback should be problematic.

As I explained in Chapter 10, in terms of translation revision specifically, the reviser needs to have the communication and interpersonal skills to provide their feedback in a professional and neutral tone; the feedback also needs to be necessary and justified, not just a matter of personal preferences and idiosyncratic style. At the other end, the translator receiving feedback needs to be an active listener and try to understand the feedback rather than jump to self-defence while at the same time being assertive enough to justify their translation approach when they believe it is best. In both cases, tact, empathy and, where relevant, intercultural competence are needed to avoid workplace conflict and keep the team intact for future projects.

The AUSIT Code of Ethics includes the principle of professional solidarity, which is defined and explained as follows:

> Interpreters and translators respect and support their fellow professionals, and they uphold the reputation and trustworthiness of the profession of interpreting and translating.
>
> **Explanation:** Practitioners have a loyalty to the profession that extends beyond their individual interest. They support and further the interests of the profession and their colleagues and offer each other assistance.
>
> (AUSIT, 2012: 6–7)

Furthermore, interpreters and translators support one another, resolve disputes in a collegial and constructive manner when they arise (AUSIT, 2012: 12). Disagreements are inevitable, but effective teams address conflicts constructively. Respectful dialogue, active listening and compromise lead to better outcomes. An important part of attitudinal competence consists of perceiving multidisciplinary teams as aides, not as competitors or critics.

As mentioned in Chapter 10, the AUSIT-FECCA Revision Guidelines also include a section on maintaining collegial relationships between professional translators and revisers: 1) including the translator in the feedback and revision process so that they can respond to suggested amendments; 2) using the same communication channel to request and provide suggested translation revisions (this avoids direct contact between reviser and translator if the revision request was received through a language service provider or should otherwise be anonymous); 3) limiting corrections to those that are necessary and justified; and 4) providing feedback in a professional and neutral manner (AUSIT-FECCA, n.d).

Box 11.2 gives some questions to consider in the context of teamwork and collaboration in community translation.

196 *Translation and Community*

Box 11.2   Questions to consider

1) Teamwork on a translation project can lead to a disorganised and inconsistent translation. If team members divide up parts of the assignment and each one works on their part independently, without opportunities or strategies to bring the pieces of the puzzle together, the risk is that the final product will be disorganised and might not look consistent and coherent. Whose responsibility is it to ensure that the entire translation work is well organised and consistent? What mechanisms, strategies and communication processes should be implemented to achieve this goal?

2) Clear communication among team members is extremely important, for both interpersonal relationships and successful completion of the project at hand. Poor communication can lead to a fragmented final product, unmet expectations and friction among team members. However, the concept of 'clear communication' is relative and varies from one culture to another. What are the basic parameters of clear communication in relation to a translation project in your culture? What would you do to bridge the cultural gap in this respect if your colleagues identify with a different culture and have different expectations in terms of clear communication?

3) You work as a community translator at a town council. You have a translation partner who looks disorganised. Their papers and reference works are all over the place. For them, this is not a problem as long as the final product is a good quality translation. You find their behaviour and work style irritating. What would you do?

4) A translator has posted a comment on social media saying that as a freelance translator, they cannot put something like "excellent teamwork skills" on their resumé, as such a claim would be derisible. How do you feel about this statement?

5) A local organisation has invited you as a community translator to form part of a team drafting awareness materials for multilingual and multicultural communities. Your contact advises that your role will consist of advising the team in charge of drafting the resources on any issues that might arise in relation to cultural sensitivities or conceptual or structural complexity. Would you accept work on such a team? Would you have any concerns? What actions would you take to ensure that you and the other team members have the same understanding of roles and expectations?

11.3   Community engagement for community translators

Community translators need to be in close contact with the sociocultural contexts of the communities they serve. They need to immerse themselves, as much as possible, in a community's culture, traditions and dynamics by developing links with

Teamwork and community engagement   197

relevant community organisations and leaders and engaging in community events, gatherings and activities. By doing so, they are likely to connect with community members, understand their needs and build trust. Such community engagement will also contribute to the translator's community language maintenance, especially when a target community is small and the translator has few organic opportunities to keep up to date with sociolinguistic developments in their minority language. Languages evolve over time, and community translation users may come from different national and socioeducational backgrounds, so community translators need to keep abreast of changes, new vocabulary, and shifts in usage.

Community engagement should start in the community translation classroom for those undertaking formal education in this area. This can be done, among other things, through situated learning and work integrated learning. Situated learning is "a theory that holds as its foundational tenet that individuals learn by engaging in experiences in authentic environments" (Miner and Nicodemus, 2021: 23). It generally refers to "a context-dependent approach to translator and interpreter training under which learners are exposed to real-life and/or highly simulated work environments and tasks, both inside and outside the classroom" (Enríquez-Raído and González-Davies, 2016: 1). Work-integrated learning refers to "on-campus and workplace learning activities and experiences which integrate theory with practice in academic learning programs" (Jackson, 2013: 99). Engaging in situated learning experiences in authentic environments requires authentic materials and activities, appropriate resources and tools, social interactions with peers and other stakeholders and a real-world context students can relate to where they can apply their learnings (Miner and Nicodemus, 2021: 33). Work-integrated learning activities

> can range from the more traditional format of full-time immersion in the workplace, such as work placements and internships, to other forms of engagement with an external stakeholder on campus such as work-related projects, student consultation projects, or an external stakeholder as a client.
>
> (Lai and Gonzalez, 2023: 221)

Where opportunities exist, students can also intern at community organisations or language services or join their education providers in translation partnerships with relevant organisations. Alternatively, they can at least practice community translation with authentic texts that are relevant to the community and that have not been translated before. Learning activities that consist of or include practice with translating public service texts for local communities and service-learning placements also provide students with opportunities to enhance their translation abilities; develop their intercultural, interpersonal and professional competences and cultivate a sense of civic responsibility (Rueda-Acedo, 2018: 62–63).

A good example is the service learning that students undertake in the translation program at the University of Texas at Arlington. As Rueda-Acedo (2018) explains, the program has a partnership with *Proyecto Inmigrante*, a non-government organisation offering administrative, legal and language services to ensure social equity for migrants by working with a Spanish-speaking community in central Texas.

198 *Translation and Community*

The partnership allows students to translate authentic documents (mainly personal official documents) which the agency uses to help clients complete real-life applications for citizenship, Temporary Protected Status and Deferred Action for Childhood Arrivals; employment authorizations; provisional or other waivers; consular processing; FBI records; resident card renewal and other administrative and legal processes. In this program that operates in a state bordering Mexico, the final intended learning outcome on this list from one of the program's courses is worth noting:

1) Practice legal translation in class and outside class.
2) Demonstrate the ability to provide professional translations at *Proyecto Inmigrante*.
3) Gain professional and work experience at *Proyecto Inmigrante*, Inc.
4) Demonstrate an understanding of the Hispanic immigrant community needs in terms of immigration-related issues (Rueda-Acedo, 2018: 44).

This service learning entails not only translating authentic documents but also attending staff presentations from the host organisation, as well as social events, which creates useful opportunities not only for employability but also for building knowledge about the community. One student provided the following reflection on their experience:

> Indeed it was worthwhile investment. It was significant because I was able to use what I have learned in class to apply it in real life, helping real people who are in desperate need of the attention and care they deserve. The experience was not comparable to being able to speak Spanish in the classroom, in a restaurant, or with fellow Hispanic friends.
>
> (Rueda-Acedo, 2018: 58)

Another example is the internship program under the Master of Intercultural Communication, Public Service Interpreting and Translation degree offered by the University of Alcalá, Spain. The internship consists of approximately 100–125 hours of translation and interpretation work completed onsite, remotely or both. With a large number of partnerships with government institutions, schools, hospitals, language services and non-government organisations, the program gives students many opportunities to engage in supervised work including translation, translation revision, original writing, interpreting and compilation of glossaries, among other activities (University of Alcalá, 2024). Non-government organisations, ethnic community associations and cultural centres particularly contribute to students' immersion in the sociocultural context of their relevant communities. In addition to introducing students to professional practice, developing their understanding of workplace culture, enhancing their self-confidence and increasing their employment opportunities (Lai and Gonzalez, 2023), such practicum placements enable students to obtain first-hand knowledge about the people and communities they plan to work with.

Teamwork and community engagement 199

Community translators come from different backgrounds and have varying life trajectories. Some are migrants or refugees or their descendants; others are native-born citizens who belong to a minority group or majority members who have learned a minority language at school and/or university. The experiences and relationships of these different categories with their communities of translation users will vary, and so will their language experience and resources. For all of them, ongoing contact with the community, ongoing community language learning and updated knowledge of social and cultural trends in the community are essential to informed translation practice.

Communities are dynamic, and their language use and communication needs evolve over time. By maintaining links, community translators can adapt their language service to address evolving needs and expectations. Whether it is an English–Arabic translator who arrived in Australia as an adult three decades ago, a Chinese–English translator who has not visited China in the last 20 years or a British-born Urdu translator who has never been to India or Pakistan, they must remain engaged with their working communities (as well as with online resources) to maintain their working language competence and their current understanding of local sociocultural contexts and the sociolinguistic profiles of community translation users.

Summary

Teamwork and community engagement are essential for both community translation students and community translators. Teamwork enables students and translators to work more effectively and productively, as it allows team members to combine efforts and skills to produce a larger translation product in less time. Community engagement enables current and future community translators to create and maintain social and institutional networks which can increase their knowledge about the communities they serve (e.g., their profiles, needs, language use and literacy levels) and enhance mutual trust between them. For both teamwork and community engagement, interpersonal and psycho-physiological or attitudinal competences are indispensable. For translation students, these skills can be developed further during their training program, through simulated teamwork (project-based learning) and, where possible, in supervised internships.

Suggested activities

1) Search for publications released locally by your relevant community organisations, preferably in your community/minority/minoritised language (newspaper, magazine, newsletter, event schedule, etc.). Read a few and write a 500-word report about new aspects or details you have learned about the community (e.g., the languages or dialects they speak, community life and events, special challenges they face).

200   *Translation and Community*

2) Identify three community organisations or language service providers where you would like to undertake a translation internship. Write a list of reasons for your choice. Discuss this with your tutor, subject coordinator or academic program director. Even if an internship is not a requirement in your program, take the initiative and be assertive. You can try approaching relevant staff at your institution and at the organisations you have chosen.
3) Summarise the text recommended in 'Further reading' in 500 words approximately. The summary may include a paragraph on how the paper relates to your own training program and experience.

Further reading

- Olvera Lobo, María Dolores; Robinson Fryer, Bryan John and Gutiérrez Artacho, Juncal (2018). Generic competences, the great forgotten: Teamwork in the undergraduate degree in Translation and Interpretation. https://digibug.ugr.es/handle/10481/50199

In this paper, the authors discuss teamwork and intra-team interactions as part of project-based learning and cooperative/collaborative learning for translation students. They report the results of classroom activities and assessment tools used in the translation and interpreting program at Granada University, Spain.

References

AUSIT (2012). *AUSIT code of ethics and code of conduct.* https://ausit.org/wp-content/uploads/2020/02/Code_Of_Ethics_Full.pdf.

AUSIT-FECCA (n.d.). *Revision guidelines and parameters for community translations.* https://ausit.org/ausit_fecca_translation_guidelines

Bilovesky, Vladimir (2023). Interpersonal skills in the development of translation competence. *AWEJ for Translation & Literary Studies*, 313–326. DOI: 10.24093/awejtls/vol7no1.23.

Carnevale, Anthony P. and Smith, Nicole (2013). Workplace basics: The skills employees need and employers want. *Human Resource Development International*, 16(5): 491–501. DOI: 10.1080/13678868.2013.821267.

Enríquez-Raído, Vanesa and González-Davies, Maria (2016). Situated learning in translator and interpreter training: Bridging research and good practice. *The Interpreter and Translator Trainer*, 10(1): 1–11.

Gummerus, Eivor and Paro, Catrine (2001). Translation quality: An organizational viewpoint. In Gambier, Yves and Gottlieb, Henrik (Eds.), *(Multi)Media translation*. Amsterdam and Philadelphia: John Benjamins: 133–142.

Hurtado Albir, Amparo (Ed.) (2017). *Researching translation competence by PACTE Group.* Amsterdam and Philadelphia: John Benjamins.

Jackson, Denise (2013). The contribution of work-integrated learning to undergraduate employability skill outcomes. *Asia-Pacific Journal of Cooperative Education*, 14(2): 99–115.

Kelly, Dorothy (2002). Un modelo de competencia traductora: Bases para el diseño curricular. *Puentes*, 1: 9–20.

Kelly, Dorothy (2005). *A handbook for translator trainers: A guide to reflective practice.* Manchester: St. Jerome.

Kelly, Dorothy (2018). Education for community translation: Thirteen key ideas. In Taibi, Mustapha (Ed.), *Translating for the community*. Bristol: Multilingual Matters: 26–41.

Lai, Miranda and Gonzalez, Erika (2023). The multilingual community translation classroom: Challenges and strategies to train profession-ready graduates. In González, Erika; Stachowiak-Szymczak, Katarzyna and Amanatidou, Despina (Eds.), *Community translation: Research and practice*. Abingdon and New York: Routledge: 212–229.

Lucas, Kaneshya and Grebing, Robin (2023). Hiring managers' perceptions of the employability of career and technical education graduates. *Community College Journal of Research and Practice*. DOI: 10.1080/10668926.2023.2293159.

Miner, Annette and Nicodemus, Brenda (2021). *Situated learning in interpreter education: From the classroom to the community*. Cham: Palgrave Macmillan.

Rueda-Acedo, Alicia (2018). From the classroom to the job market: Integrating service-learning and community translation in a legal translation course. In Taibi, Mustapha (Ed.), *Translating for the community*. Bristol: Multilingual Matters: 42–68.

Taibi, Mustapha (2018). Quality assurance in community translation. In Taibi, Mustapha (Ed.), *Translating for the community*. Bristol: Multilingual Matters: 7–25.

University of Alcalá (2024). *Prácticas*. https://uahmastercitisp.es/practicas/.

Author Index

Abdallah, Kristiina 37, 50
Adler, Mark 19
Alcaráz Varó, Enrique 85
Amanatidou, Despina 162, 165
American Translators Association (ATA) 26, 137
Ashworth, David 28
Australian Institute of Interpreters and Translators (AUSIT) 25, 26, 33, 71, 96, 103, 104, 106, 107, 108, 111, 137, 138, 144, 148, 175, 181–185

Baker, Mona 11, 51–56, 76, 103, 108, 129, 159
Barron, Anne 19, 59, 60, 62
Bell, Allan 65–66
Bell, Erica 111
Bell, Roger 45
Biber, Douglas 124, 125
Bielsa, Esperanza 9
Brown, Penelope 105
Burke, Jean 1, 19, 70, 71, 119

Campbell, Stuart 35
Cao, Deborah 85
Carroll, Mary 129, 131
Chan, Sin-wai 163
Chesher, Terry 136
Chesterman, Andrew 34, 48, 67
Córdoba Serrano, María Sierra 1, 8, 11, 22
Cornelius, Eleanor 18
Corsellis, Ann 10
Crezee, Ineke 72
Cronin, Michael 9

Darbelnet, Jean 51–55, 103
Díaz-Cintas, Jorge 128, 129, 131
Drugan, Joanna 35

Enríquez Raído, Vanessa 163, 197
Evans, Jonathan 11

Fernández, Fruela 11
Fuentes Luque, Adrian 139
Fukari, Alexandra 31
Fukuno, Maho 1, 33, 36, 37, 38

Gallego-Hernández, Daniel 159
Gambier, Yves 128, 130, 131
García, Ignacio 8, 9, 13, 14
Gentzler, Edwin 36
Gerber, Leah 123
González-Davies, María 197
González, Erika 1, 162, 165, 197, 198
Greenbaum, Sidney 125, 126

Hajek, John 120–122
Halliday, Michael 68, 95, 124
Hasan, Ruqaya 68
Hatim, Basil 32, 34, 35, 46, 47, 66, 82, 95, 100
House, Juliane 95, 106, 124, 144
Hughes, Brian 85
Hurtado Albir, Amparo 188

Ivarsson, Jan 129, 131

Katan, David 18, 30, 99, 105, 106, 107, 116
Kelly, Dorothy 8, 13, 188, 189, 191
Ko, Leong 10, 172
Koby, Geoffrey 176, 177
Koskinen, Kaisa 10, 81, 85–90, 96
Kress, Gunther 124, 128

Lai, Miranda 197, 198
Lambert-Tierrafría, Sylvie 142

Author index 203

Lesch, Harold 8, 9, 12, 14, 18, 33
Levinson, Stephen 105
Liang, Haiyan 172, 173, 174
Liddicoat, Anthony 30, 31, 99, 104
Lung, Rachel 108, 109

Määttä, Simo 1, 8, 18
Marais, Kobus 11
Martín Ruano, Rosario 110
Mason, Ian 32, 34, 35, 46, 47, 66, 82, 95, 100
Mayoral Asensio, Roberto 135, 138, 141, 144, 145, 151
Mellinger, Christopher 163, 174
Molina Martínez, Lucía 51, 53, 54, 55, 56, 57, 103
Mossop, Brian 77, 89, 172–175, 177, 178, 179, 181, 186

National Accreditation Authority for Translators and Interpreters (NAATI) 95, 137, 144, 145, 146, 147, 177, 178
National Health and Medical Research Council 20, 120, 121
Nelson, Gerald 125, 126
Nord, Christiane 16, 43, 44, 45, 47, 49, 50, 62, 124, 138, 144

O'Hagan, Minako 9, 28, 162
Olvera Lobo 200

Paloposki, Outi 10, 11, 32
Pokorn, Nike 163
Prieto Ramos, Fernando 140, 141
Pym, Anthony 14, 17, 34, 44, 45, 99

Qian, Hong 164

Reiss, Katharina 16, 43–47
Remael, Aline 128, 129, 131
Rueda-Acedo, Alicia 13, 197–198

Samuelsson-Brown, Geoffrey 28, 155
Schäffner, Christina 9, 85, 86, 88, 89, 97
Schipper, Karen 19, 20, 121
Scollon, Ron 105, 106
Seale, Holly 72
Shannon, Claude 123
Sharkas, Hala 52
Shin, Wonsun 121
Simms, Karl 114, 116
Snell-Hornby, Mary 55, 99, 100, 159
Song, Jay 121
Sosoni, Vilelmini 162
Suojanen, Tytti 12, 17, 18, 20, 65, 66
Svoboda, Tomáš 86, 162

Taibi, Mustapha 18, 30, 99, 105, 106, 107, 116
Tannen, Deborah 125, 126
Tanskanen, Sanna Kaisa 68, 125
Tomozeiu, Daniel 8, 12, 64, 65, 67, 79
Tymoczko, Maria 9, 11, 31
Tyulenev, Sergey 10, 16, 31

Van Leeuwen, Theo 128
Venuti, Lawrence 30
Vermeer, Hans 16, 43–47
Vinay, Jean Paul 51–55, 103

Way, Catherine 10, 12
Weaver, Warren 123
Wolf, Michaela 9, 31
Wong Soon, Hoy Neng 72

Zhang, Jia 64, 164, 165

Subject Index

accessibility 12, 16, 17–19, 62, 63, 67, 120, 129, 130, 180
accuracy 27, 34, 36, 67, 77, 85, 88, 92, 94, 109, 131, 140, 141, 144, 176, 178, 182, 183
agency 10–11, 13, 19, 31–32, 35–37
Arabic 18, 20, 29, 52, 53, 54, 66, 70, 71, 76, 89, 105, 107, 108, 121, 183
artificial intelligence 162–165
audience design 12, 64–66
Australia 19, 20, 25, 33, 35, 70, 71, 95, 103, 121, 136, 137, 139, 142, 145, 147, 175

Canada 35, 86
Chinese 29, 30, 89, 96, 106, 108, 109, 121, 164, 174, 183, 186
cohesion and coherence 68–70, 125, 182
community engagement 196–200
community preferences 20, 50, 120–122
COVID-19 53, 60, 119, 121, 123, 175
cultural appropriateness 71–72, 104, 176, 180, 181
cultural assumptions 102–103
cultural mediation 29–31, 37, 99–114
cyberbullying 72–77

dictionaries 154–157
dissemination 19–20, 70–71, 119–134, 182
domestic violence 110–112

encyclopaedias 157–159
ethics 26–28, 33–37, 44, 49, 50, 90, 110, 115, 138, 140, 141, 149, 164, 190, 195
extract translation 142–143, 146, 148–150

Fight the Fog 19
France 70, 137

full translation 146, 150
functionalism 11, 12, 16, 36–37, 42–50, 55, 56, 62, 67, 124, 140–142, 177, 178

genre 30, 32, 34, 45–47, 56, 61, 71, 82, 86, 95, 125, 179

institutional translation 85–88, 97
International Conference on Community Translation 8
interpersonal skills 175, 176, 188–193, 194, 195, 197

Japanese 33, 38, 54

KISS and KILC styles 30

language appropriateness 12, 16–17, 67, 68, 71, 77, 85, 95, 176, 184
language variety 20, 70–71, 110, 122, 128, 178
legal translation 85–88, 135, 139, 140, 141

machine translation 162–165
Mexico 137, 198
modes of communication 36, 122, 123–128
Morocco 137

naturalness 71, 177
New Zealand 1, 19
non-professional 9, 13, 14

offensive language 72, 75, 108, 109, 110, 113–114
official documents 135–152

parallel texts 159–160
persona 12, 64–66
Plain Language Movement 19, 62

Subject index

politeness 105–106
political correctness 77, 92, 102, 107–108, 113, 181, 182
postediting 164, 165, 167, 172, 173
public messaging 19, 20, 33, 45, 49, 59–78, 82, 106, 110, 125, 184
published translations 160–162

quality 12, 15–17, 62, 95, 124, 130–131, 144

regulatory texts 81–96, 110, 113, 115
religion 29, 103, 107, 112–113, 190
resources 154–167
revision 17, 77, 92, 165, 167, 171–186
role 25–38, 70, 72, 104, 106–107

Saudi Arabia 63, 179–180
sexual abuse 108–111
sexuality 99, 108–109
Skopos theory *see* functionalism
social role 9–20

South Africa 19, 35, 72, 74, 109
Spain 29, 35, 70, 71, 137

taboo *see* offensive language
teamwork 193–196
template translation *see* extract translation
text type 36, 45–47, 60, 71, 82, 110
thesauri 154–157
training 13, 15, 164–165, 167, 197–198
transcreation 12, 36, 45, 72
translation approach 11–12, 16–17, 31–37, 42, 50, 88–91, 140–142
translation brief 16, 47–51
translation strategies 50–55, 76–77, 85, 128–130

UK 60, 71, 79, 102
University of Alcalá 198
University of Texas at Arlington 197–198
USA 19, 22, 35, 71, 94, 119, 137, 139

Western Sydney University 6, 8

Printed in the United States
by Baker & Taylor Publisher Services